SHORT PLAYS
for
CHILDREN

Short Plays
for
Children

*A collection of royalty-free
comedies, mysteries, folk tales
and holiday plays for boys and girls*

by

HELEN LOUISE MILLER

Publishers   PLAYS, INC.   *Boston*

CAUTION

NOTICE FOR AMATEUR PRODUCTION

NOTICE FOR PROFESSIONAL PRODUCTION

Library of Congress Catalog Card Number: 68-57840.

MANUFACTURED IN THE UNITED STATES OF AMERICA

CONTENTS

v

SHORT PLAYS
for
CHILDREN

One To Grow On

Characters

KING KINROSS
QUEEN QUINELLA
MR. JOLLY ⎫
ALPHONSO ⎪
CHANCELLOR CURLICUE ⎪
NURSE PILLANPLASTER ⎪
LADY LEONA ⎬ *members of the Court*
PROFESSOR POPPINJAY ⎪
LADY LEARNINGWELL ⎪
LORD INCHWORM ⎭
PRINCE FLORIO
GODMOTHER GREENSLEEVES
BILL ⎫
BETTY ⎭ *American guests*
MRS. CUSTARD, *the cook*
MUSTARD ⎫
FLUSTERED ⎭ *the maids*
SIX CHILDREN, *prisoners*
TWO GUARDS

SETTING: *The Court of King Kinross. Two thrones and a high stool are on a raised platform at center, and there is a folding screen on either side of the platform.*

At Rise: King Kinross and Queen Quinella are seated on their thrones. Mr. Jolly, the court jester, stands near King, holding a thick notebook, and Chancellor Curlicue is standing beside his throne. A Guard is stationed in front of each screen. King is addressing the members of the Court, who are assembled before him.

King: Lords and ladies, we are assembled for a very special occasion.

All: Prince Florio's birthday!

Queen: We trust that everything is in order for the celebration.

Chancellor: All is in readiness, Your Majesty.

King: Humph! We'll soon see about that! Mr. Jolly, what jokes and riddles have you prepared for His Royal Highness?

Mr. Jolly (*Opening notebook*): Oh, I have a splendid assortment, Your Majesty. I've been collecting them all year.

King: Then let's have a sample.

Mr. Jolly: First let me ask you a question, sire. Does your watch tell time?

King: What a silly question! Of course, my watch tells time!

Mr. Jolly: How amazing, Your Majesty! I have to *look* at mine! (*All laugh.*)

King: Very good, Mr. Jolly. The Prince will like that one.

Queen: And he adores riddles. Do you have any riddles, Mr. Jolly?

Mr. Jolly: I have dozens of riddles, Your Majesty. Tell me, when is a door *not* a door?

Queen (*Pondering*): When is a door *not* a door? Dear me! That *is* difficult. (*To King*) Do you know the answer, my lord?

KING: Haven't the faintest idea, my love. We give up, Mr. Jolly.

MR. JOLLY: When it is ajar! (*They all laugh heartily.*)

KING: Splendid! Splendid! Do you get it, Quinella? When it is A JAR!

QUEEN: Of course, I get it. Oh, do let's have another, Mr. Jolly.

MR. JOLLY: This one is a real teaser. If a boy in a sailor suit grows three inches in one month, six inches in two months, twelve inches in three months, how big will he be by the end of the year?

KING (*Rising in anger*): Stop! Stop! Off with his head! Guards, arrest this man! (GUARDS *step forward and seize* MR. JOLLY.) Bind him hand and foot and take him to the dungeons at once. Tomorrow at sunrise he dies!

MR. JOLLY (*Falling to his knees*): Please, sire, have mercy! At least tell me what crime I have committed.

QUEEN (*Sobbing wildly*): Take him away! I can't bear to look at him!

MR. JOLLY: But what have I done?

KING: You have committed the worst crime of all, the unpardonable offense of mentioning the word "grow" in our royal presence.

MR. JOLLY: But, sire, it was only a joke. If Your Majesty would only wait for the answer.

QUEEN: I don't want to hear the answer! Take him away!

KING: As you very well know, our beloved son, Prince Florio, has not grown an inch for the past three years. And that is no joke!

MR. JOLLY: Please forgive me, Your Majesty. I did not mean to offend you.

CHANCELLOR (*Stepping forward*): Please, sire, may I say a word on his behalf?

KING: You have our royal permission to speak, Chancellor Curlicue.

CHANCELLOR: I merely wish to point out, sire, that the death of Mr. Jolly would be a great loss to the Prince. They have become very good friends.

ALPHONSO (*Approaching the platform*): I, too, wish to plead for Mr. Jolly, Your Majesty. My mystic calculations of the path of the planets lead me to believe that the spell will be broken this year.

KING: Your words bring us great hope, Alphonso. But what is the basis of your prediction?

ALPHONSO: As the court astrologer, I have consulted the stars, which indicate the next twelve months as a year of growth for Prince Florio.

QUEEN: The stars be praised! Perhaps you should reconsider, my lord.

KING: Very well, if you say so, my love. Guards, unhand the prisoner. (GUARDS *release* MR. JOLLY *and resume their positions in front of screens.*)

MR. JOLLY (*Bowing to* KING *and* QUEEN *in turn*): Thank you, sire. Thank you, gracious lady.

QUEEN: Now you may continue your riddle.

MR. JOLLY: Perhaps I had better skip it, Your Majesty.

KING: No, no. Now that our royal nerves are somewhat calmer, we insist on trying to guess the answer. Let me see—if a boy in a sailor suit grows three inches in one month, six inches in two months, twelve inches in three months, how big would he be by the end of a year? That's a very difficult riddle.

QUEEN: How big would he be, Mr. Jolly?

MR. JOLLY: He would be entirely too big for his britches, Your Majesty! (*All laugh.*)

KING: Very good, Mr. Jolly, but you will have to remove it from your birthday list. Unless a miracle happens, Prince Florio would not find it amusing. But enough of this! We must proceed to our annual reports.

QUEEN: I wish to have a report on my son's health from Nurse Pillanplaster.

NURSE PILLANPLASTER (*Stepping forward*): The Prince is in excellent health, Your Majesty. He has the appetite of a horse, the eyes of a hawk, the ears of a cat, and the heart of a lion. He swims like a fish, runs like a deer, and is as strong as an ox! (*Steps back*)

MR. JOLLY (*Aside*): This boy belongs in a zoo!

QUEEN: What's that? What did you say?

MR. JOLLY: Nothing, Your Majesty. I merely remarked that our young prince belongs in a zoo.

KING: How dare you insult the Prince Florio! (*To* GUARDS) Off with his head!

MR. JOLLY: Please, sire, let me explain. Every now and zen, I speak wiz zee foreign accent. I meant to zay, zire, zat zee Prince belongs in a ZOO-PERIOR class! A boy of zo many talents!

KING: Well, that sounds better, but try to speak more plainly in the future. We will now hear from Professor Poppinjay.

PROFESSOR POPPINJAY (*Coming forward*): Prince Florio is doing famously in music and dancing, sire. He sings like a lark, plays the flute like a nightingale, whistles like a magpie, and is as graceful as a swallow. (*Steps back*)

MR. JOLLY (*Aside*): This prince is really quite a bird!

KING: What was that? What did you say?

MR. JOLLY: I said, sire, that our prince must be quite a bird! Quite a bird of paradise, sir, so brilliant, so colorful, so accomplished!

QUEEN: Thank you, Mr. Jolly, that was a very nice compliment.

KING: But I am more concerned about Prince Florio's progress in the classroom. Suppose we hear from Lady Learningwell.

LADY LEARNINGWELL (*Stepping forward*): I am happy to report that the Prince has a most active mind. In fact, he sometimes asks questions that even I cannot answer.

QUEEN: Can you give us an example?

LADY LEARNINGWELL: Only yesterday he wanted to know if you multiply feet by feet and get *square* feet, can you multiply eggs by eggs and get square eggs. (*All laugh.*)

QUEEN: But is he doing his homework?

LADY LEARNINGWELL: Oh, yes, Your Majesty. Monday night he spent twelve hours over his arithmetic book!

MR. JOLLY: That was the night it fell under his bed! (*All laugh.*)

KING: I am afraid your report is not very satisfactory, Lady Learningwell, but perhaps Lady Leona, our librarian, can give us a more encouraging report on his reading. (LADY LEARNINGWELL *steps back.*)

LADY LEONA (*Stepping forward*): The Prince is still a great reader, sire. Just this month he has read *Barney Blake in Borneo, Barney Blake in Brazil, Barney Blake in Britain, Barney Blake at Bat, Barney Blake in a Balloon,* and *Barney Blake, Bootblack.* We have two hundred Barney Blake books in the library, and he has read them all.

QUEEN: I think that's wonderful!

MR. JOLLY: Your Majesty, do you know what is black and white and "red" all over?

KING: What is black and white and red all over? (*Thoughtfully*) I can't answer that riddle, Mr. Jolly.

MR. JOLLY: A newspaper, Your Majesty. (*All laugh.*)

QUEEN: Now what does Lord Inchworm, our Minister of Weights and Measures, have to say?

LORD INCHWORM (*Stepping forward*): Alas, Your Majesty, I have nothing to report. Prince Florio's measurements are exactly the same as last year's, down to one quarter of a millionth of a half inch! (*Offstage fanfare is heard.*)

ALL (*Ad lib*): The Prince is coming! Make way! Prince
Florio is coming. (*Etc.*)

KING: To your places, everyone. Sit down, everyone—you,
too, Mr. Jolly. No one must be any taller than the
Prince. (*All sit on low stools and cushions which are
around platform.* MR. JOLLY *sits on platform near* KING.
PRINCE FLORIO *rides in on a bicycle. His crown hangs
around his neck on an elastic band. He rides up to the
platform and dismounts, assisted by the* TWO GUARDS,
who wheel the bicycle off right.)

ALL (*Ad lib*): Hail to Prince Florio! Long live the Prince.
Hooray for Prince Florio! (*Etc.*)

KING *and* QUEEN: Happy birthday, Florio.

QUEEN: Come and take your place beside your father.

PRINCE FLORIO (*Mounting platform and sitting on high
stool*): Let the revels begin! (*All sing "Happy Birthday."*)

KING: Excellent, excellent!

PRINCE: Thank you, ladies and gentlemen. You sing very
well.

MR. JOLLY: Speaking of singing, Your Highness, what has
eight legs and sings?

PRINCE: I don't know, Mr. Jolly.

MR. JOLLY: A quartet! (*All laugh.*)

QUEEN: And now, dear boy, it's time for your presents.
(GUARDS *wheel in a tea wagon piled high with presents.*)

1ST GUARD: To dear Prince Florio of the Court of Kinross.

2ND GUARD: Our very best wishes!

BOTH GUARDS: Happy Birthday to you!

MR. JOLLY: Let me give you your presents, sire.

PRINCE: Just a minute, Mr. Jolly. Godmother Greensleeves
promised she had more talking presents for me.

KING: Of course! The guards will bring them in at once.
(GUARDS *exit.*)

PRINCE: I can hardly wait to see them. I do hope Godmother Greensleeves has brought me some smarter ones than the ones she brought this morning.

QUEEN: I'm sure she has done her best, child. (GUARDS *usher in* BILL *and* BETTY, *each blindfolded and each carrying a book. They are followed by* GODMOTHER GREENSLEEVES)

PRINCE: Two of them! A boy and a girl!

GODMOTHER GREENSLEEVES: Happy Birthday, Prince Florio. How do you like your talking presents?

PRINCE: They look wonderful, Godmother Greensleeves, but please remove their blindfolds so I can see them better. (GUARDS *remove blindfolds.*)

BILL *and* BETTY: Where are we?

GODMOTHER: Now, now, don't be frightened, children. You are in the Kingdom of Kinross.

KING: I am King Kinross, this is Queen Quinella, and this is our son, Prince Florio.

PRINCE: You have come to my birthday party.

BILL: But how did we get here?

BETTY: I want to go home.

GODMOTHER: Come, child, where are your manners? You've just arrived.

BETTY: But I don't understand. One minute we were sitting in the library, reading . . .

BILL: And the next minute everything turned green.

PRINCE: That was Godmother Greensleeves.

BETTY: And then everything went bumpety-bumpety-bump, and here we are.

GODMOTHER: All safe and sound and ready for the party.

PRINCE: You're just in time for the presents.

BILL: Presents?

BETTY: Dear me! We didn't bring any. We didn't know we were coming.

PRINCE: Oh, that's all right. Sit down and make yourselves at home.

QUEEN: But we should know the names of our honored guests.

GODMOTHER: Their names are William Stanley and Betty Jones, straight "A" students at Garfield School, Boontown, Pennsylvania, U.S.A.

ALL: U.S.A.!

PRINCE: Splendid! We've never had anyone from the United States.

VOICES (*From behind screen*): Let us out! Help!

BETTY (*Frightened*): What was that?

GODMOTHER: Oh, nothing at all. Those are some other children we thought would make good talking presents for Prince Florio's birthday.

BILL: Other children?

BETTY (*Fearfully*): Oh, Bill, let's get out of here!

GODMOTHER: Perhaps you had better explain, Prince Florio. (*Shouts from behind screen continue.*)

PRINCE: Guards, can't you keep those children quiet?

1ST GUARD: I'm sorry, Your Highness. They're getting restless.

2ND GUARD: And they hear strange voices.

KING: I suppose we'll have to let them out. Remove the screens. (*GUARDS remove screens, revealing two cages, in each of which three CHILDREN are imprisoned. They continue to shout.*)

CHILDREN (*Ad lib*): Let us out! Help! Take us home! (*Etc.*)

BILL: You let those children out right away, or we'll call the police! (*Members of Court laugh loudly.*)

PRINCE: Oh, dear, oh, dear! That's very funny. Chancellor Curlicue, will you please explain the arrangements for our guests?

CHANCELLOR: I'll be happy to do so, Your Highness. (*To BILL and BETTY*) You see, my friends, we have a problem here in the Kingdom of Kinross. So every year on the Prince's birthday, his Godmother brings him a special guest or two from the outside world to help us find a solution. These children behind the bars were not smart enough when we tried them out this morning, so we had to put them in prison.

BETTY: And if we fail, are you going to put Bill and me in with the others?

GODMOTHER: Oh, but you won't fail, my pretty little dears. All your teachers say you are highly intelligent.

BILL: But what *is* the problem?

PRINCE: I am! Three years ago someone cast an evil spell over me which stopped my growth.

BETTY: Have you tried vitamins?

NURSE: We buy them by the case!

BILL: What about exercises?

PRINCE: I swim, I run, and I ride my bicycle.

BILL: But what about baseball and football, and stretching and bending and weight-lifting?

BETTY: And the high jump and the broad jump and deep knee bends and push-ups?

PRINCE: Please, please! None of those! They're much too strenuous. If that's all you can suggest, you might as well go into the cages at once.

QUEEN: Not before the refreshments, dear boy. That wouldn't be polite.

KING: And we might as well let the others out for the cake and ice cream. Guards, release the prisoners. (GUARDS *pretend to open doors of cages, and* CHILDREN *step out and rush to* BILL *and* BETTY.)

1ST CHILD: Oh, do please try to think of something!

2ND CHILD: If you manage to break the spell, we can all go home.

BETTY: You poor children! Are they cruel to you here?

3RD CHILD: Well, no, not exactly cruel.

4TH CHILD: We eat from golden plates.

5TH CHILD: And rest in golden beds.

6TH CHILD: And drink milk from golden goblets.

CHILDREN: But we want to go home.

KING: But you can go home any time you like. All you have to do is find a way to break the wicked spell.

BILL: Perhaps if we had time to think . . .

PRINCE: Take all the time you like. Sit down, everybody, and Mr. Jolly will hand me my presents.

MR. JOLLY (*Handing him a loosely wrapped package*): This one is from me, Your Highness.

PRINCE (*Tearing off wrapper*): Thank you, Mr. Jolly! Just what I wanted! A parakeet! (*He holds up a bird cage.*)

MR. JOLLY: When I bought it, I asked the clerk to send me the bill, but he said I'd have to take the whole bird. (*All laugh.* MR. JOLLY *hands him next package.*)

CHANCELLOR (*As* PRINCE *unwraps it*): A book on law and government, Your Highness. It's time you learned about the laws of our kingdom.

PRINCE: Thank you, Chancellor, but I'm afraid it's much too hard for me.

ALPHONSO (*As* MR. JOLLY *hands* PRINCE *the next package*): This one is from me, Your Highness—a map of the heavens with all the signs of the zodiac.

PRINCE: How nice! But I'm afraid I'd never understand it.

NURSE (*As* MR. JOLLY *hands* PRINCE *next present*): Some new vitamins, sir, in the form of chocolate sauce.

PRINCE: Thank you, Nurse. I'll have some on my ice cream.

LADY LEARNINGWELL (*As* PRINCE *takes next gift*): An adding machine, Your Highness, pocket-size, so you can catch up on your arithmetic.

PRINCE: Just what I need, Lady Learningwell.

PROFESSOR (*Handing* PRINCE *package*): A new book of music, Your Highness.

PRINCE: Thank you, Professor, but I like to play and sing my old pieces.

LADY LEONA (*Handing package to* PRINCE): A new book, Prince Florio.

PRINCE: Another Barney Blake book!

LADY LEONA: I'm sorry, Your Highness, but there are no more Barney Blake books. You've read them all.

PRINCE: Then Scribble and Scratch must write some more.

LADY LEONA: But they've run out of ideas. After all, two hundred books is a big dose of Barney Blake.

PRINCE: But they know I never read anything else. Father, can't you do something about this?

KING: Indeed, I can, son. I'll have Scribble and Scratch shut up in the tower on bread and water until they produce another Barney Blake book.

PRINCE: Good! (*Opening last present*) Ah! This must be from you, Lord Inchworm.

LORD INCHWORM: It's a magic tape-measure, Your Highness. It measures you any size you want to be.

PRINCE: Thank you, Lord Inchworm, and thank you all for your wonderful presents. And now, Mother, will you please ring for Mrs. Custard? It's time for the refreshments.

QUEEN (*Ringing bell*): Mrs. Custard has prepared a very special cake for you this year. (MRS. CUSTARD *enters, followed by* MUSTARD *and* FLUSTERED, *the maids, who wheel in a tea wagon on which is an enormous cake, decorated with eleven candles. They wheel the cake to center as* GUARDS *remove the empty tea wagon which held the presents.*)

PRINCE: It's a beautiful cake, Mrs. Custard.

MRS. CUSTARD: I hope it's good, Your Highness. Eleven layers, one for each year.

MUSTARD: White dough, yellow dough, chocolate, strawberry, orange.

FLUSTERED: Pineapple, lemon, spice, raisin, angel food, and devil's food!

MRS. CUSTARD: If Your Highness will cut the cake, Mustard and Flustered will serve it to your guests. (*Hands* PRINCE *silver knife, as he descends the steps*)

PRINCE: But first I must blow out the candles.

BILL: Wait! How old are you?

PRINCE: This is my eleventh birthday.

BILL: But there aren't enough candles.

PRINCE (*Pointing*): One, two, three, four, five, six, seven, eight, nine, ten, eleven!

BETTY: But there should be twelve.

PRINCE: I told you I'm only eleven years old.

BETTY *and* BILL (*Dancing up and down in excitement*): That's it! That's it!

KING: That's what? What are you shouting about?

BETTY: That's why the Prince has stopped growing.

BILL: There aren't enough candles.

BETTY: There isn't a candle to grow on.

ALL: What?

BILL: A proper birthday cake must always have a candle to grow on.

PRINCE: Come to think of it, I always did have a candle to grow on until Mrs. Custard came.

QUEEN: Then it's all her fault.

KING: Take her away! To the dungeon with her! (GUARDS *seize* MRS. CUSTARD.)

MRS. CUSTARD (*Breaking away and throwing herself at the foot of the throne*): Mercy! Spare me, O King! I never meant to do any harm. I never heard of a candle to grow on! Nobody ever told me!

ALL (*Rising, shouting and shaking their fists*):
Boil her, stew her, fry her, bake her!
She's the wicked troublemaker!

KING: Silence! Guards, do your duty! And take those two maids with you. They are also to blame.

BILL: Wait a minute, Your Majesty. I think you are making a mistake.

KING: Mistake? What mistake?

BILL: I'm sure Mrs. Custard is telling the truth. She looks like a kindhearted woman who wouldn't hurt a fly. Maybe the Prince didn't have a candle to grow on, but the rest of you are also to blame.

ALL: You mean me?

BILL: I mean all of you, including the Prince himself.

PRINCE: How can you blame me?

BILL: You haven't tried very hard. You don't even stand up straight.

PRINCE: How dare you talk to me like that?

BETTY: It's time somebody told you a thing or two.

BILL: Straighten up! Throw out your chest, pull in that stomach! (*He does so.*)

BETTY: Why, you look taller already.

BILL: And what are you doing with that crown around your neck? It belongs on your head.

PRINCE: But it gives me a headache.

BETTY: You'll have plenty of headaches if you're going to be a king. Put it on!

KING (*As* PRINCE *puts on crown*): He's beginning to look like a king.

BILL: And it's high time he started acting like one. If he's going to be a king, he'll have to grow up.

PRINCE: From now on I'm sure to grow up, if I have the right number of candles on my cake.

BILL: The candle to grow on is important, but don't forget you may be six feet tall and still not be grown up.

BETTY: Growing up is hard work. It takes lots of time and effort and study. You don't even want to try anything new. You want to play the same music, read the same books.

BILL: How can you expect to grow up if you keep on reading those Barney Blake books year in and year out?

BETTY: You need more than a candle to grow on. You need some books to grow on. (*Handing him her book*) Here, try this one.

BILL (*Handing book to* PRINCE): And this.

PRINCE: But they don't have any pictures, and the words are too big. These look like grown-up books.

BILL: Exactly. And you'd better start doing some grown-up reading.

BETTY: You need to exercise your brain as well as your body.

KING: Where did you two learn all this?

BILL: At school.

BETTY: Our teacher says anybody can be ten feet tall if he reads the right books.

QUEEN: Lady Leona, do we have grown-up books in our library?

LADY LEONA: Certainly. We have encyclopedias, dictionaries, books on science, history, government, law, travel, biography, and all types of fiction, but Prince Florio won't even take them off the shelves. He just wants Barney Blake.

KING: Blast Barney Blake! I never want to hear that name again. And from now on, every one of us must do all we can to help Prince Florio grow up.

QUEEN: Dear me! Then he won't be a baby any more.

KING: That's right, my dear. I guess you and I are as much to blame as Mrs. Custard. Guards, you may release your prisoner.

MRS. CUSTARD: Oh, thank you, thank you, sire. Mustard and Flustered will bring the candle to grow on at once. (*Maids exit.*)

1ST CHILD: Is the spell broken, Your Majesty?

2ND CHILD: May we go home now?

KING: I am not so sure there was a spell in the first place, but if there was one, our American visitors have broken it.

ALPHONSO: My prophecy has come true.

GODMOTHER: I told you they were highly intelligent, sire.

3RD CHILD: When may we go home, Your Majesty?

KING: As soon as we've had the cake and ice cream.

PRINCE: Here comes my candle to grow on. (MUSTARD *and* FLUSTERED *re-enter and place twelfth candle in center of cake.*) Now I can make my birthday wish. (*He shuts his eyes tightly and recites.*)

> I wish I may,
> I wish I might . . .
> I wish to reach
> A proper height.
> But tall or short
> Or short or tall,
> I wish for wisdom
> Most of all.

(*He stands up very straight, throws back his shoulders, and walks to cake, as all crowd around. He blows out the candles.*)

KING: He looks taller already!

ALL (*Ad lib*): Hooray! He looks taller already! Long live Prince Florio! (*Etc.*) (*All cheer as curtains close.*)

THE END

Shirley Holmes and the FBI

Characters

SHIRLEY HOLMES	ALF
DONNA	ADAM
KATE	BABY FACE BOYD
JEN	CURLY SMITH
CANDY	OFFICER HIGGINS
JERRY MASON	OFFICER RYAN
BRUCE	VOICE FROM RADIO
LARRY	

SETTING: *An abandoned garage-workshop.*
AT RISE: *The stage is dark. Then,* BABY FACE BOYD *and* CURLY SMITH *play their flashlights around the walls.*

BABY FACE: It must be here someplace, Curly.

CURLY (*Sarcastically*): Oh, sure! All we have to do is find it.

BABY FACE: That shouldn't be too hard with Gentleman Joe's directions.

CURLY: Oh, come off it, Baby Face! I'll bet the cops have gone over every inch of this place.

BABY FACE: You're forgetting that Gentleman Joe was a pretty smooth operator. He made sure there were no clues to connect this hideaway with the great Fairview

19

holdup. Remember, he was five miles outside of town when they caught him. Now let's get moving before they send out a general alarm on our escape.

CURLY: It's so dark in here. There must be a light switch somewhere. (*He gropes along walls and door frame for switch.*)

BABY FACE: What do you expect in a garage with no windows? Besides, there wouldn't be any lights here.

CURLY (*As he flips switch and lights go on*): Who says there's no juice in this place?

BABY FACE: That's funny. I never expected electricity! But come on, let's have a look at Gentleman Joe's instructions. (*They turn off flashlights and put them in their pockets. Both are wearing half masks.*)

CURLY (*Spreading a paper out on workbench*): Here it is, but it's Greek to me. Why couldn't he have told you straight out where he hid the money?

BABY FACE: He never expected us to escape and go looking for it. Besides, Gentleman Joe liked to think he was smarter than the rest of us. He never figured I could dope out his secret code. (*Reading*) Um-m-m—"Four CS . . . One CM . . . One LB."

CURLY: What does CS stand for?

BABY FACE: Take a look at these walls, Curly. What do you see?

CURLY: Cinder blocks. Now I get it. C stands for *cinder* or maybe *cement*. But what about S?

BABY FACE: S is for *slabs* or *stones*. If we're right, "Four CS" means *four cement slabs*. Start counting, Curly.

CURLY: But where do we start? From the right? From the left? From the bottom? Or from the top?

BABY FACE: We'll try them all. (*Consulting paper*) "Four CS"—*four cement slabs*. "One CM" . . . Aha! *One cement moves!* In other words, we count four of these cement blocks, and the next one moves. That must be where he hid the money!

CURLY: What about the next letters—LB? What does LB mean?

BABY FACE: *Lift block,* stupid! Now start counting. I'll take this side. You take the other.

CURLY: But what if somebody comes? We're unarmed.

BABY FACE: And we're going to stay that way so nobody gets hurt. Besides, who would come poking around an abandoned garage on a vacant lot?

SHIRLEY *(Offstage)*: Hurry and open the door! What's the matter? Won't the key work?

CANDY *(Offstage)*: Hold your horses!

BABY FACE: Hey, someone's coming. We have to get out of here.

CURLY: Too late. Duck! *(They crouch.)*

CANDY *(As door swings open)*: There, that does it. *(She starts to enter and suddenly sees* BABY FACE *and* CURLY, *and drops pail she is carrying.)* Help! Help! Robbers!

SHIRLEY *(Pushing past* CANDY, *she enters carrying mop and pail; impatiently)*: Oh, for goodness' sake! Be quiet, Candy! *(*JEN, DONNA *and* KATE *follow* SHIRLEY *into garage carrying mops, pails, and boxes.* JEN *holds folder of papers.* SHIRLEY *sees* BABY FACE *and* CURLY *and speaks to them scoffingly.)* Robbers, indeed! I must say you two have a lot of nerve. Maybe you can fool Candy and the others with those masks, but not me. I'd know you anywhere.

CURLY *(Getting up and moving toward door)*: Let's beat it! The kid is wise to us.

SHIRLEY: You bet I'm wise to you, so don't bother to put on any cheap gangster act! I never thought Jerry Mason would stoop to sending his big brother and his buddy to spy on us! No wonder you're wearing masks, you big bullies! You should be ashamed to show your faces.

BABY FACE: Now wait a minute, little girl!

SHIRLEY: What do you say, girls? Now that we have these two big, brawny high school boys in our midst, let's put them to work.

BABY FACE (*Outraged*): High school boys!

JEN: A good idea, Shirley. They can help us clean up this place. (JEN *puts folder of papers on the workbench. The other girls put down boxes and push pails and mops toward* BABY FACE *and* CURLY.)

CANDY: They really had me fooled for a minute.

DONNA: I was scared, too, Candy. What's the big idea of the masks?

SHIRLEY: Part of the big plan to scare us off! Jerry and his Super-Sleuths are determined to have this old garage for their meeting place, but the FBI got here first.

CURLY (*Alarmed*): The FBI?

KATE: Female Bureau of Investigators!

SHIRLEY: As if they didn't know! Well, don't just stand there! (*Pointing*) Stack those boxes along the wall, (*Prodding gangsters with mop*) and hurry up!

CURLY (*To* BABY FACE): Boy, this is a switch!

JEN: I honestly don't see how you recognized them, Shirley.

SHIRLEY: Elementary, my dear Watson! Elementary!

JEN: Oh, don't be so smart! And stop calling me *Watson!* Just because your name is Shirley Holmes, you don't have to talk like *Sherlock* Holmes. My name is Jen.

SHIRLEY: But your last name *is* Watson, and you *are* my first assistant detective, and . . .

CURLY: Detective! What is she talking about?

BABY FACE: Easy, boy! It's just some game they're playing.

DONNA: Is that so?

CANDY: I'll have you know we're real, honest-to-goodness investigators with half a dozen mysteries to our credit.

DONNA: And our business is growing. That's why we need this garage for our headquarters.

SHIRLEY: And we're going to have it, too. In spite of Jerry Mason and his Super-Sleuths. (*Offstage howl of sirens is heard through next few lines.*)

BABY FACE: What's that?

CURLY: Police sirens! Run for your life!

BABY FACE: Pardon our hasty departure, ladies, but for once my partner is right. We have urgent business elsewhere. (*CURLY and BABY FACE dash out and slam door shut.*)

DONNA: Well, what was that all about?

KATE: I don't know, but there goes our extra help.

CANDY: Something tells me, Kate, that we're just as well off without that pair.

JEN: You're right, Candy. Even Shirley can't explain how she recognized them.

SHIRLEY: I have my methods, but if we stand here talking all day, we'll never get this place straightened up. (*Offstage knocking in rhythmic pattern is heard.*)

DONNA: Do you think they've come back?

SHIRLEY: Open the door and see. (*As DONNA opens door, JERRY steps in waving a white flag on a stick.*)

DONNA: Jerry Mason, you get out of here and stay out.

JERRY: Have a heart, Donna! Look! We come under a flag of truce.

KATE: Do you have the rest of your outfit?

JERRY: Sure thing! Didn't you hear our bicycle sirens? (*Over his shoulder*) Super-Sleuths, advance and report. (ALF, LARRY, BRUCE and ADAM *enter.*)

ALF: Alf Lyman reporting, sir.

LARRY: Larry Briggs reporting, sir.

BRUCE: Bruce Harmon reporting, sir.

ADAM: Adam Powers reporting, sir.

JERRY: All present and accounted for! Now what can we do to help?

DONNA: Help?

JERRY: Sure, that's why we came. We thought we could lend a hand.

SHIRLEY: A likely story!

JEN: After that mean trick you just played on us?

ALF: Trick? What trick?

LARRY: We haven't been near this place all day.

CANDY: Oh, don't act so innocent!

KATE: You ought to be ashamed of yourselves.

SHIRLEY: Sending Jerry's big brother and his buddy to scare us away from here.

JERRY: What is all this? My brother is away on a basketball trip and so are most of his buddies.

DONNA (*Sarcastically*): Then I guess we only imagined we saw two big boys in here with masks tied over their faces.

BRUCE (*To* JERRY): They must mean those two guys who almost knocked me over just now, when we were parking our bikes in the alley.

JERRY: But they were no friends of ours.

ADAM: We never saw them before.

SHIRLEY: Are you telling the truth?

LARRY: We sure are!

SHIRLEY: But I could have sworn I recognized them. I could see their high school letters on their shirts, showing through their sweaters—SPHS!

CANDY: Maybe they weren't high school boys. Maybe they were robbers after all.

JERRY: Did they take anything?

ALF: Is anything missing?

DONNA: Let's take a look. (*All scatter to look in various places.*)

SHIRLEY: There is so much junk in here, we would hardly know if anything is missing or not.

ALF (*Looking in box*): This is full of pots and pans and groceries.

JEN: That's mine. I was going to make some fudge.

BRUCE: Fudge!

JERRY: I thought this was to be a business office, official headquarters for your silly FBI meetings.

CANDY: They are not silly!

KATE: And there's no law against making fudge.

DONNA: We wanted to try out the electric hot plate.

SHIRLEY: Businessmen are always taking coffee breaks, so we decided on a fudge break.

BRUCE: I'm all for it!

ADAM: Me, too. Let's stick around!

ALF (*Picking up box*): I'll put this up on the bench for you. (JERRY *picks up folder of papers and robbers' instruction sheet from workbench.*)

JERRY (*As he looks at paper left by robbers*): Wait a minute. What's this? (ALF *sets box down on workbench and looks at paper in* JERRY's *hand.*)

ALF: Um-m. Looks like some sort of code.

JERRY: Right! (*Reading*) "Four CS, One CM, One LB, One CC, Two SQCB."

JEN (*Snatching paper away from him*): Secret code, poppycock! That's my fudge recipe!

JERRY: Fudge recipe!

JEN: It's a new one Mother found in a magazine. She typed it for me this morning. I guess it fell out of my folder.

ALF: You could have fooled me. I thought it was a cryptogram.

JEN: That's how much you boys know about cooking! CS is cups of sugar, CM is a cup of milk and LB is a lump of butter.

KATE (*Scanning paper*): I guess CC is a cup of cocoa.

DONNA: Two SQCB. That must be two squares of chocolate, but what's the *B*?

CANDY: *B* for *Bitter*. Even I know you always use bitter chocolate for fudge.

BRUCE: All this is making me hungry. Why don't you go ahead and make the fudge while we pitch in on the clean-up job?

JEN: O.K. I only hope this hot plate is in working order. (*Pretends to turn it on*) It seems all right.

CANDY (*Joining her*): Let me help you, Jen. (*Girls start to make fudge.*)

ALF: If this radio is working, we can have some music while we work. (*Fiddles with radio; static is heard.*)

SHIRLEY: I still don't understand this great burst of generosity.

KATE: Neither do I, not when you were so determined to have this place for your Super-Sleuths meetings.

BRUCE: There's an old saying: "When you can't lick 'em, join 'em!"

SHIRLEY: Nothing doing! The FBI is strictly female, and it's going to stay that way.

JERRY: Oh, come now, Shirley, you know the best detectives in the business are men.

DONNA: Is that so? How about the Mystery of the Missing Notebook, and the Case of the Kidnapped Kitten? We solved those without any help from you.

JERRY: Kid stuff! Now we Super-Sleuths—(VOICE *is heard from radio*)

VOICE: We interrupt this program to bring you a special news bulletin.

ALF: This old radio works pretty well.

VOICE (*Continuing*): Fairview Police have just been alerted to be on the lookout for Baby Face Boyd and Curly Smith, who escaped from the State Prison Hospital Squad early this morning. Prison officials have reason to believe the two men may be heading for Fairview in an attempt to recover the money from the great payroll holdup last spring. The missing prisoners are described as short, slight, and extremely youthful in appearance—easily mistaken for teen-agers. A reward of five thousand dollars is offered for their capture or information leading to their arrest.

CANDY: Shirley, those two weren't high school boys—they were the bandits! I know they were. (ALF *turns off radio.*)

JERRY: Some detectives! You and your Female Bureau of Investigators!

ADAM: FBI! Ha, ha! Flea-Brained Idiots would be more like it!

ALF: You had those two guys right here, and you let them get away.

SHIRLEY: How could I have been so stupid! Those letters I saw on their shirts—SPHS—I thought they stood for South Penn High School, not State Prison Hospital Squad!

DONNA: But what were those two bandits doing in this garage?

ADAM: Looking for hidden money. What else?

JERRY: Then it must still be here. Come on. Let's turn this place inside out! (*They all begin to look about frantically, except* JEN, *who continues stirring fudge.*)

ALF: Hey, Larry, give me a hand with these stepladders and this lumber. (*They move ladders and lumber aside and reveal a cupboard.*)

SHIRLEY (*Astonished*): I never knew that old cupboard was there. (JEN *comes forward carrying pan of fudge.*)

JEN (*Shaking her head*): Look at this mess. Something's wrong with this fudge.

JERRY: Never mind the fudge now—not at a time like this.

JEN: But look at it—I can hardly stir it. I don't understand what happened to it.

CANDY: You must have made a mistake in the recipe. (*She*

walks over to bench and begins to leaf through papers in folder.)

JEN: I put in everything the recipe called for.

SHIRLEY: The recipe. Where is it, Jen?

JEN: Right there next to the hot plate. What are you all excited about?

SHIRLEY (*Picking up recipe excitedly and scanning it quickly*): Jen, you've solved the mystery!

JEN: I've done *what?*

SHIRLEY: Your fudge has solved the mystery. Jerry was right. This *is* a secret code. Oh, why didn't I notice this before?

LARRY: Notice what?

SHIRLEY: The proportions are all wrong. No wonder the fudge is too thick! Just one cup of milk would never dissolve four cups of sugar! And why would you use cocoa and bitter chocolate in the same recipe?

JEN: Then it's not the right recipe.

CANDY (*Excitedly, as she pulls piece of paper from folder and begins waving it around*): That's not a recipe at all. Look, Jen. I just found this in your folder. It's labeled "Recipe for Chocolate Fudge."

JEN: Don't tell me I tried to make fudge from a secret code!

BRUCE: If we can crack that code, we'll find the money.

DONNA: If this paper is really the clue to the hidden money, those men will come back.

KATE: I'm scared! Let's get out of here.

JERRY: You're right, Kate. This is a man's job. You girls go home, and let the Super-Sleuths take over.

SHIRLEY: Not on your life! Kate, you run to the nearest phone and call the police. Donna, you go down to the corner and try to find Officer Higgins. I'll lock the door after you. (DONNA *and* KATE *leave.*)

JERRY: If we can only figure out this crazy code. (*Reading*)

"Four CS"—those letters must stand for something right here in this garage.

BRUCE: C! C! What begins with the letter C? Ceiling . . . cement . . . counter . . .

SHIRLEY: Cupboard! *Cupboard* starts with a C! Quick, let's look!

ALF: But it says "Four CS." There's only one cupboard.

SHIRLEY: But maybe it has four shelves.

JERRY: That's it! "Four CS"! Fourth cupboard shelf!

LARRY (*Climbing on packing box*): Let me look!

JEN: Do you see anything?

LARRY: A lot of cobwebs. Wait a minute. There's something shoved back here. (*Takes down a bag, and hands it to* BRUCE.) Don't drop it. It's heavy.

BRUCE: It's made of some heavy material.

ADAM: Probably canvas.

SHIRLEY: Of course! It all fits. CM—*canvas mailbag.*

BRUCE (*Opening bag*): Wow! It's stuffed full of money!

ALL (*Ad lib*): We've found it! The holdup money! It's here! (*Etc.*)

LARRY (*Still groping on shelves*): Here's a big flat book of some kind. (*Hands book to* JEN)

JEN (*As she takes it from him*): It's a ledger book. That must be what LB stands for. (*She opens ledger.*) Look! More money hidden between the pages!

BRUCE (*To* LARRY): Anything else up there?

LARRY (*As he gropes in cupboard*): I think so. Yes, here's a can. (*Hands it to* CANDY)

CANDY: It's a coffee can. There's the CC we thought was a cup of cocoa! (*Opens can and looks inside*) Here's more money!

LARRY: I guess that's all. (*Makes final sweep of shelves with his hand*) No, wait a minute. Here are two boxes. (*Takes them down and hands them to* ALF)

ALF: Cigar boxes.

JEN: Two squares of chocolate—bitter turn out to be two square cigar boxes. (*There is a sound of rattling at door.*)

ADAM: Sh-h! Someone's at the door.

CANDY: Maybe the girls are back with the police.

SHIRLEY: No. They would have given us the signal.

CURLY (*Calling from offstage*): Open up in there.

JERRY: You girls take cover. (*There is a loud banging on the door.*)

BABY FACE (*Calling from offstage, angrily*): Open up, I say, and be quick about it!

CANDY (*As banging continues*): They may break down the door.

SHIRLEY (*Seizing canoe paddle from table*): Then let's get ready for them! Jen, you take the baseball bat. Candy, you get that tennis racket.

CURLY (*Calling from offstage*): This is a countdown! Ten seconds, and we're coming in!

BRUCE: They mean business!

JERRY: Quick. Set up those ladders at either side of the door. (ALF *and* ADAM *set up ladders as* CURLY *begins a slow countdown from offstage.*) I think we're about to make the catch of the season.

ALF: What are you going to do?

JERRY (*Tossing volleyball net to* ALF): You and Adam get up on the ladders, stretch this net across the doorway and drop it over their heads as they come through the door. (ALF *takes net from* JERRY, *hands one end to* ADAM. *They mount ladders and stretch net across doorway.* BRUCE *and* LARRY *each grab a mop, as girls line up at either side with their "weapons."*)

SHIRLEY: We're ready for them now, Jerry.

JERRY (*Looking over group*): All set? (*Pause*) Here we go! (JERRY *opens door, and* BABY FACE *and* CURLY *plunge through doorway.* ALF *and* ADAM *drop volleyball net over them, and both robbers become entangled in it. The others rush at them, bringing them to floor; as they struggle to free themselves, they become completely trapped.*)

BABY FACE *and* CURLY: Help! Help! (JERRY *sits astride* CURLY, *and* BRUCE *sits on* BABY FACE.)

JERRY: Had enough?

CURLY *and* BABY FACE (*Ad lib*): Yes! Let us up! Get off my back! (*Etc.*)

KATE (*As she enters, followed by* DONNA, OFFICER HIGGINS *and* OFFICER RYAN): I hope we're in time.

HIGGINS: What in the world is all this about?

RYAN: What's going on here, anyway?

DONNA (*Suddenly seeing* BABY FACE *and* CURLY *trapped in net*): There they are—the men I told you about! They're the prisoners you're looking for! (JERRY *and* BRUCE *get up, and* BABY FACE *and* CURLY *sit up, still covered with net.*)

HIGGINS (*Bending over prisoners and examining them closely*): They answer the description all right.

JERRY (*Pointing to table*): And you'll find the missing money right there, too. (BABY FACE *and* CURLY *finally free themselves from net and stand up.*)

BABY FACE: They found the money! They broke Gentleman Joe's code!

CURLY: How did you kids ever figure out that "Four CS" meant *four cement slabs?*

SHIRLEY: It didn't. It stood for *fourth cupboard shelf,* and that's where we found all the money.

BABY FACE: It beats me. The cupboard wasn't even here when we were looking.

RYAN: I wish you kids would fill us in on this code business. I have to put it all in my report.

DONNA: Well, we surprised these two holdup men here in the garage, but mistook them for high school boys playing a joke.

SHIRLEY: They ran off when they heard the sirens and left a piece of paper here with what turned out to be a code that led us to the money.

ALF: I turned on the radio and we heard the special news bulletin about the escape of these two characters.

JERRY: And Shirley broke the code and led us to the loot . . . with the help of her Female Bureau of Investigators.

SHIRLEY: But it was you and your Super-Sleuths who figured out how to trap Baby Face and Curly in the volleyball net.

HIGGINS: I must say *that* was a new idea to me.

JERRY: Not very new, Officer! Have you ever seen pictures of Roman gladiators trapping their enemies in nets?

HIGGINS: Now that you mention it, I did see something like that in a movie last week. But just the same, you can take credit for making it work on a modern problem . . . (*As he takes prisoners' arms*) and these two certainly are "modern problems"!

RYAN (*As he starts to stack money into carton*): And this is the money from the payroll robbery all right. You kids deserve a lot of credit.

HIGGINS (*Starting toward door with* CURLY *and* BABY FACE): Come on, Ryan. We have to get this pair down to Headquarters. (*Turning to* JERRY *and* SHIRLEY) And we'll want some of you to come down later and tell the whole story to the Chief.

RYAN: And there's the matter of the reward, you know. (*He picks up carton and walks over to prisoners and takes one by the arm.*)

ALL: Reward! We forgot all about it!

HIGGINS: Sure thing—five thousand dollars—and you boys and girls have certainly earned it.

RYAN: Let's go, Higgins. (*To* BABY FACE *and* CURLY) Come on, you two. March! (HIGGINS *and* RYAN *lead prisoners to door.*)

BABY FACE (*As he goes off*): Trapped by a bunch of kids! (*Exits*)

CURLY (*Following*): And they made everything sound so easy! (*Exits*)

HIGGINS (*Turning at door*): I'll send a squad car for you kids in about twenty minutes. (HIGGINS *and* RYAN *exit.*)

ALF: Wow! If we get all that money, the Super-Sleuths can build a super-duper clubhouse!

KATE: And what about the FBI?

SHIRLEY: I've been thinking about the FBI, Kate. Maybe we should make a few changes. It's pretty nice to have some husky boys around, when you need them.

JERRY: And I've been thinking, too, Shirley. I doubt if the Super-Sleuths could solve a mystery with a pan of fudge.

JEN: Are you talking about a merger?

SHIRLEY: That's what I have in mind.

CANDY: But we'd have to change our name. We couldn't call ourselves the Female Bureau of Investigators if we took in boys.

SHIRLEY: I think I've had about enough of mysteries and investigating. If we get the reward, there's something else we could do.

ALL: What?

SHIRLEY: Well, there are lots of boys and girls in Fairview who have no meeting place for their clubs and societies.

JERRY: I get the idea! Maybe if we talked to the Town Council or the Recreation Department, we could build a clubhouse for the whole town.

SHIRLEY: Jerry, you're a mind reader. How about it, girls?

JEN: I like the idea, Shirley. But I hate to give up our name.

JERRY: It could still be the FBI, you know . . .

SHIRLEY: Only the letters would stand for Fairview Bureau of Improvements.

JEN: Fairview Bureau of Improvements!

LARRY: That sounds great!

JERRY: Let's put it to a vote!

SHIRLEY: All in favor, say "Aye." (*Loud chorus of "Ayes" as the curtain falls.*)

THE END

The Case of the Giggling Goblin

Characters

JUDGE JACK-O'-LANTERN
CAPTAIN CORNSTALK
SERGEANT SCARECROW
GLADYS, *the Giggling Goblin*
MR. GOBLIN. ⎱ *her parents*
MRS. GOBLIN ⎰
MISS WITCH HAZEL, *court stenographer*
THREE WITCH SISTERS
DR. SPOOK
MISS OLGA OGRE
PHANTOM OF THE OPERA
DR. DRACULA
EIGHT HOBGOBLINS
DAMON DEMON, *a reporter*
HARRY HAUNT, *a photographer*
PETE
JOE

SETTING: *Judge Jack-o'-Lantern's underground courtroom in the abandoned Bloody Bones Mine. The Judge's high desk is on a raised platform up center. To the right of the desk is the prisoner's box, and to the left is the witness stand. A long table with chairs is placed diagonally*

at right, and chairs are arranged in diagonal rows at left.
At Rise: Judge Jack-o'-Lantern, *wearing spectacles,*
orange robe, and orange wig, is sitting at his desk. Captain Cornstalk *stands to his right and* Sergeant Scarecrow *stands to his left.* Gladys, Mr. *and* Mrs. Goblin
and Miss Witch Hazel *are seated at the table.* Dr.
Spook, Miss Ogre, Three Witch Sisters, Phantom of
the Opera, Dr. Dracula, *and* Eight Hobgoblins *are*
sitting in chairs at left. Judge *raps three times with his*
gavel.

Judge: This court is now in session! Since this is not a
formal trial, but an informal hearing on the case of the
Giggling Goblin, we will dispense with formalities. We
have asked Mr. and Mrs. Gorgon Goblin to appear be-
fore us this morning with their daughter Gladys, whose
constant and unmannerly giggling has branded her a
public nuisance to the citizens of Hauntsville. Are the
Goblins present?
Goblins (*Rising*): We are here, your Honor. (*They sit.*)
Judge: Very well then, we will proceed.
Miss Witch Hazel (*Waving her notebook*): Excuse me,
Judge Jack-o'-Lantern . . .
Judge: Yes, what is it, Miss Witch Hazel?
Witch Hazel: Forgive me for interrupting, but you don't
have your extra heads.
Judge: How very careless of us. Captain Cornstalk, Sergeant Scarecrow, our extra heads, if you please. (Cornstalk *exits right and* Scarecrow *exits left.*) Since two
heads are always better than one, we make it our policy
to bring our full powers to bear on every case. (Cornstalk *and* Scarecrow *re-enter, each bearing a jack-o'-*
lantern on a tray—one jack-o'-lantern is grinning, the
other frowning.) Captain Scarecrow, our smiling face, if
you please! (Scarecrow *offers grinning jack-o'-lantern,*

which JUDGE *places on one side of his desk.*) This represents our naturally friendly and jovial self. And now the other. (*Places frowning face on other side of desk*) This represents our more serious and judicial nature. (CORNSTALK *and* SCARECROW *return to their places.*) We will now ask the accused to approach the bench.

MR. GOBLIN (*Nudging* GLADYS): He means *you!*

GLADYS (*Rising*): But where's the bench? (*Giggling*) I don't see any bench.

JUDGE (*With a bang of gavel*): The prisoner will approach the bar!

GLADYS (*Giggling louder*): There isn't any bar either. Why is he talking about a bench and a bar?

JUDGE (*As spectators laugh mildly*): Order in the court! (*To* GLADYS) We mean you are to come here (*Indicating prisoner's box*) and sit beside us so we can ask you some questions.

GLADYS (*Giggling*): Why didn't you say so? (*She goes to prisoner's box.*)

JUDGE: Now, don't be nervous, child.

GLADYS: Oh, I'm not nervous, Judge Jack-o'-Lantern.

JUDGE: Good. Now tell me, what is your full name?

GLADYS (*Slowly, with a giggle between each name*): My name is Gladys . . . Glendora . . . Gwendolyn . . . Guinevere . . . Goblin! (*Tries to stifle giggles*) I'm sorry, your Honor, but I have to giggle every time I say it.

JUDGE: We must admit it *is* a most unusual name, but nothing to send you into hysterics. (*As she continues to giggle*) May we ask what you are giggling about now?

GLADYS: Oh, dear! *Must* I answer that?

JUDGE (*Firmly*): You must!

GLADYS: Well, sir (*Giggles*), if you really must know, it's . . . it's your wig!

JUDGE (*Clapping his hand to his head*): My what?

GLADYS: Your wig, sir. It's slipped to one side, and, well, it just tickles me!

JUDGE: Miss Goblin, please control yourself. (*Adjusts wig, making it worse*)

GLADYS: Yes, your Honor. Oh, dear! Here I go again! (*Giggles*)

JUDGE: Now what is it?

GLADYS (*Overcome and pointing to him*): Those glasses, your Honor. They keep sliding down your nose.

JUDGE (*Pounding with gavel as audience laughs*): Order in the court!

GLADYS: I'm sorry, your Honor, I really am. But when this tickling starts in the pit of my stomach, it just comes up and up till it gets into my throat and finally comes out in a giggle. It's hard to explain, but I'm sure you know what I mean. Don't you ever get tickled, your Honor?

JUDGE: That question has no bearing on the case. As Judge of the Court of Common Pleas . . .

GLADYS (*Shrieking with laughter*): Oh, that's the funniest thing I've ever heard! The Court of Common *Fleas!*

JUDGE: Who said anything about fleas?

GLADYS (*Still laughing*): You did! You said you were Judge of the Court of Common Fleas!

JUDGE: *Pleas!* The Court of Common Pleas! (*As audience laughs*) Order! (*Uses gavel*) We warn you for the first and last time against unseemly laughter in this court. (*As laughter subsides*) Miss Witch Hazel, you will strike all mention of fleas from the record!

WITCH HAZEL: Yes, your Honor.

JUDGE: We will now talk with the parents of this incredible child. Mr. and Mrs. Goblin, fleas . . . I mean, *please!* (CORNSTALK *escorts* MR. *and* MRS. GOBLIN *to the witness stand.* MRS. GOBLIN *sits.* MR. GOBLIN *stands beside her.*) As the parents of the accused, how do you account for her behavior?

MRS. GOBLIN: I'm sure I don't know, your Honor. This tickling she mentioned started when she was just a baby.

MR. GOBLIN: I always said she swallowed a feather when we left her with that Bird-Woman baby-sitter!

MRS. GOBLIN: We've tried everything, your Honor. We've followed Dr. Spook's book on Goblin Guidance, and when that didn't work, we even spanked her.

MR. GOBLIN: But she still giggles in spite of everything!

DR. SPOOK (*Rising*): Outrageous! Judge Jack-o'-Lantern, may I be allowed to speak?

JUDGE: We will be glad to hear your opinion, Dr. Spook.

DR. SPOOK (*Coming forward*): In my judgment, this unfortunate little Goblin suffers from *giggilia nervosa*, or nervous giggles. I recommend that she be allowed to giggle whenever she feels like it.

MISS OGRE (*Rising*): Nonsense!
For giggling there's a time and place;
Untimely giggles bring disgrace.
This Goblin child should hide her face—
It's pure bad manners in her case!

JUDGE: And who are you to interrupt the court in this fashion?

MISS OGRE: My name is Olga Ogre. Giggling Gladys is one of my pupils at the Academy for Sprites and Spirits.

JUDGE (*To* MR. *and* MRS. GOBLIN): If you will step down, Mr. and Mrs. Goblin, we will question Miss Ogre. (MISS OGRE, *carrying a thick book, takes her place on witness stand. The* GOBLINS *and* DR. SPOOK *sit at table.*) I am sure you can tell us how Gladys behaves in school, Miss Ogre.

MISS OGRE: I can tell you she has been sent out of the room three times this week for giggling. Only yesterday . . .

GLADYS: Oh, please, Judge Jack-o'-Lantern, let me tell you about that. Miss Ogre asked Billy Banshee to name three cool drinks made from fruits, and guess what he said!

JUDGE: Hm-m. Lemonade, orangeade and limeade?

GLADYS (*Giggling*): No, sir. He said, "Lemonade, orange-ade and *masquerade!*" I thought I'd die laughing.

MISS OGRE: You see, your Honor? Bad manners. It says right here on page 72 of our textbook, *Manners for Monsters*—(*Opening book*)

For well-bred monsters it's a sin
To laugh, or giggle, or to grin
At others' blunder or mistake;
This is a habit you must break!

JUDGE: Has she broken any other rules in that book?

MISS OGRE: Practically all of them. (*Leafing through book*) Here's one she breaks all the time:

Never laugh at monsters' clothes,
Coats or hats, or shoes or hose.
Never laugh at monsters' faces,
Noses, ears, or lack of graces.
Never giggle—if you do
Someone, someday, may laugh at you!

JUDGE: What proof do you have of this?

WITCH HAZEL: My sisters and I have proof, your Honor.

JUDGE: The Witch Sisters will come to the bench. (WITCH HAZEL *and* THREE WITCH SISTERS *go to center and face audience.*)

WITCH HAZEL: She laughed at my wart.

1ST SISTER: She laughed at my chin.

2ND SISTER: She laughed at my nose.

3RD SISTER: And my toothless grin.

WITCH HAZEL: And that's not all!

WITCHES:

She watched as we danced in the dark of the moon,
And her laughter rang out like the cry of a loon.

GLADYS: But you should see them dance, your Honor. They're hysterical!

JUDGE: There will be no dancing in the courtroom.

DR. SPOOK: How can you judge without evidence, your Honor?

JUDGE: Hm-m. Well spoken, Dr. Spook. I will consult with my advisers. (*Pantomimes conversation with jack-o'-lanterns*) We have agreed your point is well taken. We will admit the Witches' dance as evidence. Sergeant Scarecrow will attend to the music. (SCARECROW *exits.* WITCHES *take traditional ballet poses and when recorded music starts, perform an exaggerated and comic ballet routine. Witnesses suppress giggles and* JUDGE *tries not to laugh at conclusion*) Your efforts are appreciated, ladies, and I will weigh this evidence most carefully. You may be seated. (*They return to places.* SCARECROW *re-enters.*) Miss Witch Hazel, do we have any other plaintiffs present?

WITCH HAZEL (*Consulting her notes*): The Phantom of the Opera has signed a complaint, your Honor.

JUDGE: In that case, we will excuse Miss Ogre and call the Phantom to the stand. (MISS OGRE *takes her place as* PHANTOM OF THE OPERA *takes the stand.*) Now, sir, what charges do you prefer in this case?

PHANTOM: More giggling. She has dared to laugh at *me,* the toast of Paris, London and Vienna.

JUDGE: Since we have admitted the Witches' dance as evidence, will you oblige us with a sample of your art?

PHANTOM: My pleasure, your Honor. (*He bursts into an operatic aria, singing in falsetto with exaggerated gestures. Everyone is convulsed with laughter.* JUDGE *hides his face in his arms.*)

JUDGE (*Removing spectacles and wiping eyes*): A most moving performance, sir. You are excused. Next witness. (PHANTOM *returns to his seat.*)

WITCH HAZEL: There are no more witnesses, your Honor,

but the court physician wishes to make a statement.

JUDGE: Excellent. Will Dr. Dracula please come forward?

DR. DRACULA (*Going to stand; carrying black bag*): I have reason to believe, your Honor, that the case of the Giggling Goblin can be cured.

JUDGE: Explain your theory, Doctor.

DR. DRACULA: It's very simple. Remove the giggle and the cure will follow.

GLADYS: No! My giggle is part of me!

JUDGE: Quiet, child. Proceed, Dr. Dracula.

DR. DRACULA (*Producing folding cardboard skeleton from bag*): If Captain Cornstalk will assist me, I will demonstrate. (CORNSTALK *holds up skeleton by string and* DR. DRACULA *uses a pointer as he speaks*) Now the patient says . . .

GLADYS (*Shouting*): I am *not* his patient!

DR. DRACULA: Very well. The *Goblin* says the tickling starts here (*Points to midriff*) and proceeds upward through the lungs and laugh canal until it reaches the oral cavity where it explodes into a giggle. Obviously, if we remove the giggle, and block the laugh canal, her problem will be solved.

GLADYS: But I'd never laugh again. Please, your Honor, I'd rather be shut up in a dungeon than never laugh again.

JUDGE: We agree the treatment seems a bit drastic.

DR. DRACULA: To remove a giggle would make medical history.

JUDGE: No doubt. But it's not medical history we want— it's justice. (DR. DRACULA *replaces his equipment and returns to his place.*) Now if there are no further witnesses or questions, we are ready to pronounce our verdict.

DR. SPOOK (*Standing*): If it please the court, I would like to suggest that we hear from the younger generation. So far we have heard only the testimony of adults.

JUDGE: An excellent suggestion. If there are any hobgoblins present, will they please come forward? (EIGHT HOBGOBLINS *approach the bench*.) Are you hobgoblins in the same class with Gladys in school?

ALL: We are, your Honor.

JUDGE: And do you like to play with her?

ALL (*Loudly*): No!

JUDGE: Why not? (HOBGOBLINS *line up facing audience*.)

1ST HOBGOBLIN: She laughs at me and calls me fat.

2ND HOBGOBLIN: She laughs when I strike out at bat.

3RD HOBGOBLIN: She laughed when teacher scolded me.

4TH HOBGOBLIN: She laughed when I upset my tea.

5TH HOBGOBLIN: She laughs whenever I'm in tears.

6TH HOBGOBLIN: She giggles at my deepest fears.

7TH HOBGOBLIN: She laughed when I fell down the stair.

8TH HOBGOBLIN: She laughs at everything I wear.

ALL:

And when we plan a secret play,

Her giggles give us all away.

DR. SPOOK: I am sadly disappointed. I thought her friends would speak well of her! (HOBGOBLINS *return to their seats*.)

JUDGE: Well, Gladys, what do you have to say for yourself?

GLADYS: Nothing, I guess, only I never really meant to hurt anyone's feelings.

JUDGE: Can you think of any good your giggling has accomplished?

GLADYS: Not exactly, your Honor, but yesterday when I was walking through the woods, I saw two men snooping around the Bloody Bones Mine and I think my giggles scared them away.

JUDGE: What sort of men? What were they doing?

GLADYS: They were just ordinary men, the two-legged kind. They weren't really doing anything, but they were each carrying a bundle of cigars.

JUDGE: Cigars! How extraordinary! No one ever comes near this mine. It's been abandoned for years. That's why it's such a perfect place for our courtroom. Are you sure they were coming here?

GLADYS: Oh, yes, sir. I heard them talking about the Bloody Bones Mine.

JUDGE: What did they say?

GLADYS: Nothing much, except that they bet there was still gold in "them thar hills."

JUDGE: Very interesting, but of no use whatever as your defense. Having heard all the evidence, we will now confer with our advisers on a verdict. (*Consults in pantomime with jack-o'-lanterns, then looks up*) We have reached our decision. (*Removing smiling jack-o'-lantern*) Although our jovial and jolly self appreciates your sense of humor, our more serious judgment prevails. We find the citizens of Hauntsville justified in declaring you a public nuisance. You will rise and face the court. (JUDGE *and* GLADYS *rise.*)
A little laughter now and then
Is relished by the gravest men.
But you must learn the "where and when"
Before you make mistakes again!

GLADYS: I'll try, your Honor, I really will.

JUDGE: We have not finished.
Until improvement can be seen,
Until you wipe your record clean,
And learn what manners really mean,
We banish you from Halloween!

GLADYS (*Weeping*): Oh, no, your Honor. Anything but that. What's the good of being a Goblin if you can't play tricks on Halloween? (*There is a scuffle offstage as* DAMON DEMON *and* HARRY HAUNT, *who has a camera, try to force their way past* CORNSTALK *and* SCARECROW.)

CORNSTALK: Halt, in the name of the law!

SCARECROW: Court is in session. No one is allowed to enter.

DAMON: This is a matter of life and death!

HARRY: Thank goodness we have arrived in time.

JUDGE: What is the meaning of this? Who are you?

DAMON: I am Damon Demon, reporter for the *Hauntsville Happenings*.

HARRY: I am Harry Haunt, news photographer for the same paper.

JUDGE: Out! No reporters or photographers allowed. This hearing is strictly private.

DAMON: You must listen to us, Judge! You must clear this courtroom at once.

HARRY: Two men are on their way here to dynamite the mine.

BOTH: You will be blown to smithereens.

JUDGE: I don't believe it.

GLADYS: It could be true, Judge. Remember the two men I saw with bundles of cigars. Maybe those cigars were sticks of dynamite.

HARRY: Everybody out! (*All scramble to their feet.*) Wait! Listen! (*All stop.*) I think they've already reached the entrance.

DAMON: Hide, everyone. We'll douse the lights. (*Lights go out; all hide behind pieces of furniture. Lights come up slightly, so stage is dimly lit.* PETE, *carrying flashlight, and* JOE, *carrying sticks of* "*dynamite,*" *enter.* PETE *throws beam around stage.*)

PETE (*In a stage whisper*): All clear, Joe. Nothing here but a lot of junk the mining company left behind.

JOE (*Shuddering*): This place gives me the creeps. It wasn't called the Bloody Bones Mine for nothing, you know.

PETE: Take it easy, pal. We'll hightail it out of here as soon as we light the fuse on this dynamite. Remember, if we open up a new vein of gold, we'll be on easy street for life. (*They kneel at center and arrange sticks of dynamite.*)

JOE: Did you ever hear that the mine is haunted?

PETE: Tell that to your grandmother.

JOE: Just the same, Pete, you ran plenty fast yesterday when you heard that weird cackling.

PETE: Maybe I did, but this is no time for the shakes. Here, let me try that fuse.

JOE (*Jumping to his feet and pointing*): I think I saw something move over there!

PETE: Quit being so nervous. (*A long, loud, piercing laugh is heard.* PETE *jumps up.*)

JOE (*Shaking*): What was that?

PETE (*Starting to exit*): I'm not waiting to find out.

JOE: But the fuse isn't lit.

PETE: You light it. I'm getting out of here. (*Second peal of laughter is heard, as* PETE *runs out.*)

JOE: Hey! Wait for me! (*Exits running. Lights come up.* DAMON *stands up.*)

DAMON: Where is everybody?

JUDGE: Right here. (*Crawls up from behind desk*)

DAMON: Come out, come out, wherever you are. The coast is clear! (*All cautiously emerge from hiding.*)

HARRY: That was a close call, Judge.

DAMON: What a story this will make! And for once, we have all the facts.

JUDGE: Not quite all the facts, my friend. There is one question that demands an answer. Who let out that terrible giggle? (*Silence*) Who dared laugh in the face of such danger? Gladys, was it you?

GLADYS: Yes, sir, it was.

JUDGE: But why? Why should you laugh at such a time?

GLADYS: Because I was scared silly, and when I feel silly, I giggle!

JUDGE (*To* DAMON *and* HARRY): Now there's your real story, boys! "Giggling Goblin Saves Bloody Bones Mine!" Gladys, you are the Halloween heroine of all time!

DAMON: I'll see that you are written up in *Who's Who at Halloween*.

HARRY: Your picture will be in all the papers!

GLADYS: But Judge Jack-o'-Lantern has just banished me from Halloween.

JUDGE: In view of the circumstances, we may reverse our decision. That is, if the plaintiffs wish to withdraw their charges? What say you, citizens of Hauntsville?

ALL: Withdraw!

JUDGE: Since all charges against you are withdrawn, the Case of the Giggling Goblin is dismissed!

ALL: Hurrah!

JUDGE: Well, Gladys, how do you feel?

GLADYS: I don't know, sir. It's funny, but now that I am innocent I feel guiltier than before. I—I just can't forget how I have insulted my friends and neighbors. Truly I never meant to hurt anyone's feelings.

DR. SPOOK: Now, now, Gladys. Don't let's have a guilt complex! (MR. *and* MRS. GOBLIN *go to* GLADYS.)

MRS. GOBLIN: Come along, dear.

MR. GOBLIN: We'll take you home and you can forget the whole thing.

GLADYS: But I don't want to forget. I want to remember when to laugh and when *not* to laugh. I don't want to be called the *Giggling Goblin* any more. I think I'll change my name to *Gloomy Gladys*.

JUDGE: We don't want you to be gloomy, my dear. You should be grateful for your sense of humor.

GLADYS: That's it, Judge Jack-o'-Lantern! That's my new name! From now on I'll be the *Grateful Goblin*. Grateful to you for your kindness, grateful to my parents for putting up with me, and grateful to my friends for giving me another chance. (*Putting her hand to her mouth*) Oh, dear! There's that tickling again!

MRS. GOBLIN: What's the matter now?

GLADYS: Nothing, Mother, except I'm suddenly so happy, I'm even grateful for my giggle!

JUDGE (*Striking three times with gavel*):
The Court of Hauntsville's now adjourned,
And many lessons have been learned.
We will not point them out to you,
Because you have observed them, too.
So now before we say "ta-ta,"
Please join me in one big *Ha! Ha!*
(*All laugh long and loud as the curtains close.*)

THE END

Simple Simon's Reward

Characters

SIMPLE SIMON	JACK
PATTY PASTRY	DICK
PIEMAN, *her father*	LADY
COUNTESS OF CLOROX	GENTLEMAN
LORD AJAX	WOMAN
HERALD	TWO CHILDREN
BOB	THREE GIRLS
FRED	

SETTING: *The road to the Fairground. An open booth is at center, with many pies on the counter, and a sign reading* PIES FOR SALE. *Several tables with chairs and benches are left and right of the booth.*

AT RISE: PATTY PASTRY *is sitting in the booth, waving a flyswatter over the pies.*

PATTY (*Singing*):
Shoo fly, don't bother me,
Shoo fly, don't bother me,
Shoo fly, don't bother me,
For I belong to somebody!

SIMON (*Entering left*): Hello, Patty, how's business?

PATTY: Terrible, Simon! Simply terrible! I haven't made a sale all morning.

SIMON: With so many people going to the Fair, you'd think some would stop for a bite to eat.

PATTY: I guess they're saving their money for the Fair, but by the time they come home, their pockets will be empty.

SIMON (*Looking at pies on counter and sniffing*): Um-m-m! They look delicious!

PATTY: Want one?

SIMON: Not till I've earned some money. I don't have a cent.

PATTY: That doesn't matter. What will you have—apple or cherry?

SIMON: Neither one, Patty, thanks just the same. Your father wouldn't like it.

PATTY: Oh, he wouldn't care, and besides, he's not here. He went back to the bakery for more pies. He seems to think we'll do a big business today. (PIEMAN *enters left, pushing a cart loaded with pies*)

PIEMAN (*Calling*): Pies for sale! Fresh pies for sale! A penny a pie! Pies for sale! (WOMAN *enters left with* TWO CHILDREN)

1ST CHILD: Look, Mom, look! Pies for sale!

2ND CHILD: Yum! They smell so good!

1ST CHILD: Let's get some! I'm hungry!

WOMAN: You can't be hungry. You just had your breakfast.

2ND CHILD: But they're only a penny apiece.

1ST CHILD: I have a penny, Mother.

WOMAN: Then save it. You'll be wanting a ride on the merry-go-round and goodness knows what else! Now come along. (WOMAN *hustles* CHILDREN *off right.*)

PIEMAN (*Shrugging his shoulders*): That's the way it goes.

SIMON: Better luck next time, Mr. Pastry.

PIEMAN: Oh, hello, Simon. Want a free sample?

SIMON: No, thank you, sir. I'm on my way to the Fair to try to earn some money. But when I come back, I'm going to buy a stack so high! (*Indicating*) Be sure to save some for me.

PIEMAN (*Looking at booth*): At the rate we're going now, there will be plenty left.

PATTY: Don't be discouraged, Father. (BOB, DICK, FRED, *and* JACK *enter left*) Here are some more customers.

SIMON (*Fearfully*): I don't want those boys to see me here. (*Hides behind booth*)

BOB: Hurry up, can't you? We don't want to miss anything!

DICK: What's the rush? Getting there is half the fun! Hello, Patty! Good morning, Mr. Pastry.

PATTY: Hello, boys. How about a nice, fresh, juicy pie?

PIEMAN (*Hopefully*): Only a penny!

FRED: That's cheap enough! (*Reaching into pocket*) I'll take a raspberry tart.

BOB (*Impatiently*): Not now! There isn't time. Come on!

PIEMAN: Prices will be much higher inside the Fairground.

JACK: Maybe so, but we're in a hurry. (*Tugging at* FRED's *sleeve*) Come on.

FRED: Sorry, Patty. How about coming with us to the Fair?

PATTY: Thanks, but I must stay here and help my father. (SIMON *steps out from behind booth*)

SIMON: I'll tend the stand for you, Patty, if you really want to go.

BOYS: Well! If it isn't Simple Simon!

SIMON (*Furiously*): Don't you dare call me that! Don't you dare!

BOYS (*Laughing and chanting mockingly*):
Simple Simon met a pieman going to the Fair.

PATTY: Stop it! Stop it!

BOYS (*Continuing*):
Says Simple Simon to the pieman,

"Let me taste your ware."

PIEMAN: Now, now, boys! That's enough!

JACK: He was too simple to know that pies cost money.

PIEMAN: Simon was only a small boy when that happened.

PATTY: Much too young to understand about money. So stop shouting that silly rhyme.

DICK: But he was old enough to know better last summer, when he went fishing in his mother's pail.

BOYS (*Mockingly*):
Simple Simon went a-fishing for to catch a whale;
All the water he had got was in his mother's pail.

BOB: How simple can you be?

SIMON: It was *not* simple!

FRED: Not simple to go fishing in a pail?

SIMON: I wasn't fishing! I was conducting an experiment.

JACK (*Laughing*): An experiment!

DICK: What kind of experiment?

SIMON: Oh, what's the use? You wouldn't understand.

JACK: I suppose you were conducting another experiment when you went looking for plums on thistles?

BOB (*Chanting*):
Simple Simon went to look if plums grew on a thistle!

BOYS (*Continuing*):
He pricked his fingers very much, which made poor Simon whistle!

SIMON: I was *not* looking for plums! I was looking for thistle flowers. They're called *plumes,* not plums!

DICK: You'll have to think of a better story than that, Simple Simon.

PIEMAN: Now look here, fellows, fun is fun, but I can't have you tormenting a customer.

BOYS (*Laughing*): Simple Simon, a customer?

PATTY (*Angrily*): Yes, a customer! And one of our very best! (*Handing SIMON a pie*) Here, Simon, here is your pie. I hope you enjoy it.

FRED: Better make him show you his penny.

PIEMAN (*Sternly*): I told you boys once—that's enough—and I mean it! Now clear out of here! Every one of you! Go on! Move!

BOB: We were only teasing, sir.

PIEMAN: Then go tease each other! I'll have no more name-calling around here. Now, off with you!

DICK: Very well, sir, we'll go. But you'll find out for your-self just how simple Simple Simon really is. (*To boys*) Come on, gang! (*Boys exit right*)

SIMON: Thanks for standing up for me, Mr. Pastry. I'd better go, too.

PIEMAN: You're a good lad, Simon. Besides, I don't approve of name-calling. I can still remember how the boys called me pie-face when I was about your age.

PATTY: Don't go, Simon! You haven't eaten your pie.

SIMON (*Returning pie to counter*): Thanks, Patty, but I don't want it unless I can pay for it.

PIEMAN: If you really feel that way about it, why not stay here and work for me?

SIMON: I'd like to, but you don't have any customers, Mr. Pastry.

PATTY (*Looking off left*): Yes, we do. Look! A lady and gentleman are heading this way. (LADY *and* GENTLEMAN *enter left*)

SIMON (*With a bow*): Good morning, ma'am. Good morn-ing, sir. How about a freshly-baked pie to eat at the Fair?

GENTLEMAN: Sorry, boy. Pie doesn't agree with me. Always gives me indigestion.

SIMON: Perhaps the lady . . .

LADY: No, indeed! No pie for me. I'm on a diet! (LADY *and* GENTLEMAN *exit right*)

SIMON: I'm afraid I'm not much of a salesman. (THREE GIRLS *enter left*)

1ST GIRL: Oh, look, girls! Look at those gorgeous pies!

2ND GIRL: What kind do you have, Mr. Pieman?

PIEMAN:
> I've apple and cherry,
> And lemon and berry,
> And custard with cream on the top!

SIMON:
> Your money's not wasted,
> For once you have tasted,
> You'll never be able to stop!

PATTY:
> There's pumpkin and mince pie,
> And peach pie and quince pie,
> And all of 'em baked fresh today!

PIEMAN:
> I've rhubarb and raisin,
> And what is amazin',

ALL THREE:
> There's only a penny to pay!

1ST GIRL: What do you think, girls?

2ND GIRL: Not now. Better wait till we come back.

3RD GIRL (*As they exit right*): We'll try not to spend all our money.

PATTY: This just isn't our lucky day.

SIMON: There must be a way to get these folks to buy.

PIEMAN: You think of something, lad, and I'll make you a partner in the business.

SIMON: I have it! Why don't we move the booth inside the Fairground? That's where people are spending their money.

PATTY: I wish we could, Simon, but we don't have a permit.

SIMON: Then we'll get one!

PIEMAN: That's just the trouble. We can't.

SIMON: Why not?

PATTY: Because of a terrible thing that happened long before I was born. The Pastry family always sold pies at the Fair until the day the old Duchess of Cleanser broke a tooth on a cherry stone in one of our pies. Every year since then, our request for a permit has been denied.

SIMON: The Duchess of Cleanser? She died years ago.

PATTY: Yes, but her granddaughter, the Countess of Clorox, is even worse. She drives us frantic with what she calls her health inspections. If she ever found a speck of dirt in the bakery, I think she'd put us out of business for good.

SIMON: She'll never find any dirt in your bakery. It's the cleanest shop in town.

PIEMAN: We try to keep it clean, but the Countess is never satisfied. This very morning she was poking her nose into the sugar bags and flour sacks. Even lifting the lids of the kettles, and peeking into the ovens.

SIMON: What about Lord Ajax? Doesn't he issue town permits and licenses?

PATTY: The Countess has Lord Ajax under her thumb. Her word is law. (HERALD *enters left, carrying a long staff.*)

HERALD (*Loudly*): Make way for the Countess of Clorox and Lord Ajax! Make way! Make way! Make way for the Countess of Clorox and Lord Ajax!

PIEMAN: Quick, Patty! Put the covers on the pies! (SIMON *helps* PATTY *spread a cloth over pies on counter as* PIEMAN *covers those on cart.* HERALD *moves right as* COUNTESS *and* LORD AJAX, *who has a thick beard, enter left and pause.* LORD AJAX *points to the booth, and whispers to the* COUNTESS. *They walk to the booth.*)

COUNTESS: Ah, I see you have set up your stand as close as possible to the Fairground, Mr. Pastry.

PIEMAN (*Bowing*): We are well within our legal rights, milady.

PATTY: I trust you found everything satisfactory when you visited our bakery this morning, milady.

COUNTESS: Passable! Passable!

LORD AJAX (*Inspecting the booth*): You have done well to protect your pies from dust and dirt.

COUNTESS (*Running her finger along the counter*): But what is this? Something sticky!

SIMON (*Wiping the counter with his handkerchief*): That was my fault, Countess. I must have spilled some cherry juice.

COUNTESS: Indeed! And who are you? What are you doing here?

SIMON: My name is Simon, ma'am.

COUNTESS (*Thoughtfully*): Simon . . . Simon . . . I've heard that name before.

PATTY: Simon is our new helper, Countess.

COUNTESS (*To* SIMON): In that case, let me see your hands. (*Inspecting them*) They appear to be clean enough. Now let me see your nails. (*Inspecting*) Hm-m-m! Lord Ajax, what do you think?

LORD AJAX (*Joining her*): I agree. His hands are quite clean.

SIMON (*Kneeling*): Please, Countess, please, I beg of you to grant me a favor.

COUNTESS: Speak up, lad. What is it?

SIMON: I beg of you to grant Mr. Pastry a permit to sell his pies inside the Fairground.

LORD AJAX (*Angrily*): What kind of simpleton are you to make such a request?

COUNTESS: Simpleton! Now I know where I heard that name before! You must be the Simple Simon I hear the children mocking in the village.

PATTY: But he is *not* simple, milady! Really, he isn't!

COUNTESS: He's worse than simple to ask such a favor. Never, never, never will I forget what happened to my beloved grandmother when she ate one of your dreadful pies!

SIMON: Not dreadful, milady! Delicious! And far better than any of the other pastries to be found at the Fair.

LORD AJAX (*Haughtily*): Silence! How dare you argue with the Countess?

COUNTESS: What impudence! (*Putting her hand to the side of her head*) It gives me a headache to listen to him! (*She screams.*)

LORD AJAX: What is it, my dear? What is it? Do you feel faint?

COUNTESS: My earring! My diamond earring! It's gone!

LORD AJAX: It can't be!

COUNTESS (*Frantically*): I've lost it! It's worth a fortune! (*Shaking her skirt*) Help me look for it.

LORD AJAX (*Searching the ground on hands and knees*): Now, don't upset yourself, my dear. We'll find it. (PATTY *searches the counter.* PIEMAN *walks around, inspecting the ground*)

SIMON: Maybe you weren't wearing both earrings today, Countess.

COUNTESS: *Simple* Simon is a good name for you! I know I was wearing both of them when I left the palace.

PIEMAN: I'm sure you didn't drop it here.

LORD AJAX (*Rising from hands and knees*): We'll retrace our steps, my dear. We will also offer a reward. The more searchers we have, the sooner we'll find it. (*To* HERALD) Herald, proclaim the news of the lost earring, and offer one hundred pounds' reward for its return.

COUNTESS (*Impatiently*): Hurry! Hurry! There's no time to lose! (COUNTESS *and* LORD AJAX *exit left*)

HERALD (*Striding up and down*): Hear ye! Hear ye! The Countess of Clorox offers one hundred pounds' reward for the return of her lost diamond earring! (*Moves off right repeating announcement*)

PIEMAN (*Standing up*): Trouble and more trouble!

SIMON: Maybe not, sir. Maybe this is the stroke of good luck we've been waiting for.

PATTY: We'll never be lucky enough to find that earring. Never!

SIMON: Suppose it should happen to be inside one of your pies.

PATTY *and* PIEMAN: Impossible!

SIMON: Suppose the Countess lost her earring while she was inspecting your bakery this morning.

PIEMAN: But my wife would have noticed. She would have seen it.

SIMON: Not if it fell into the sugar, or the flour, or even into a kettle of custard cooking on the stove.

PIEMAN: Ye gods! That's all we need to ruin us forever! (WOMAN *enters right with* Two CHILDREN)

WOMAN (*To* CHILDREN): You heard what the man said. A hundred pounds' reward for that diamond earring. Now look sharp! Keep your eyes open.

SIMON: Quick, Patty! A pie! (*He bites into the tart she hands him and offers a second tart to the* WOMAN.) Would you care for a pie, ma'am?

WOMAN: This is no time for pie, boy. We're looking for a diamond earring!

SIMON (*Still eating*): So am I, ma'am! So am I.

1ST CHILD (*Laughing*): Isn't that just like Simple Simon?

2ND CHILD (*Mockingly*): Looking for an earring in a pie!

SIMON: Maybe I'm not so simple, after all. It so happens the Countess was inspecting Mr. Pastry's bakery early this morning, so if she lost her earring there . . .

WOMAN: Ridiculous!

PATTY: But if it dropped into a bag of sugar . . . or a sack of flour . . . no one would have noticed.

PIEMAN: We baked all of our pies after she left the shop.

CHILDREN (*Excitedly*): Mother! Mother! The pies! The pies!

WOMAN: What an idea! But it could be possible. (*To* PATTY) Hurry, girl! I'll take six of those pies right away.

PATTY: What kind would you like? We have apple, cherry, custard. . . .

WOMAN (*Hastily*): Any kind. It doesn't matter. (*She takes six tarts from counter, takes coins from her pocket and gives them to* PATTY.) Here you are.

CHILDREN: Let's eat!

PIEMAN: You may sit here and eat (*Indicating tables*), if you wish.

WOMAN (*Sitting at table with* CHILDREN): Now be sure to eat slowly and carefully. Chew every mouthful! (BOB, DICK, FRED and JACK enter right)

BOB: Have you heard the news, Patty?

DICK: The Countess of Clorox is offering a hundred pounds to anyone who finds her diamond earring.

FRED: We're off to look for it!

JACK: Want to come along?

PATTY: No, thank you. (*Biting into a tart*) We're conducting our own search right here.

PIEMAN: The Countess was in our shop this morning, and Simon says . . .

BOB: Don't tell me you'd listen to Simple Simon.

SIMON (*Taking a tart from the cart*): You won't think I'm so simple if you bite into a pie and find the missing earring. After all, the Countess was snooping about in the bakery this morning, just before these pies were baked.

BOB: Hey! That's a great idea, fellows!

PATTY: You'd better hurry before someone else finds the earring. (*Indicating* WOMAN *and* CHILDREN) Those people have already bought six pies.

FRED: We'll take six more! (*He takes tarts from counter.*)

JACK (*Taking more*): Make it twelve! We can easily eat three apiece.

DICK (*Giving coins to* PATTY): I'll pay for them, and you can settle with me later. (*Boys sit at a table as* LADY, GENTLEMAN *and* THREE GIRLS *enter right*)

LADY: I can't go another step! My feet are killing me.

GENTLEMAN: But think of the reward! One hundred pounds!

SIMON: Excuse me, sir, but if you are looking for the lost earring . . .

GENTLEMAN: Don't tell me someone has found it already!

SIMON: Not yet, sir. But all of these folks are buying pies because they think the Countess may have dropped her earring at the bakery this morning. It may have fallen into the flour or the sugar. (*He bites his pie carefully*)

GENTLEMAN: Zounds! What an amazing possibility! Quick! Quick! Let me have six of those pies at once! (PATTY *and* PIEMAN *give him the pies and take money*)

LADY: At last I can sit down! (LADY *and* GENTLEMAN *sit at a table*)

1ST GIRL (*Eagerly*): And I'll take three! Any flavor will do!

2ND GIRL: Give me four . . . all custard! They're easier to eat.

3RD GIRL: Three for me, if you have any left.

PIEMAN (*Giving them pies and taking money*): You've just about cleaned us out. But we still have a few left. (HERALD *enters right, wiping his brow*)

SIMON (*To* HERALD): How about a pie, sir? You must be tired and hungry by now.

PATTY (*Handing* HERALD *a pie*): Do have a pie, sir! You may be the lucky one to find the earring.

HERALD: Earring? How could an earring be in a pie?

SIMON: Let me explain. (*He whispers into* HERALD's *ear as* COUNTESS *and* LORD AJAX *enter left.*)

COUNTESS: Look at that! All those lazy, greedy people, stuffing themselves on pie, when they should be looking for my earring. (*Seeing* HERALD) Even my own servant!

HERALD (*Swallowing hard*): But, milady . . .

LORD AJAX: Eating on duty! I'll deal with you when we get back to the palace.

HERALD: Please, sir, it's my duty to eat, sir. (*Pointing to* SIMON) This lad just whispered to me that the Countess dropped her earring at the bakery and it was baked into a pie.

COUNTESS (*To* SIMON, *indignantly*): How dare you!

SIMON: I swear to you, Countess, I merely suggested that such a thing might have happened.

PIEMAN: After all, you *were* poking into our flour and sugar.

PATTY: And looking into our kettles!

COUNTESS: Oh, Lord Ajax, do you really think it's possible?

LORD AJAX: Possible? It's highly possible! Pieman, hand over the rest of those pies.

SIMON: Please, sir, there is no need for further search. You see, the earring has been found.

ALL (*Ad lib*): Found! The earring!

COUNTESS: Who? Who found it? Where is it?

LORD AJAX: Why has it not been returned?

SIMON: The Countess shall have her earring in just a moment, sir. You see, milady, I am the one who found it.

ALL: You!

COUNTESS: Then give it to me at once! What are you waiting for?

LORD AJAX (*Opening his purse*): I am quite prepared to pay the hundred pounds.

SIMON: Oh, no, sir. It's not that. I could never accept the reward.

COUNTESS (*Haughtily*): Why not, may I ask?

SIMON: Because the earring was never *lost!*

LORD AJAX: How could you find it, if it was never lost?

COUNTESS (*Impatiently*): Young man, I order you to return that earring at once!

SIMON: Perhaps Lord Ajax will oblige you.

LORD AJAX (*Astonished*): What are you talking about?

SIMON: About the earring, Lord Ajax. It is in your possession.

COUNTESS: How dare you imply that Lord Ajax is a thief?

SIMON: I didn't say he was a thief, Countess. I merely said he has your earring.

LORD AJAX: It's a lie! A lie!

SIMON: I never lie, sir. And if you will examine your beard carefully, you will find I speak the truth. (LORD AJAX *pinches his beard, then pulls out the earring*)

LORD AJAX (*Displaying earring*): By Jove! The boy is right!

COUNTESS: My earring! To think it was there all the time!

LORD AJAX: It must have caught in my beard when I whispered something to you earlier. (*To* SIMON) You are a sharp lad to notice it.

COUNTESS: You shall be rewarded for your cleverness.

GENTLEMAN (*Rising and advancing*): He deserves no reward. He is a trickster! A cheat!

WOMAN: He tricked us into buying all these pies!

BOB: He knew all the time where to find the earring!

SIMON: No! I swear to you I just noticed it now, when the diamond glittered in the sun.

WOMAN: I don't believe you. I'm onto your salesman's tricks.

PIEMAN: If you insist that we tricked you, I will refund your money.

PATTY: Oh, no, Father! They bought the pies of their own free will, and from the way they gobbled them up, I'm sure they enjoyed every bite.

LADY: So we did, my dear. The pies were delicious. Far better than any I have ever eaten at the Fair. Don't you agree, Countess?

COUNTESS: I wouldn't know. I've never tasted them.

HERALD: In that case, milady, I invite you and Lord Ajax to be my guests. (*Offering each a pie*) The pastry melts in your mouth, and the filling is divine.

COUNTESS (*Stepping back*): No, no, thank you! I couldn't, really!

LORD AJAX: But they look so good! Indeed, I am almost tempted. . . .

SIMON (*Kneeling*): Please, milady. You offered to reward me for the return of your earring. Let this be my reward. Just taste one of the pies.

LORD AJAX: Fair enough, my dear! The lad has earned the reward.

COUNTESS (*Reluctantly*): Very well. (*To* HERALD) We accept your offer. (*All watch anxiously as* COUNTESS *and* LORD AJAX *taste the pies.*) Um-m-m! Marvelous! Marvelous! I had no idea a pie could be so delicious!

LORD AJAX: I agree. It would be a crime to deprive the Fair-goers of such a treat.

COUNTESS: Quite right! Mr. Pastry, from this day forth your request to sell your pies on the Fairground will be granted.

ALL (*Cheering*): Hooray! Hooray!

LORD AJAX: But what about your grandmother, the Duchess of Cleanser?

COUNTESS: All I can say is that her broken tooth was well worth the price. And from what I have seen of Mr. Pastry's bakery, I am sure there will be no more danger of cherry stones.

PIEMAN: Oh, thank you, thank you, milady!

COUNTESS: Don't thank me, Mr. Pastry. Thank *Sir* Simon.

ALL: *Sir* Simon?

COUNTESS: That's what I said! (*To* SIMON, *who is still kneeling*) Rise, Sir Simon, and assume your rightful place as a knight of the realm.

SIMON (*Rising*): Thank you, milady.

FRED: Just imagine! Simple Simon—a knight!

COUNTESS (*Angrily*): No more of that! Never call him by that name again! (*To* HERALD) Herald, make a note! The name of Simple Simon is henceforth and forever abolished, under the penalty of the law.

HERALD: Very good, milady. And now, if I may be so bold, I suggest that you and Lord Ajax continue on your way to the Fair. Your people are expecting you.

LORD AJAX: Come, Countess. We must not keep them waiting. (HERALD *leads the way as* COUNTESS *and* LORD AJAX *exit right.*)

DICK: Congratulations, Simon! You're not so simple after all.

JACK: Let me be the first to admit you're smarter than any of us.

PATTY: I could have told you that!

BOB: We apologize for calling you . . .

FRED (*Quickly*): Don't say it! Don't say it! It's against the law!

JACK: How will we ever remember? We've said that rhyme so often, it's bound to slip out.

PIEMAN: Then learn a new one to take its place.

BOB: A *new* rhyme about Simon?

PIEMAN: In addition to being a pieman, I am also a poet— in a small way. And I have just composed a verse in honor of Sir Simon and this occasion. (*Reciting*) Once Sir Simon met a pieman going to the Fair.

Said *Clever* Simon to the pieman, "Let me taste your ware!"

The pieman said to Clever Simon, "You'll never need a penny!

"You eat your fill, and free of charge, as long as I have any!"

Now repeat the verse until you know it by heart! (*All recite the verse as* PIEMAN, *with a flourish and a bow, gives* SIMON *a pie. Curtain.*)

THE END

Circus Daze

Characters

CLANCY
MR. DARNUM, *owner of the circus*
LEON, *the lion tamer*
HUGO, *the human bullet*
SANCHO, *the sword-swallower*
CARLOS, *of the Flying Crashendos*
GAUCHO THE GREAT, *the knife-thrower*
MADAME COBRA, *the snake-charmer*
VIC
SAM
ROY
ALF
SANDY
PATTY
MR. CUMMINGS, *Vic's father*

BEFORE RISE: ROY, ALF, VIC, SAM, SANDY *and* PATTY, *all wearing jeans, enter right.* ROY *and* ALF *lie down on floor at left and peek under curtain as* SANDY *and* PATTY *do the same at right.* VIC *goes to center and peeks through opening of curtain, with* SAM *standing beside him, arguing for his turn. Offstage circus music is heard.*

SAM: Come on, Vic. You've looked long enough. It's my turn!

VIC: Not till the end of this act, it isn't. Boy, oh boy, Sam. You should see those elephants!

SAM: How can I see anything with you hogging the best peephole? (*With a shove*) Come on! Move over! (*As boys struggle,* CLANCY *enters left, unnoticed by others. He is dressed in old-fashioned policeman's costume, and wears a false nose and mustache. He clowns for audience, then tiptoes to center, and suddenly reaches out and collars* VIC *and* SAM.)

CLANCY: Aha! Caught in the act! (*The other children scramble to their feet.*) Stop! Stay right where you are! Don't move a muscle!

ALL (*Ad lib*): Please! Please, Officer! We haven't done anything! (*Etc.*)

CLANCY: Tell it to the judge.

SAM: Please, sir, don't arrest us.

VIC: We really didn't see much of the show. Honest.

CLANCY: It's against the law to sneak into a circus without a ticket.

SANDY: But we weren't sneaking, Officer. We were only peeking.

CLANCY: Same thing in the eyes of the law.

ALF: But we hardly saw anything.

ROY: Mostly people's feet and legs.

PATTY: If you let us go, we'll never do it again.

CLANCY: That's what they all say.

SAM: But we mean it!

ALL: Honest!

VIC (*With great importance*): Besides, I have an uncle in this circus.

CLANCY (*With sarcasm*): Is that so?

VIC: Yes, that's so!

CLANCY: And who is this uncle of yours, young man?

VIC (*Floundering*): Well, sir, that's the tough part. I don't exactly know his name.

CLANCY: Ha! You don't know the name of your own uncle!

VIC: Well, you see, he's not *exactly* my uncle.

CLANCY: And I suppose he doesn't *exactly* belong to the circus, and I suppose you're not *exactly* telling the truth.

VIC: But I *am* telling the truth. This uncle of mine, who isn't really my uncle, was a friend of my dad's when they were little boys, and he married a second cousin of my mother's aunt who lives in Peoria.

CLANCY (*Trying not to laugh*): And that's supposed to make him your uncle, is it?

VIC (*Doubtfully*): Well . . . yes . . . in a way.

CLANCY: A mighty funny sort of way, I'd call it. Young man, what is your name?

VIC: Victor—Victor Cummings the Third. And this is my friend, Sam Gallagher, and—

CLANCY: Save it, youngster. You can report your names at headquarters.

SANDY (*Starting to cry*): Oh, dear! What will my mother say?

PATTY (*Also crying*): I want to go home!

CLANCY: You'll go home soon enough, young lady. But first, you're coming with me.

ROY: Are you really taking us to Police Headquarters?

CLANCY: Who said anything about the police? I'm marching you right into Darnum and Daily Circus Headquarters. You can speak your piece to Mr. Darnum himself. Now line up and get moving! (*He lines up children facing left and herds them off ahead of him. He prods the last boy with his rubber stick, as he looks over his shoulder and winks at the audience. The curtains open.*)

*   *   *

SETTING: *Mr. Darnum's office. Several folding chairs and a*

table with circus props on it are at one side. A cardboard weight labeled 2,000 lbs. is on the floor.
AT RISE: MR. DARNUM *is seated at a desk at center, as children, followed by* CLANCY, *enter.*

MR. DARNUM (*Looking up, annoyed*): What's all this, Clancy? I gave strict orders I was not to be disturbed during show time.

CLANCY: An emergency, Mr. Darnum. I just caught these young scamps trying to sneak in under the Big Top. I knew you would want to see them at once.

MR. DARNUM: You did quite right, Clancy! Now, let's have your names, starting with this young man. (*Pointing to* SAM)

SAM: My name is Sam Gallagher, but honest and truly we weren't trying to sneak into the circus, sir. (MR. DARNUM *writes down name.*)

MR. DARNUM: When I want any explanations, I'll ask for them. Now, you. (*Pointing to* ROY) What's your name?

ROY: Roy—Roy Baker, Your Honor.

MR. DARNUM (*Writing*): You don't have to call me "Your Honor." This isn't a court of law. Next!

ALF: I'm Alf—Alfred Arthur Algernon Anderson.

MR. DARNUM (*After writing down the name slowly and carefully and looking up at the two girls*): Now you two! I must say I'm surprised to see two little girls mixed up in such a matter.

VIC: We told them not to come, sir.

MR. DARNUM: Silence! Each one of you will speak for yourself.

SANDY: I'm Sandy Lou Davis.

PATTY (*Between sobs*): I'm Patricia Ann Evans, and I want to call my mother.

CLANCY (*Producing handkerchief*): Here, blow your nose, and sit down on that chair. Both of you better sit down.

(Seats girls on folding chairs and puts his hand on VIC's *shoulder)* This fellow seems to be the ringleader, Mr. Darnum. Calls himself Victor Cummings the Third and claims he has an uncle working with our show.

MR. DARNUM: Cummings, eh? Where do you live?

VIC: 918 Columbia Boulevard.

MR. DARNUM *(Writing)*: This uncle of yours—what does he do in our circus?

VIC: Well, sir, I don't exactly know. We haven't heard from him in a long time.

CLANCY: And he says he isn't *exactly* his uncle either, and he doesn't *exactly* know his name.

VIC: But I do know that Dad always called him "Sawdust" and that's how he used to sign the postcards he sent us.

CLANCY *and* MR. DARNUM: Sawdust!

CLANCY: That's a sure-enough circus term, but there's nobody here by that name.

SAM: We should have known Vic was only kidding us.

ALF: That's really why we came here . . . to meet Vic's uncle.

ROY: Vic said he might even give us a job with the circus.

MR. DARNUM: A job! You mean you kids really want to leave home and join the circus?

ALL: Sure!

ROY: It would beat going to school.

SANDY: And doing the dishes.

MR. DARNUM: But what about your parents?

ALF: Oh, they wouldn't mind . . . not after we become famous.

PATTY: And we'd let our mothers know where we were so they wouldn't worry.

MR. DARNUM: Hm-m-m! *(To* CLANCY) Well, Clancy, if these boys and girls really want jobs, maybe we can put them to work. *(Writes on pad, folds up two notes and gives them to* CLANCY) Here, follow the instructions in this memo. Several of our performers have spoken about needing assistants. As soon as these people have finished their acts, bring them to my office. And then take care of the other note.

CLANCY: Very good, sir. (CLANCY *exits right.*)

MR. DARNUM (*Leaning back in his chair*): Now then, let's see what you can do. Do any of you have any experience in show business?

ROY: I did a tumbling act in our school circus.

MR. DARNUM: Fine! Let's have a demonstration.

ROY: You mean right now? Here?

MR. DARNUM: No time like the present. (ROY *does a few feeble somersaults and attempts a cartwheel which is not very successful.*) Hm-m-m. (*Makes a note*) What about you? (*Pointing to* ALF)

ALF: I've been practicing weight lifting in the gym.

MR. DARNUM: Good! (*Pointing to weight*) See what you can do with that. (ALF *tugs and heaves but can't budge it.*)

ALF (*Wiping his brow*): That's a bit out of my class, Mr. Darnum. I do better with dumbbells and Indian clubs.

MR. DARNUM: I'll make a note of that. (*Points to* SAM) Now *you!* What can you do?

SAM: I have a book on juggling, but I've read only the first chapter.

MR. DARNUM (*Pointing to stack of plates on prop table*): Help yourself to those plates and give it a try.

SAM (*Attempting to juggle three plates and dropping all of them*): I guess I need more practice.

MR. DARNUM: Hm-m-m! I agree. Now we'll see what Victor Cummings the Third can do.

ROY: Show him your clown routine, Vic.

VIC: I—I'm afraid I don't feel very funny right now.

MR. DARNUM: A true circus clown is funny whether he feels like it or not. Go ahead. Make me laugh.

VIC: O.K., Mr. Darnum. I'll try. (*He does a few exaggerated steps, trips over his own feet and falls flat.*)

MR. DARNUM (*Writing*): Well, I'll give you credit for trying and maybe you *would* be funnier with a costume and make-up. Let's see if the girls have any circus talent. (*Pointing to* SANDY) Do you have any accomplishments?

SANDY: I've had some dancing lessons, but I don't know too many steps. (*Does a few ballet steps with a twirl or two*)

MR. DARNUM: Hm-m-m! Not bad! Do you think you could do some of those steps on a high wire . . . say maybe fifty feet above the ground?

SANDY: Oh, dear me, no! I get dizzy on top of a stepladder.

MR. DARNUM (*Writing*): O.K.! That's out. That leaves you, little lady. (*Pointing to* PATTY) And I hope you're good.

PATTY: I do baton twirling, but I don't have my baton.

MR. DARNUM (*Indicating prop table*): There's one on the table. Help yourself. (PATTY *gets baton and does a short exhibition of baton twirling.*) Maybe you have some possibilities, my dear. A lighted torch on either end of your baton would make your act more spectacular.

PATTY: Oh, no, Mr. Darnum! I'm scared to death of fire. And my mother would never let me try such a thing.

MR. DARNUM: Then that's out. Well, children, I must admit I have not been too impressed with what you have shown me in the way of talent. But since I believe in giving young people a chance, we'll see if any of our performers can use you. (LEON, *the lion tamer, enters right. He wears a shirt which is badly ripped.*)

LEON: You sent for me, Mr. Darnum?

MR. DARNUM: Yes, Leon. Do come in. I want you to meet

some real circus fans. But perhaps you had better see about those scratches first.

LEON: Oh, they're nothing, Mr. Darnum. The lions were a bit on the cranky side today, but nothing to worry about.

MR. DARNUM: Boys and girls, this is Leon, our lion tamer. (*Children acknowledge introduction.*) Leon has been looking for someone to give him a hand with the big cats. (*Pointing to* ALF) This young man has been developing his muscles with weight lifting, Leon. I thought you might want to look him over.

LEON (*Inspecting* ALF): Well, he does look like a strong lad, and I do need someone with strong shoulder muscles to work out that new wrestling act I've been planning with Tina the Tigress.

ALF (*Swallowing hard*): I—I don't really think I'm the type, Mr. Leon. I've never had much experience with animals.

LEON: Oh, don't worry about that. Tina's still young and playful, and you could sort of grow up together. A few hours a day in her cage and you might get along fine. On the other hand, if she didn't take a liking to you—well! You know how she acted with that last boy we tried, Mr. Darnum.

MR. DARNUM: You mean the one who's still in the hospital? He just wasn't her type. Now this lad seems to have nerves of steel.

ALF: Oh, no, sir, not really! My mother says I'm a very nervous child.

MR. DARNUM: What a pity. Well, think it over, Leon. (HUGO *enters right. He wears a torn jacket and his face is badly smudged*) Oh, excuse me a minute! Here's Hugo.

LEON: Hi, Hugo! What happened to you?

HUGO: Something's wrong with that confounded cannon.

The gunpowder exploded before I was ready. I tell you, Mr. Darnum, this business of being shot out of a cannon twice a day is too much. I just have to have an assistant.

MR. DARNUM: That's why I sent for you. Children, this is Hugo, the human bullet.

CHILDREN: How do you do?

MR. DARNUM (*Pointing to* ROY): This boy has been showing me some of his acrobatic stunts. Maybe you can use him in your act.

ROY: But I don't want to be shot out of a cannon.

HUGO (*Looking him over*): Humph! Not bad! And just about the right size. I like 'em young and limber.

ROY: My father always told me to stay away from guns.

HUGO: Oh, sure! Guns are dangerous, but a cannon . . . well, a cannon is different. You never need to worry about being *hit* by a bullet, when you *are* the bullet. Understand?

ROY: No, sir, I don't understand, and anyhow—

SANCHO (*Offstage*): Help, help!

MR. DARNUM (*Half-rising*): Wait a minute. Someone is in trouble! (SANCHO, *the sword-swallower, enters right. He is dressed in Spanish costume with a long cape which conceals a full-length sword in his belt. He pretends to be struggling with a wooden sword hilt protruding from his mouth.*)

LEON: Oh, boy! Sancho's sword is stuck again. Here, let me help. (*He turns* SANCHO *around with his back to the audience and after much struggle removes the long sword from under the cape, making it appear as if he has pulled it from his mouth.* SANCHO *conceals the short sword handle under cape.*) There we are! (*Patting* SANCHO *on back and turning him to face audience*) Feel better?

SANCHO (*Rubbing his throat and swallowing several times*): Much better, thanks. But my throat still feels a little scratchy.

MR. DARNUM: Sancho, you're in luck. I think we've found the assistant you've been asking for. (*Pointing to* SAM) This is Sam Gallagher. He wants to be a juggler, but I think he'd make a better sword-swallower . . . with a little training.

SANCHO: Good! (*Clapping* SAM *on shoulder*) You come with me, lad.

SAM: No! I don't want to swallow a sword!

SANCHO: Nonsense! I have a six-inch dagger that will do for a start. It's easy . . . much easier than fire-eating.

SAM: No! No! You let go of me!

MR. DARNUM: Take it easy, Sancho. Give him a few minutes to get used to the idea. By the way, have you seen any of the Flying Crashendos?

SANCHO: I just passed Carlos on my way in here. Ah, here he is! (CARLOS *enters right.*)

CARLOS: You sent for me, Chief?

MR. DARNUM: Yes, I want you to meet Vic Cummings— Victor Cummings the Third. Vic, this is Carlos, one of the famous Flying Crashendos.

VIC: How do you do, sir?

MR. DARNUM: Vic wants to be a clown, and you've been talking about adding some humor to your act.

CARLOS: A great idea, Chief. (*Looking at* VIC) He's just about the right weight, too, I think.

HUGO: How do you plan to use him?

CARLOS: When Gringo and I are hanging by our heels from the two high bars, we can toss him back and forth between us.

VIC: Oh, no, you won't! Not me!

CARLOS: Every now and then we can miss the catch and

Milo can grab him from the center trapeze ring. That
should get a laugh. How about it, sonny?

VIC: Nothing doing! Let me out of here! (*He attempts to
dash out right, but is stopped by the entrance of* CLANCY
and GAUCHO THE GREAT, *who are wheeling in a big
sheet of cardboard with the outline of a girl on it.*)

MR. DARNUM: Aha! Here comes Gaucho the Great with
something for the ladies.

GAUCHO (*To* MR. DARNUM, *as* CLANCY *wheels the cardboard to center, facing the audience*): Your message
came at the right moment, sir. My partner has just quit.
Walked out on me without notice.

MR. DARNUM: I am quite sure that either one of these girls
will be proud and happy to work with Gaucho the Great,
the most amazing knife-thrower of all time.

CLANCY: We brought his equipment along, sir, so the little
ladies can try it for size.

SANDY *and* PATTY (*Cringing*): No! No! Not me! Not me!

GAUCHO (*Taking* SANDY *by the hand*): This one! She will
be perfect. (*Pulling her into place so that she is standing
against the outline on the cardboard*) Look! A perfect fit!

SANDY (*Screaming*): No! Let go of me! Help!

GAUCHO: Don't be nervous, my child. I am Gaucho,
Gaucho the Great. I never miss! Never! Not even when
I am blindfolded.

PATTY: What about your partner? Why did she quit?

MR. DARNUM: Never ask awkward questions, child. We
circus folk do not discuss each other.

CLANCY: And we carry heavy insurance on all our performers.

SANDY: I don't want any insurance. I want to go home!
(*Struggling*) You let go of me!

GAUCHO: Steady, steady, my dear! Your first lesson is not to
wiggle. (MADAME COBRA *enters right. A large stuffed*

green snake is coiled around her body. In one hand she carries a large covered reed basket.)

MADAME COBRA: Sorry I'm late, Mr. Darnum, but I couldn't disappoint my public. What an audience! We had to go back in the ring for thirteen bows.

MR. DARNUM: Ah, Madame Cobra, we've been expecting you.

ALF (*Yelling and pointing*): Look! Look! It's a live snake!

ALL (*Screaming; ad lib*): A snake! Look out! A snake! (*Etc.*)

MADAME COBRA: Of course it's a snake. What would you expect from a snake-charmer? Now do be quiet. You're disturbing Melinda. (*Stroking snake*) There, there, darling. There's nothing to be afraid of. These silly children won't hurt you. (*To* MR. DARNUM) You said you had an assistant for me. (*Pointing to* PATTY) Is that the one?

PATTY: No! Help! Let me out! (CLANCY *bars her way as she tries to run off.*)

CLANCY: Here, now! None of that!

MADAME COBRA: And stop that screaming! You're waking Cuddles and he needs his rest. I can feel him stirring in his basket. (*As* PATTY *backs away*) Here! (*Offering basket to* PATTY) Take him and let him hear you sing. He likes anything slow and soothing.

PATTY: No! I won't touch it.

MADAME COBRA: This is an outrage, Mr. Darnum! These hoodlums are upsetting my pets!

MR. DARNUM (*Shouting*): Quiet! Quiet! (*Circus performers catch and hold children.*) Now listen to me. I must say I am sadly disappointed in all of you. I've given you your chance to appear with some of the greatest stars of the Big Top and you act like a bunch of scared rabbits. I now have no choice but to turn you over to the authorities. (MR. CUMMINGS *enters left. He goes to* MR. DARNUM *with outstretched hand.*)

MR. CUMMINGS: As I live and breathe, it's old Sawdust Dalrymple in the flesh! I came as soon as I got your message! How are you, you old rascal! (*They shake hands and pound each other on the back.*)

MR. DARNUM: It's great to see you again, old scout.

VIC (*Running to his father*): Dad! Get us out of here!

CHILDREN (*Swarming around him*): Please, Mr. Cummings, take us away!

MR. CUMMINGS: For heaven's sake! Vic! Sam! Patty! What are you youngsters doing here?

MR. DARNUM (*Laughing*): They're doing just what you and I did when we were kids, Victor. Clancy caught 'em trying to sneak in under the Big Top.

VIC: That's not so, Dad! We were only taking a peek.

CLANCY: Sneak or peek. It's all the same.

MR. DARNUM: Well, either way, it was a lucky thing. I've wanted to get in touch with you for years, old friend. Didn't even know you lived here till your boy gave me the tip. So I sent Clancy around with a note.

MR. CUMMINGS: Too bad we lost track of each other, Sawdust. I had no idea the Darnum and Daily Circus belonged to you. When did you change your name?

MR. DARNUM: Years ago. "Dalrymple" was too long to fit on a circus poster.

MR. CUMMINGS: Vic, this is your Uncle Sawdust I've been telling you about ever since you were a little boy.

VIC: Golly! Are you really my Uncle Sawdust?

MR. DARNUM: I sure am, boy. The minute you said you were Victor Cummings the Third, I knew you were the son of my old friend.

ALF: Then why did you let that policeman arrest us?

CLANCY (*Taking off his false nose and mustache*): Arrest you? I couldn't arrest a fly! I'm just a circus clown and this getup is part of my act.

PATTY: But you dragged us in here as if we were prisoners.

CLANCY: Still part of the act, dear. And I know Mr. Darnum has such a soft heart for kids that he always likes to give them a real circus thrill.

ROY: He sure gave us a thrill all right!

SAM: Scared the living daylights out of us!

MR. DARNUM: I didn't really mean to scare you. But I do want to point out that running away to join a circus isn't always what it's cracked up to be.

VIC: We understand now, Mr. Darnum . . . er . . . I mean Uncle Sawdust.

LEON: And just think . . . you can tell all your friends at school that you've met some real circus stars.

HUGO: I'll be glad to give you my autograph.

SANCHO: And I'll really let you in on some of my sword-swallowing secrets.

CARLOS: I'll introduce you to the rest of the Flying Crash-endos.

GAUCHO (*Bowing and kissing* SANDY's *hand*): I only regret that I cannot have such a charming lady as my partner.

MADAME COBRA: If you want to, I'll let you look at Cuddles. He's really sweet.

CHILDREN: No, thank you!

MR. CUMMINGS: It's been great to see you, Sawdust. When can we get together and talk about old times?

MR. DARNUM: Bring your family around to my tent after the show tonight, and we'll have a real get-together. Clancy, suppose you hand out these free passes for the next performance. Give them enough for their whole class—the teacher, too!

ALL: Gee! Thanks, Mr. Darnum. (*They thank* CLANCY *as he distributes passes.*)

ROY: Boy, oh boy! Now that I know I'm not going to be shot out of a cannon, this has been a great experience.

ALF: I can hardly wait to tell the rest of the kids that I met a real lion tamer.

SAM: And a sword-swallower.

PATTY: And a snake-charmer!

SANDY: But they'll never believe us!

MR. CUMMINGS: They will, if you show them a picture. (*Pulling camera out of his pocket*) I think we should have one for the record.

MR. DARNUM: Everybody get into the act. (MR. DARNUM *and* CLANCY *pose at center as each performer takes his place with a child beside him.*) All set?

MR. CUMMINGS (*Sighting through camera*): Come on now, relax! Smile! You all look as if you're in a daze!

VIC: You're so right, Dad! We're in a real daze—a circus daze—and I don't think I ever want to wake up! (MR. CUMMINGS *snaps picture as curtains close.*)

THE END

Captain Castaway's Captives

Characters

CAPTAIN CASTAWAY
MATE
BOSUN BONES
HELMSMAN
SAM SNOOP ⎤
SILAS SNEAK │
THOMAS TATTLE ⎬ *spies*
PAUL PRY │
NOSEY PARKER ⎦
WING FOO
LADY DORINDA
GIL
MIKE
COLIN
DEBBY
TEDDY LOU
GLORIA

SETTING: *A pirate ship.*
AT RISE: HELMSMAN *stands at helm, right, peering intently off right.* CAPTAIN CASTAWAY *stands center, scanning the horizon through a spyglass.* MATE *sits on a coil of rope, whittling.*

CAPTAIN: Still no sign of the landing party. Something must have gone wrong. (*Cupping his hands and shouting to* HELMSMAN) Helmsman, ahoy! Are you holding steady on your course? (HELMSMAN *turns, smiling broadly. He first shakes his head no, then nods yes, and finally shrugs his shoulders*)

MATE: He can't hear a thing you say, sir, but we've been patroling the coastline for more than an hour.

CAPTAIN: If I weren't so tenderhearted, I'd throw that fellow to the sharks. (*To* MATE) Tell me, who is in charge of the jolly-boat?

MATE: Bosun Bones, sir, and you know you can count on him.

CAPTAIN: Nevertheless, I'm worried.

MATE: No need to worry, sir. Bosun Bones knows his business. He'll bring back the prisoners you've ordered.

CAPTAIN: I hope so. I've grown rather fond of Bones. I should hate to see him swinging from the yardarm.

BOSUN (*Offstage*): Ship ahoy! Ship ahoy!

MATE (*Rising*): There! That's him. I—er—begging your pardon, sir. That is *he* now!

CAPTAIN: You saved yourself that time, Mate. But I'm warning you, another slip like that may cost you your life.

MATE: Aye, sir. I can still hear poor Codfish, the cabin boy, screaming, *It is I! It is she! It is he!* as he walked the plank. But it was too late, poor lad. Now he lays—I mean *lies*—in a watery grave.

CAPTAIN: If you can make that Helmsman understand you, tell him to heave to and slow down till the jolly-boat pulls along side. Then order the crew to lower the landing ladder.

MATE: Aye, aye, sir. (*Crosses to* HELMSMAN *where he pantomimes giving orders and receives* HELMSMAN's *salute. As he starts to exit left, the* CAPTAIN *stops him.*)

CAPTAIN: One moment, Mate. Where is the Lady Dorinda?

MATE: Still locked in her cabin, sir. She refuses to come out.

CAPTAIN: A stubborn lass, that one. But she can't live on bread and water much longer. Are the spies in position?

MATES: Every man at his post, sir. (*He exits left*)

CAPTAIN: I'll check to make sure. (*Takes small notebook from pocket; reads names*) Paul Pry.

PAUL PRY (*Popping up from barrel labeled* APPLES, *left*): Here, sir.

CAPTAIN: Sam Snoop.

SAM SNOOP (*Unrolling himself from canvas on floor*): Here, sir!

CAPTAIN: Silas Sneak.

SILAS SNEAK (*Rising from keg labeled* POWDER, *up left*): Here, sir.

CAPTAIN: Nosey Parker.

NOSEY PARKER (*Raising lid of chest labeled* TREASURE, *up center*): Here, sir.

CAPTAIN: Thomas Tattle.

THOMAS TATTLE (*Appearing from behind pile of crates down left*): Here, sir.

CAPTAIN: Good. All present and accounted for. Are your notebooks ready?

ALL (*Holding up notebooks*): Ready, sir.

CAPTAIN: Splendid! Now remember to keep your ears open, and make careful notes on all conversations. Don't miss a single mistake, or I'll have your heads.

ALL: Aye, aye, sir!

CAPTAIN: Take cover. The prisoners are approaching. (*Spies return to hiding places as* BOSUN BONES *enters right, followed by* GIL, MIKE, COLIN, DEBBY, TEDDY LOU, *and* GLORIA. *All carry school books*)

BOSUN: Here they are, sir. Just what you ordered.

CAPTAIN: What are their names?

BOSUN: Permit me to introduce them. Teddy Lou Crandall, Debby Graham, Gloria Green, Gilbert King, Colin Moore, and Michael Kelley. (*Children nod as introduced.*)

CAPTAIN: And I am Captain Castaway, at your service. Welcome aboard.

CHILDREN (*Together*): Thank you, sir.

GIL: I can't believe you're real!

GLORIA: Or that any of this is happening to us.

TEDDY LOU: When Bosun Bones invited us to visit a pirate ship, we thought it was a joke.

COLIN: Or a masquerade.

CAPTAIN: You will soon find out it is neither.

MIKE: But *why,* sir? Why did you choose *us?*

CAPTAIN: Let's say I thought a sea voyage might do you good. A change of air.

DEBBY: But we can't leave home. Our parents won't know where we are.

CAPTAIN: They will be notified in due time.

TEDDY LOU (*Looking off right*): We're moving faster and faster.

CAPTAIN: Yes, the wind is freshening. We'll make good time. I promise you the voyage will be a short one. In fact, it will be over before you know it.

DEBBY (*Doubtfully*): Well, just so we're home in time for supper.

CAPTAIN: That reminds me. You must be hungry. Bosun Bones, go below and tell Cook to prepare some light refreshments.

BOSUN: Aye, aye, sir. (*Exits left*)

CAPTAIN: And now, if you will excuse me, I must retire to my cabin. I am expecting some important messages. (*Glances meaningfully at hiding places of spies*) Meanwhile, explore the ship and enjoy yourselves . . . while you have the chance. (*Exits left*)

GIL: I don't get it! (SAM SNOOP *untangles himself from canvas and writes in notebook*) I don't get it at all.

MIKE: Me neither. (PAUL PRY *rises from barrel to make a note*) Why did he invite *us,* when there's so many other kids he could have asked?

TEDDY LOU: So what? (SILAS SNEAK *rises from keg to write*) Let's do like the man says and enjoy ourselves. I move we explore the ship.

DEBBY: It's just like that book we read in school, *Treasure Island,* by Mark Twain. (THOMAS TATTLE *appears from behind crates, and writes furiously*)

GLORIA: You're right. Even to the apple barrel. Remember how Long John Silver hid in the apple barrel? (TATTLE *continues to write.*)

COLIN: Maybe somebody is hiding there now. Let's take a look.

DEBBY: No, Colin, no! It's not polite to go snooping around when you're a guest.

MIKE: Debby is right. You shouldn't be so *acquisitive!* (NOSEY PARKER *lifts lid of chest and makes a note.*)

COLIN: Just the same, I'd like to look around. There's something fishy about this whole deal. (SAM SNOOP *makes a note*) For some reason, I don't trust that captain.

GLORIA: Why not? He seems to be a perfect gentleman.

GIL: Then why is he a pirate?

COLIN: Search me. (SAM SNOOP *writes again.*) But Captain Kidd was once a respected merchant and ship owner, and he turned pirate.

MIKE: I agree with Colin. There's something wrong here. And if there's stolen treasure aboard, it's our duty to find it.

GIL: Come on. Let's open that chest. (*As boys move to chest,* LADY DORINDA *runs in from left.*)

LADY DORINDA: No, no! Stop! Don't take another step.

GIL (*Flustered*): I'm sorry. We were only . . . we just meant to . . .

LADY DORINDA: Don't bother to explain, but stay away from that chest.

DEBBY: Who are you?

LADY DORINDA: I am Lady Dorinda. I have come to save you.

MIKE: Save us from what?

GLORIA: Are you a lady pirate?

TEDDY LOU: Or the Captain's wife?

LADY DORINDA: Heaven forbid! I am a captive, like yourselves.

ALL: A captive!

DEBBY: But we're not captives. We are *guests*. The Captain himself invited us aboard.

LADY DORINDA (*With sarcasm*): I'm sure he did, but, nevertheless, you are his prisoners.

GLORIA: I don't believe it.

TEDDY LOU: He said the voyage would be over before we knew it.

LADY DORINDA: Which means that none of you will leave this ship alive.

ALL (*Loudly*): What?

LADY DORINDA: Sh! Not so loud. (*In a half whisper*) We are surrounded by spies.

ALL (*Ad lib*): Spies? Where? (*Etc.*)

LADY DORINDA: Wait a minute. (*Running to each hiding place, she sprinkles white powder on each one*) There! That should do the trick.

GLORIA: What trick?

LADY DORINDA: Listen! (*Spies snore loudly.*) Do you hear what I hear?

TEDDY LOU: It sounds like snoring.

LADY DORINDA: Exactly. My sleeping powder never fails. Now we can talk.

COLIN (*Pointing to* HELMSMAN): What about him?

LADY DORINDA: Don't worry. He's deaf and he can't hear a thing. Now, listen to me. You are in the clutches of Captain Castaway, one of the most ruthless pirates who ever sailed the Spanish Main.

DEBBY: But he seems like such a nice man.

LADY DORINDA: Nice? I shudder when I think of all the captives he has put to death, most of them boys and girls like you.

GIL: But what could he possibly have against us? We never saw him until today.

LADY DORINDA: Tell me, what was your English grade on your last report card?

GIL: D-minus. But why does that matter?

LADY DORINDA: And the rest of you?

MIKE: C-minus.

COLIN: Mine was a D, but even that is better than last time.

TEDDY LOU: I had an incomplete. Forgot to hand in my book reports.

DEBBY: I passed, but by the skin of my teeth.

GLORIA: I was lucky enough to get a C, but there was a note that said, "Need for improvement."

LADY DORINDA: That Bosun Bones certainly knows how to pick the Captain's captives.

GLORIA: What do you mean?

LADY DORINDA: Captain Castaway is waging a one-man war against everyone who murders the King's English. At every port he sends the Bosun ashore to invite boys and girls like you to visit his ship, then holds them captive. When he has enough evidence against them, he makes them walk the plank.

DEBBY: Walk the plank?

MIKE: You can't be serious.

LADY DORINDA: I'm a living example.

COLIN: How come you're still alive?

LADY DORINDA: Only because I don't use expressions like, "How come?" I was captured by mistake and so far he's never been able to catch me in a single grammatical error.

MIKE: Then why doesn't he leave you go?

LADY DORINDA: Don't say that! Don't ever say that again. It's *let* me go.

MIKE: O.K. Why doesn't he *let* you go?

LADY DORINDA: Because he wants to use me as a spy.

DEBBY: But you're not a spy, are you?

LADY DORINDA: I spy on the *other* spies. That's how I know that each one carries a notebook to keep track of all your mistakes. Now is our chance to collect them and destroy the evidence against you. Quick! There's no time to lose. (*Children help her take notebooks from hiding places*) That's the lot. (*Glancing through one*) Oh, my aching adverbs! It's lucky for you the Captain will never see these. I'll throw them overboard. (*As she turns to do so,* WING FOO *enters left with tea tray on folding stand*)

WING FOO: Captain say young ladies and gentlemen plenty hungry. Wing Foo bring tea and Chinese fortune cookies. (*Seeing* LADY DORINDA) Ah, Missy Dorinda come out of cabin at last. Enjoy good fresh air and cup of tea.

LADY DORINDA (*Concealing notebooks behind her back*): Thank you, Wing Foo. You may leave the tray and I will serve our guests.

WING FOO (*Placing stand on floor*): Guests! Ha! Ha! Ha! Missy Dorinda make plenty good joke. Very, very funny. (*Points finger at* LADY DORINDA) Confucius say:
   Life's like a cooky. Take a bite,
   When you fear the end's in sight!
(*Exits left*)

MIKE: What did he mean by that?

LADY DORINDA: I'm not sure, but Wing Foo has always been kind to me. (*Places notebooks on tea tray*) Maybe he's trying to tell us something.

GLORIA (*Excitedly*): The fortune cookies!

COLIN: Let's have a look. (*Opens one and reads*) Listen to this:

You will have Wing Foo to thank
For sparing you the dreaded plank.

TEDDY LOU: He *is* trying to help us! (*Taking cooky*)
Watch your words! Make no mistakes!
Discover those the *Captain* makes.

LADY DORINDA: But he never makes mistakes. Absolutely never.

GIL: Maybe Wing Foo knows something we don't know. (*Taking cooky, reading*)
No man is perfect every day,
Not even Captain Castaway.

DEBBY (*Taking cooky*): This one says:
Heed my advice, the very best.
And put the Captain to the test.

LADY DORINDA: But, how? What kind of test?

MIKE (*Taking cooky and reading*):
If you would catch our Captain cruel,
Engage him in a verbal duel!

LADY DORINDA: But who would dare to challenge him?

GLORIA (*Taking last cooky, reading*):
One man aboard this pirate ship
Can help you give our Chief the slip.

ALL (*Ad lib*): But, who? Who could it be? (*Etc.*)

HELMSMAN (*Suddenly turning*): Me! I mean, *I!* I'm your man.

ALL (*In surprise*): You!

LADY DORINDA: But how could you hear what we said?

GLORIA: I thought you were deaf.

HELMSMAN: So does everyone else on board, except Wing Foo. He knows I hear everything that goes on. Now I can use my knowledge to get my revenge.

COLIN: Revenge? What did the Captain do to you?

HELMSMAN: Codfish the cabin boy was my nephew. Last week the poor lad walked the plank, just because he made a few grammatical errors.

DEBBY: How awful.

HELMSMAN: You will meet the same fate, unless you catch the Captain in his own trap.

MIKE: How?

HELMSMAN: Expose him to his crew as a fake and a fraud.

LADY DORINDA: But he isn't a fake. He always speaks perfect English.

HELMSMAN: Aye, but have you ever seen his *writing?*

DEBBY: You mean he can't write?

HELMSMAN: Oh, he can write a legible hand, but by Neptune, you should see his sentence structure. (*Lowering his voice*) And that's not the worst of it. (*Looking around cautiously*) He can't spell worth a sixpence!

ALL (*Shocked*): What?

HELMSMAN: Not even simple words, like (*Spelling*) t-h-e-i-r, and t-h-e-r-e.

GIL: How do you know?

HELMSMAN: Night after night I hear him muttering to himself as he paces the deck,
    "E before I, or I before E . . .
    I never can tell, for the life of me!"

DEBBY: Now my fortune cooky makes sense. "Put the Captain to the test." It means a *spelling* test.

MIKE:
    If you would catch our Captain cruel,
    Engage him in a verbal duel!
A verbal duel is a spelling match!

HELMSMAN: I have shown you the way. The rest is up to you. Now I must get back to my post. (*Returns to platform*)

COLIN: Thank goodness we brought our dictionaries. We can look up some words. (*As children run to books,* CAPTAIN CASTAWAY *enters left, with toy pistols drawn, followed by* MATE *and* BOSUN, *each brandishing a cardboard cutlass.*)

CAPTAIN: Halt! Stand where you are! (*Looking around deck*) What has happened to my spies? Why have I received no reports?

LADY DORINDA: Your spies are quite safe, Captain, as you can hear for yourself. (*Loud snores from hiding places are heard.*)

BOSUN: Blow me down, Captain! They're fast asleep. (*He pulls* SAM SNOOP *out from under canvas*) On your feet, Snoop! (SNOOP *stands, rubbing his eyes*) Wake up, Sneak! (*Pounds on powder keg*) Climb out of there. On the double! (SNEAK *climbs out of keg*)

MATE (*Pounding on apple barrel*): Wake up, Pry! Wake up and get out of there. (PAUL PRY *climbs out of barrel*) On your feet, Tattle, unless you want to wake up dead. (*Drags* TATTLE *out from behind crates*)

BOSUN (*Pulling* PARKER *from chest*): You'll answer to the Captain for this, Nosey Parker!

CAPTAIN: Line them up, Mate! They know the penalty for falling asleep on duty.

LADY DORINDA: They are not to blame, Captain. They're victims of my sleeping powder.

CAPTAIN: You'll walk the plank for this, my lady. (*To spies*) Now, you lubberly lubbers, I'll have your reports. Hand over those notebooks, before I blast you into bits.

SPIES (*Reaching into pockets; ad lib*): They're gone! Stolen!

Vanished! (*Etc.*) (GIL *moves stealthily toward notebooks on tea tray and reaches for them*)

PAUL PRY: There! There they are, sir. Right behind you.

CAPTAIN (*Wheeling and pointing pistols at* GIL): Stop! One more step, and you're on your way to Davy Jones's locker. (*Picks up notebooks*) Aha! At last, the evidence I've been waiting for. Mate! Bosun! Keep them covered. (*Hands a pistol to each*) Now, we're ready for business. (*Distributes notebooks to spies*) I am ready for your reports.

SAM SNOOP (*Pointing to* GIL): That one said, "I don't get it! I don't get it at all!" That's slang, isn't it, sir?

CAPTAIN: Right! And he will be our first victim.

PAUL PRY (*Pointing to* MIKE): That one said, "Me neither."

CAPTAIN: Guilty!

PAUL PRY: But there's more, sir. He also said, "Why did he invite us when there's so many other kids he could have asked."

CAPTAIN: There *is* instead of there *are, kids* instead of *children, could have* instead of *might have.* Guilty on three more points.

SILAS SNEAK (*Pointing to* TEDDY LOU): She said, "So what. Let's do like the man says."

CAPTAIN: Guilty! *So what* is bad enough, but using *like* as a conjunction is unforgivable. Next!

THOMAS TATTLE: The young ladies don't know their literature, sir. (*Pointing to* DEBBY) That one said *Treasure Island* was written by Mark Twain, instead of Robert Louis Stevenson. And that one (*Pointing to* GLORIA) named Long John Silver instead of Jim Hawkins as the character in the book who hid in the apple barrel.

CAPTAIN: Both guilty. Next!

NOSEY PARKER: That boy (*Pointing to* MIKE) used the

word *acquisitive,* meaning *greedy,* when he meant *inquisitive,* meaning *curious!*

CAPTAIN: It's the plank for him.

SAM SNOOP: There's more slang, sir. That boy *(Pointing to* COLIN) used such expressions as, "Something fishy . . . whole deal . . . search me."

CAPTAIN: Guilty! Guilty! Bosun, sound your pipe for Wing Foo. We'll need to clear the deck for the plank. (BOSUN *blows pipe and* WING FOO *enters left)*

GIL: Since I am to be your first victim, Captain Castaway, I hereby challenge you to a duel.

CAPTAIN *(Laughing):* A duel? Well, well, well! Which do you prefer, young man, swords or pistols?

GIL: Neither. I challenge you to a duel of words.

CAPTAIN: Words? You have already lost that battle.

GIL: Not entirely, sir. I admit we haven't done so well with grammar and literature, but what about writing and spelling?

COLIN: We challenge you to a spelling duel, Captain.

CAPTAIN: This is ridiculous.

TEDDY LOU: Oh, no, sir. Our English course at school includes spelling, reading and writing.

CAPTAIN: But you've never seen my writing.

WING FOO *(Bowing to* GIL): Wing Foo present evidence. *(Handing slip of paper to* GIL) Exhibit A—last week's grocery list.

GIL *(Reading from list):* Now hear this: bread *(Spelling),* B-R-E-D. *(Gasps from crew)* Cheese, C-H-E-A-S-E. Biscuits, B-I-S-C-U-T-S.

CAPTAIN: Stop! I've been betrayed. Arrest this traitor, and put him in irons.

HELMSMAN *(Joining group):* Not so fast, Captain! You have some explaining to do.

CAPTAIN *and* CREW (*Ad lib*): He can hear! He's not deaf! (*Etc.*)

HELMSMAN: By pretending to be deaf, I have heard some important secrets. Wait till you hear how our Captain got his name.

CAPTAIN: My name has nothing to do with this case.

WING FOO: Captain Castaway real for sure castaway.

HELMSMAN: Wing Foo is right. This man was cast adrift in an open boat, because his shipmates could not stand his bad grammar.

MATE: But he speaks perfect English, now.

HELMSMAN: So would you, if you were marooned on a desert island with nothing to read except a copy of *Basic Rules of English Grammar*. Unfortunately, he was rescued before he caught up on his writing and spelling.

LADY DORINDA: Who rescued him?

WING FOO: I did, Missy Dorinda. He promise to teach me English, but when he find out I can cook, he take away all my books. Make me slave over hot stove.

MATE: What do you say, Captain? True or false?

CAPTAIN: I refuse to answer.

BOSUN: Then you must be guilty.

GIL: The duel! Let's have the duel.

CAPTAIN: There will be no duel. Remember, I am still your Captain.

MATE *and* BOSUN (*Each thrusting a pistol into his ribs*): Then prove it. We serve no captain who refuses a fair fight.

CAPTAIN: This is mutiny, do you hear? Mutiny!

GIL: Spell it!

CAPTAIN: What?

GIL: Go ahead and spell it!! *Mutiny*. That's your first word.

MATE *and* BOSUN (*Poking him again with pistols*): Spell it, Captain, or you're done for.

CAPTAIN (*Spelling slowly*): M-U-T- (*Pauses*), M-U-T-T, M-U-T-T-A . . . I can't. I never could spell, not even the easiest words.

HELMSMAN (*With a sneer*): And you're the great Captain Castaway who made your prisoners walk the plank because of their grammar.

CAPTAIN: But spelling isn't grammar.

LADY DORINDA: No, but it's a very important part of our language. It's not enough to speak good English. You must also be able to write it correctly as well, before you set yourself up as an expert.

BOSUN: Well, lads, what shall we do with him?

MATE: Throw him overboard.

SPIES: Feed him to the sharks! (*They grab* CAPTAIN) One . . . two . . .

GIL: No! Stop!

COLIN: Let's give him another chance.

MATE: What?

MIKE: Why not? A few more years on a desert island and he may learn to spell.

DEBBY: Here, Captain, you may have my spelling book. (*Hands him a book*)

TEDDY LOU: And my dictionary. (*Hands him a book*)

GLORIA (*Handing him a notebook*): You'll need a pencil, and lots of paper. Twenty-five words a day should do the trick.

CAPTAIN (*Struggling*): No! No!

MATE: What do you say, mates?

ALL: Aye, aye!

WING FOO: Wing Foo get can of fresh water and tin of biscuits. (*Exits left*)

MATE: This way to the boat! (*They hustle* CAPTAIN *off left*) And the nearest desert island!

LADY DORINDA: So that's the end of Captain Castaway.

HELMSMAN: I doubt it. Sooner or later someone will rescue him, and he will be worse than ever.

MIKE: You're right. If he perfects his writing and spelling, he'll be a holy terror.

DEBBY (*To* HELMSMAN): Oh, please, sir, take us home again.

GLORIA: We must warn the others.

GIL: How?

TEDDY LOU: By describing the dreadful fate that awaits them if they don't mind their P's and Q's.

COLIN: Do you think they'll believe us?

LADY DORINDA: We can soon find out.

MIKE: How?

LADY DORINDA (*Pointing to audience*): Do you see all those boys and girls out there watching us?

MIKE (*Looking at audience*): Yes!

LADY DORINDA: We'll tell them a story that they'll never forget. I'll begin.

> Once there was a little boy
> Who laughed at grammar rules,
> And said he wouldn't use the speech
> Approved by proper schools.

GIL:

> He said it made no difference
> If he used "I seen," or "ain't,"
> He liked to use the kind of slang
> That made his teachers faint.

MIKE:

> But once when he was showing off
> With *lie* and *lay* and *lied,*
> A certain pirate captain
> Was standing by his side.
> "My name is Captain Castaway,"
> He heard the pirate shout.

ALL:

And the Captain will get *you*,
If you don't watch out.

GLORIA:

Once there was a little girl
Who said she didn't care
About the rules of grammar,
So she said, "This here! That there!"

DEBBY:

And as for verbs and pronouns,
She didn't give a hang,
Till one fine day she heard a knock
And then the doorbell rang.

TEDDY LOU:

And there stood Captain Castaway
To take her off to sea,
Along with other captives
Who were just as bad as she.

LADY DORINDA:

And no one heard her holler,
And no one heard her shout,

ALL:

And the Captain will get *you*,
If you don't watch out.

COLIN:

So when you study grammar,
Though you find it rather hard,
Beware lest Captain Castaway
Present his calling card.

DEBBY:

And if you are the careless type
Who says he doesn't care,
You'd better heed this warning
That you study, and beware

Of making stupid errors
In your writing and your speech,

LADY DORINDA:

And be a bit more mindful
Of what your teachers teach.

GLORIA:

And be careful of your language,
And know what you're about,

ALL:

Or the Captain will get *you*,
If you don't watch out. (*Curtain*)

THE END

An All-American Thank You

Characters

BILLY BREWSTER	BETTY HOPKINS
MARY BREWSTER, *his sister*	MRS. ABBOT
CORNY, *his friend*	MRS. TILLY
AUNT PRISCILLA ALDEN	JAN BRUZINSKI
FRED HOPKINS	

TIME: *Shortly before Thanksgiving.*

SETTING: *The living room of Aunt Priscilla Alden's home.*

AT RISE: BILLY BREWSTER *is sitting at a small table, a mirror in front of him, with his back to the audience.* BILLY *is busily pasting small red dots on his face from gummed red paper, which* CORNY *is punching out with paper punch.* CORNY *sits so that his leg cannot be seen by audience.*

BILLY: How am I doing?

CORNY: Fine. But you can't stop at the neck, Billy. You have to open your collar and do your chest. Maybe you'd better take off your shirt, so you can do the whole top half of you. I have plenty of red spots.

BILLY: Yeah, but they're all the same size. Can't you use a smaller punch so we get more variety?

CORNY: Your Uncle Corny thinks of everything. One smaller punch coming up. (*Exchanges punch for a smaller one*) You can spread these tiny ones around where they'll do the most good. (MARY BREWSTER *enters left, carrying a Pilgrim dress on a hanger and a suit box under her other arm. She stops in surprise.*)

MARY: Billy Brewster! What on earth are you doing?

BILLY (*Without turning around*): Go away!

MARY: Not till I find out what you're up to. Corny, why are you punching out all those holes?

CORNY: They're not holes, Mary. They're dots.

BILLY (*Whirling around to face the audience, his face well covered with red spots*): If you *must* know, we're making measles.

MARY: Making what?

BILLY: Measles!

CORNY: Or maybe chickenpox. We're not sure yet.

MARY: What are you talking about?

CORNY: In case you don't know it, Mary, your brother is about to break out in a Thanksgiving rash.

BILLY: Quiet, Corny. It would be just like her to run and tell.

MARY: I resent that, Billy Brewster. You know I'm not a tattletale. But if you two know what's good for you, you'll stop cutting out paper dots and put on your costumes. (*Hands him a box*)

BILLY (*Innocently*): What costumes?

MARY: You know perfectly well what costumes! You and Corny and I are to represent three of the children who came over on the *Mayflower* in the procession this afternoon.

BILLY: Maybe you're going to be in the procession, Mary, but Corny and I are going to be in the Cougar cheering section at the football game this afternoon.

MARY: But you can't. Aunt Priscilla is counting on you. She has the name of every man, woman and child on the *Mayflower* passenger list and every one must be represented.

CORNY: Now, I ask you, Mary, how could I possibly march in a procession and climb up that steep hill to the old burial ground with my whole foot and leg in a bandage? (*Limps out from behind table, displaying bandaged foot and leg*) My mother would never hear of it. And surely your Aunt Priscilla wouldn't want Billy to join the procession when he has measles, would she?

MARY: So that's your little game!

BILLY: It's not a game. It's a defense.

MARY: A defense against what?

BILLY: Against getting roped into that silly procession that will keep me from seeing Big Red Bruzinski in action.

MARY: That's the most unAmerican thing I ever heard.

CORNY: What's unAmerican about measles? Everybody gets 'em sooner or later.

MARY: But you're only making up an excuse to get out of your patriotic duty. Doesn't Thanksgiving mean anything to you at all?

CORNY: Sure! It means a football game and a turkey dinner.

MARY: I'm ashamed of you both.

BILLY: Oh, come on now, Mary. You know Thanksgiving means more to me than that. But gee whiz! You're only a girl. You don't understand about Bruzinski. He's an All-American halfback.

MARY: And you're a Non-American nothing. A disgrace to the name of Brewster! If you can't show any gratitude to your country, you could at least show some gratitude to Aunt Priscilla for having us here while Mother and Dad are away.

BILLY: I am grateful to Aunt Priss. Honest I am.

MARY: But you're deceiving her just the same. And you know how much this procession means to her. She started it years ago to remind people what Thanksgiving really means.

CORNY: As if they didn't know.

MARY: Oh, they know all right, but too many are just like you. They think only about turkey dinners and football games.

BILLY: It's easy for you to talk. Girls like to get dressed up and parade around.

MARY: Well, I'm not going to stand here and argue. I have to press my costume. But I'm warning you, Billy Brewster, you'll never get away with it. Aunt Priscilla will feel those pasted-on measles the minute she touches you.

BILLY: I aim to stay out of her reach.

MARY: Ha! She'll feel your head first thing to see if you have a fever. (*Exits right*)

BILLY (*Sitting on sofa with box beside him*): You know something, Corny? Maybe she's right.

CORNY: Don't worry. We can fool your aunt as easy as pie.

BILLY: I don't mean that. I mean maybe she's right about Thanksgiving. Maybe this *is* a dirty trick.

CORNY: Forget it. Big Red Bruzinski's worth a lot more than a bunch of make-believe Pilgrims. He's real!

BILLY: But so is Thanksgiving. And my Aunt Priscilla is a real descendant of John and Priscilla Alden.

CORNY: Yeah, I was in her room in school last year. She told us all about it. (*Doorbell rings.*) Holy Ned! Here she comes.

BILLY: She wouldn't ring her own doorbell, stupid. I'll get it. (*Goes off right*) Hi, Betty! Hello, Fred. Come in. (*Ushers in* BETTY *and* FRED, *both in Pilgrim costume*)

BETTY: Good grief, Billy. What's wrong with your face?

FRED: Don't tell me you're coming down with measles!

CORNY: Not really, Fred. But thanks a lot. Now we know Bill will pass the test.

FRED *and* BETTY: What test?

CORNY: The sick-list test. With my bad leg (*Limping*) and Billy's measles, neither one of us will be able to take part in the procession.

FRED (*Touching* BILLY'*s face*): Why, you old fakers! Those measles are only pasted on. What's the big idea?

CORNY: The football game—what else? The minute everybody's out of the house, it's Spaulding Field for us!

FRED: How about that! (*Moving to table*) Say, do you have any of those spots left over?

BETTY: Fred Hopkins, don't you dare! Miss Alden's having enough trouble.

BILLY: What kind of trouble?

MARY (*Entering right in Pilgrim costume*): Oh, hello, Betty, Fred. I'm glad to see you don't have measles or a sprained ankle. But then, I know nothing would keep you out of the procession.

FRED: That's really why we came over, Mary. We wanted to ask your aunt if there's any truth in the rumor that's going around.

MARY: What rumor?

BETTY: Well, we heard the procession is being called off.

ALL: Called off!

BILLY: But why?

CORNY: Nobody would dare.

MARY (*As phone rings*): Maybe that's Aunt Priscilla now. (*Answering phone*) The Alden residence. . . . I'm sorry, sir, she's not here just now. Is there a message? . . . What! No, indeed, I'm sure she never heard of such a law! Why wasn't she told about it before? . . . You *what!* You only just heard about it? . . . Oh, I see. But surely something could be done, even now. . . . How many names did you say? . . . Two hundred! Well, no, the procession's due to start in an hour. . . . Yes, yes, I understand. Yes, sir, it will be a terrible blow to her, but I'll tell her. Thank you; goodbye. (*Hangs up*)

CORNY: What was all that about?

MARY: You can take that bandage off your leg, Corny, and help Billy peel off those spots. There's not going to be a procession.

ALL: What happened?

MARY: It's your precious football team. The manager was afraid the procession would wreck the attendance at the game, so the lawyer for the Cougars dug up an old law from eighteen hundred and something that says you can't have a parade unless you present a petition with two hundred signatures.

FRED: But the procession isn't a parade; it's a ceremony.

MARY: Mr. Sikes, the man who called me, said anything that marches through the streets is a parade.

CORNY: But they can't do this.

MARY: Why are you so steamed up about it all of a sudden? You were trying your best to get out of it.

CORNY: But I never wanted to have it called off! Why, I've been in that procession ever since I can remember . . . and even *before* I can remember. My mother carried me when I was a baby. I was Peregrine White, the first English child born in this colony. Come on, Bill, get those spots off and start moving!

FRED: What are you going to do?

CORNY: You mean what are *we* going to do! (*Picking spots off* BILLY'*s face*)

BILLY: Ouch! That hurts. Take it easy!

CORNY: Sorry, chum, but time's a-wasting! How many names did that guy say we needed?

MARY: Two hundred. And there's hardly any time left.

CORNY: Time enough, if we hop to it. Now, everybody grab a pencil and a sheet of paper and follow me. (*MARY scurries around getting pencils and paper.*)

BETTY: Where are we going?

CORNY: I'll tell you when we get there. (*Surveying* BILLY) That's good enough, Bill. You're still speckly, but you'll have to do. Come on, kids!

MARY: I'd better wait here for Aunt Priscilla.

CORNY: O.K., but don't let her panic. We'll have a procession or my name isn't Cornelius Cornwall the Third. Now, come on. Move!

BILLY (*As all but* MARY *exit left*): Better press my costume, sis. I think your "Non-American nothing" might just be wearing it!

MARY (*Picking up costume box*): I never will understand boys. One minute they're all against you, the next minute they're all for you. (*Phone rings and she answers*) Alden residence. . . . Oh, yes, Mrs. Parks. Yes, we've heard the news, but Aunt Priscilla still hasn't called off the procession. No, no, she's not home yet, but I suggest you go right ahead with your plans. . . . Yes, I know, two o'clock sharp, at the church. Thank you for calling. Goodbye. (*Hangs up phone.* AUNT PRISCILLA *enters left with* MRS. ABBOT *and* MRS. TILLY *supporting her. All are in Pilgrim dress,* AUNT PRISCILLA *wearing a coat over hers.*)

AUNT PRISCILLA: I'm all right, Susan. Really I am.

MRS. ABBOT: Better get your aunt a glass of water, Mary. She's had some bad news.

MARY (*Running to her*): Aunt Priscilla, are you all right?

AUNT PRISCILLA: Of course, I am, child. Not a bit of need for all this fuss!

MRS. TILLY: Let me take your coat, Priscilla (*Does so*), and you sit right down. You look as if you might faint. (MRS.

ABBOTT *and* MRS. TILLY *help* AUNT PRISCILLA *to a chair.*)

MARY: I'll get that water right away. (*Runs off right*)

AUNT PRISCILLA: I never fainted in my life and I'm not about to start now. I'll admit it was a bit of a shock! (*As* MARY *re-enters with water*) But the end of the procession's not the end of the world, you know.

MARY: Drink this, Aunt Priscilla. (*Gives her glass of water*) I'll get your pills.

AUNT PRISCILLA (*Sipping water*): Thank you, Mary, but I don't need any pills.

MRS. ABBOT: But you're shaking!

AUNT PRISCILLA (*Returning glass to* MARY): Nonsense! I'm as steady as Plymouth Rock. (*Doorbell rings*)

MRS. ABBOT: Don't let anyone in, Mary. Your aunt isn't fit to see anyone right now.

AUNT PRISCILLA (*As* MARY *runs off left*): But maybe it's good news, Abby.

MRS. TILLY: Now don't get your hopes up, Priscilla. You might as well face it.

MARY (*Offstage*): I'm sorry, sir. My aunt isn't feeling well.

AUNT PRISCILLA (*Calling*): Mary, if that's one of my boys, you let him come in! (MARY *enters alone.*)

MARY: It's someone who says you were his favorite teacher. Someone named Jan.

AUNT PRISCILLA (*Rising and moving left*): Jan! Jan Bruzinski! You come right in here where I can see you. Do you hear?

BRUZINSKI (*Entering left*): Yes, ma'am!

AUNT PRISCILLA (*Extending both hands*): Mercy sakes' alive! How you've grown! I never would have known you.

BRUZINSKI: I'd know you in a million, Miss Alden! You . . . you haven't changed a bit. Not in all these years.

But what's this about your not feeling well? I don't like that at all.

Mrs. Abbot: Miss Alden has had a terrible shock.

Mrs. Tilly: She's very upset.

Bruzinski (*Helping her to a chair*): Then she must sit down and tell me all about it.

Aunt Priscilla (*Sitting down*): I never thought you'd be giving me orders, Jan. Abby . . . Susan . . . this is one of the finest boys I ever had in school, Jan Bruzinski. Jan, this is Mrs. Abbot, Mrs. Tilly, and my niece, Mary Brewster.

Bruzinski: Glad to know you!

Mary: Are you really Jan Bruzinski? Big Red Bruzinski, the football star?

Bruzinski: That's me all right . . . er . . . I mean, that is, I . . . er . . . I am he . . . oh, confound it, Miss Alden, I still get mixed up in my grammar.

Aunt Priscilla: Never mind, Jan. I'd still give you an "A" for effort!

Bruzinski: Now what's all this about having a shock? What happened?

Mary: But, Mr. Bruzinski, don't you know?

Mrs. Abbot: Miss Alden has just found out we must cancel the annual Pilgrim Procession because of the football game.

Bruzinski (*Shouting*): What!

Mrs. Tilly: It seems there's some sort of law we never heard of.

Bruzinski: But that's why I came! Miss Alden, can't you do something? You always promised me when I was big enough, I could play Miles Standish.

Mary: Excuse me, Mr. Bruzinski, but I'm afraid you don't understand. It was *your* lawyer who dug up the law that says we can't have a parade unless we get up a petition with at least two hundred names.

BRUZINSKI: *My* lawyer! I don't even have a lawyer.

MARY: Not your personal lawyer, sir—the lawyer for your team. He was afraid the procession would ruin the attendance at the game.

BRUZINSKI: Mike Masters! Wait till I get my hands on him. Miss Alden, where's your telephone?

AUNT PRISCILLA (*Pointing*): Right over there, Jan. But remember the law is the law.

BRUZINSKI (*At phone, dialing*): Hello? Is this the Club House at Spaulding Field? Bruzinski, here. Get me Mike Masters, please, and on the double! This is an emergency. . . . This you, Mike? This is Red. I want to know why you're interfering with this town's Thanksgiving procession. . . . Yeah . . . yeah. . . . Well, I have news for you. That game's been postponed till *after* the big parade, as you call it. . . . Why? Because I'm going to be *in* the parade, that's why. If you want to play without me, go right ahead. And as for that old law you dug up, I have one that's a lot older. Ever hear of the Bill of Rights? Well, then you know it's illegal to interfere with the freedom of worship or the right of people to assemble in peace. O.K. Then you march yourself right down to the Town Hall and straighten things out, because our Pilgrim Procession is going to assemble in about fifteen minutes and then proceed to the Old Burial Ground for a memorial service. . . . You do that. And no more monkey business. . . . Sure, sure, I appreciate your interest, but I'll appreciate this a lot more. See you later. Bye! (*Hangs up*)

AUNT PRISCILLA: Oh, Jan, you were just wonderful. Thank you. (BILLY, CORNY, FRED and BETTY *enter left, each waving a paper.*)

CORNY: We have 'em! One hundred and ninety-nine!

BETTY: When you sign, Mary, we'll have an even two hundred!

BILLY: Look, Aunt Priscilla. Here's your petition. Now we can have the procession.

AUNT PRISCILLA: Billy, what on earth is wrong with your face? You look as if you're getting measles.

BILLY: I'm not, Aunt Priscilla, honest.

MRS. ABBOT: And your poor leg, Corny. It's all bandaged.

MRS. TILLY: What happened?

CORNY: You've heard the old saying about putting your foot in it? Well, that's what I almost did.

FRED (*Quickly*): But thanks to Corny, the petition is lined up. He knew all the places with the biggest families in town.

BETTY: I'm not sure if it's strictly legal. Mr. Patrick Aloysius Timothy Reilly signed three times, once for each name.

CORNY: But we can go ahead with the procession.

AUNT PRISCILLA: Corny, you're a real hero. To think you'd run all over town on that bad leg.

CORNY: I'm no hero, Miss Alden. There's really nothing wrong with my leg.

BILLY: Please hurry, Aunt Priscilla. Call up that Mr. Sikes and tell him we have the names.

AUNT PRISCILLA: That won't be necessary, Billy. Thanks to Jan here, the situation is already well in hand. Jan, I want you to meet my nephew, Billy Brewster, his friend, Corny, and two of my most loyal helpers, Betty and Fred Hopkins.

ALL: How do you do.

AUNT PRISCILLA: When this fellow was your age, the other children called him Jan the Juggernaut. But his real name is Jan Bruzinski.

BOYS: Not Big Red Bruzinski!

BRUZINSKI: One and the same.

Mrs. Abbot: Mr. Bruzinski is going to take part in our procession.

Corny: But what about the game?

Bruzinski: First things first, my boy. The game comes later.

Mrs. Tilly: He wants to be Miles Standish.

Aunt Priscilla: Oh, I'm sorry about that, Jan. After you've waited all these years.

Bruzinski: You mean I'm still not big enough?

Aunt Priscilla: On the contrary, you're far *too* big! Miles Standish was never as tall as you are now. But it so happens our Mr. Brewster has come down with flu, so if you'd care to take his part . . .

Bruzinski (*Laughing*): You mean I'm finally going to become a Brewster?

Aunt Priscilla (*Smiling*): I had almost forgotten how you wanted to change your name from Bruzinski to Brewster so folks would think your family had arrived on the *Mayflower,* too!

Bruzinski: And you told me the name of the ship didn't matter. It's what a man does with his own name that really counts.

Corny: You've sure brought plenty of honor to your name, sir.

Billy: Bruzinski is just as famous as Brewster now.

Bruzinski: Thank you, Billy. And you know something? That's why I made such an effort to get here in time for the Thanksgiving procession. I wanted to thank the country that gave me the chance to make Bruzinski an all-American name! (*Taking* Aunt Priscilla *by the hand and helping her to her feet*) And a very special thank you to the little lady who taught me what being a true American really means. (*Curtain*)

THE END

The Rabbit Who Refused to Run

Characters

PETER RABBIT THE GREAT
FLOPPY
FLUFFY
RUFFY } *Briar Patch bunnies*
PUFFY
GRUFFY
MAMMA RABBIT
MR. OWL
ROBBIE, *a boy*

SETTING: *A forest glade.*

AT RISE: PETER RABBIT THE GREAT *is standing on a tree stump, leading Briar Patch bunnies as they sing "Bye, Baby Bunting." As they start to sing verse for the second time,* MAMMA RABBIT *enters, very upset.*

MAMMA RABBIT: Stop it! Stop it! Stop that terrible song!

ALL (*Except* PETER): What's the matter, Mamma?

MAMMA RABBIT: Where did you learn that horrible song?

PETER: I taught the bunnies the song, Mrs. Rabbit. What's wrong with it?

MAMMA RABBIT: It's a hunting song. That's what's wrong with it. Goodness sakes' alive! It gives me bunny bumps just to listen to it.

ALL: But we like it!

FLOPPY: Let's sing it again! (*Starts song.*)

MAMMA RABBIT: One more squeak out of you, Floppy Rabbit, and you go straight to bed without any supper. Now, you little rabbits, listen to me. This is the hunting season, and hunting is nothing to sing about.

PETER: It's nothing to be afraid of either, Mrs. Rabbit.

MAMMA RABBIT: Indeed! And just who are you? Where did you come from?

FLOPPY: He's our new friend.

FLUFFY: He just moved to the Briar Patch!

RUFFY: And he knows ever so many songs and games.

ALL: He's lots of fun!

MAMMA RABBIT: But that still doesn't answer my question. (*To* PETER) What is your name? And what are you doing here, filling my children's heads with such nonsense?

PETER: My name is Peter the Great. Surely you've heard of me.

MAMMA RABBIT: Peter the Great? There are lots of Peter Rabbits in the Briar Patch . . . Peter Cottontail, Peter Pink Nose, Peter Whiskers . . . but Peter the Great! That's a silly name for a rabbit.

PETER (*Boastfully*):
I want you to know that I'm named for a king—
A brave and a bold man was he.
Since I bear his name, I'll share in his fame,
And the whole world will hear about me!

MAMMA RABBIT: Humph! Well! I've heard enough about you already. Now please go home where you belong, before you get my babies into trouble.

PETER: But I haven't any home.

ALL: He hasn't any home.

MAMMA RABBIT: No home? No home at all?

PETER: Not any more. I used to live in a big house in the

city with a boy named Robbie. Every morning he gave me a big, juicy carrot, every noon a nice, fresh lettuce leaf, and every night a big head of cabbage. But then, one day, a terrible thing happened.

ALL: What?

PETER: Robbie's family moved away.

PUFFY: Why didn't they take you with them?

PETER: They wanted to, but I fell out of the station wagon and couldn't catch up with them. I tried to find my way back home, but I never got any further than the Briar Patch.

MAMMA RABBIT: You poor little fellow!

ALL: Weren't you scared?

PETER: Scared? What would I be scared of?

FLOPPY: Weren't you scared of being all alone?

FLUFFY: Weren't you afraid of the dark?

PETER (*Disdainfully*): Of course not! I'm never afraid! (*Strutting up and down*)
I'm not afraid of anything!
(At least not very much!)
I'm not afraid to stay at night
In my dark rabbit hutch!
I'm not afraid of motor cars,
I'm not afraid of boys!
I'm not afraid of sticks and stones,
I'm not afraid of noise!

MAMMA RABBIT: That's all well and good, Peter, but here in the Briar Patch, things are different. There are dozens of things to be afraid of: foxes and weasels and bears who come out of the woods . . . dogs and cats with their sharp teeth and terrible claws . . . snakes, and . . .

ALL: And thunderstorms!

MAMMA RABBIT: And most of all . . . *men!* Those big,

two-legged creatures who prowl through the forest at this time of year, with great dogs yapping at their heels, and big sticks in their hands. . . .

ALL: Sticks that go BANG! BANG! BANG!

PETER: I must say, you make it all sound pretty bad, but it doesn't do any good to be afraid.

ALL: But we *are* afraid!

FLOPPY:

When I see a man in a hunter's red hat,
My poor little heart goes pittity-pat!

PETER (*Singing to tune of "Who's Afraid of the Big Bad Wolf"*):

Who's afraid of an old red hat, old red hat, old red hat?
Who's afraid of an old red hat?
Ho, ho, ho, not me!

FLUFFY:

When I see a fox, all slinky and sly,
I'm so badly frightened I pretty near die!

PETER (*Singing, as before*):

Who's afraid of a sly old fox, sly old fox, sly old fox?
Who's afraid of a sly old fox?
Ho, ho, ho, not me!

RUFFY:

When I see a dog in the woods by the lake,
And hear his wild barking, I shiver and shake!

PETER (*Singing, as before*):

Who's afraid of a barking dog, barking dog, barking dog?
Who's afraid of a barking dog?
Ho, ho, ho, not me!

PUFFY:

When I see a hawk in the heavens so wide,
I hop to the bushes and lie down and hide!

PETER (*Singing, as before*):

Who's afraid of a flying hawk, flying hawk, flying hawk?
Who's afraid of a flying hawk?
Ho, ho, ho, not me!

GRUFFY:

Whenever I hear a loud bang or bump,
My poor little heart goes thumpity-thump!

PETER (*Singing, as before*):

Who's afraid of a big bang-bang, big bang-bang, big
bang-bang?
Who's afraid of a big bang-bang?
Ho, ho, ho, not me!

(*Speaking*) You're nothing but a bunch of scared rabbits.

MAMMA RABBIT: It's our nature to be timid.

PETER: Not me! I decided long ago—

If Peter the Great ruled the Russians
In the far, far away days of old,
Then I'll be the King of the Rabbits,
And make them courageous and bold!

ALL (*Except* MAMMA): Can you do that?

PETER: Sure I can!

FLOPPY: Can you make my heart stop going pittity-pat?

PUFFY: Can you make me stop running away?

GRUFFY: Can you keep my heart from going thumpity-thump, thumpity-thump, thumpity-thump-thump-
thump?

PETER: Of course I can!

MAMMA RABBIT: Don't listen to him, children. Rabbits are
born to be scared.

PETER: It's easy to be brave when you know the secret.

ALL: Tell us!

PETER (*As rabbits gather round*): Well, you see, when I
first went to live with Robbie, he was afraid of everything.
Thunderstorms, and spooky forms,

And shadows in the night,
Barbers, dentists, doctors, too,
He trembled at their sight!

Afraid to pick the rose that grows,
Afraid of thorn and thistle,
But things he feared, all disappeared
When Robbie learned to whistle!

ALL: What?

PETER: You heard me! Robbie wasn't afraid any more, after he learned to whistle.

MAMMA RABBIT: What does learning to whistle have to do with bravery?

PETER: Plenty! Robbie's mother was a very wise woman, and she wanted her little boy to stop being afraid of everything. So every night she sang a song to him. It sounded like this. (*Recording of "I Whistle a Happy Tune" from "The King and I" is heard. Rabbits strut about the stage and pantomime actions indicated by song.*)

RABBITS (*Clapping their hands*): Goody! Goody! Goody! Now we can all be brave as lions.

MAMMA RABBIT: That advice may be fine for boys and girls, Peter, but it will never work for rabbits.

PETER: Why not?

MAMMA RABBIT: Because rabbits can't whistle, that's why.

ALL: But we can try! (*They try desperately but unsuccessfully to whistle.*)

MAMMA RABBIT: It's no use, children.

FLOPPY: But we want to be brave.

RUFFY: We don't want to shiver and shake.

PUFFY: We don't want to run away and hide every time we hear a noise.

MR. OWL (*Calling from offstage*): Whooo . . . Whooo . . . Whooo!

RABBITS (*Huddling around* MAMMA RABBIT): What's that?
  What's that?
MAMMA RABBIT: No need to be frightened this time, chil-
  dren. It's our good friend, the Wise Old Owl.
MR. OWL (*Entering*): Whooo . . . whooo . . . whooo
  ever heard of such a thing? Whooo . . . whooo . . .
  whooo ever heard of a whistling rabbit?
RUFFY: But we want to be brave, Mr. Owl.
GRUFFY: We're ashamed of being scared all the time.
FLOPPY: Since you're such a wise old bird, maybe you can
  tell us what to do.
MR. OWL: Whooo—me?
ALL: Yes, you!
MR. OWL: Well, now, let me think.
PETER: Rabbits should learn to stand on their own four
  feet and face up to danger.
ALL: We'd rather fight than run.
MAMMA RABBIT: Did you ever hear such talk?
MR. OWL: Before you rabbits decide to fight, here's some-
  thing to think about—
  Now dogs and cats can bite and scratch,
  And even mules can kick;
  The birds of prey have claws that snatch,
  But rabbits must be *quick!*

  The billygoat butts down his foe,
  The rhino has his horn,
  But rabbits always run away,
  'Cause that's the way they're born.

  The kangaroo kicks up a fuss,
  And bumblebees can sting.
  Most animals have some defense,
  But rabbits . . . not a thing!

Except to scamper hippity-hop,
And safely hide away,
And that's how clever bunnies
Come back another day!

FLOPPY: Then it's no disgrace to run away from danger?

MAMMA RABBIT: Certainly not! It's just common sense.

PETER: But I still think you don't have to be afraid while you're running.

MR. OWL: You have a point there, my friend, although sometimes a good healthy dose of fear makes you run all the faster.

MAMMA RABBIT (*Pointing*): Look! Look, children! I think I see a spot of red in those bushes!

PETER: Ho! Ho! Ho! It's only a bunch of autumn leaves.

FLOPPY: But it's coming nearer—

FLUFFY: And nearer—

RUFFY: And nearer!

ALL: It's a red hat!

MAMMA RABBIT: Run! Run! Run for your lives! (*Rabbits run offstage in every direction.*)

PETER (*Standing his ground*): It's no use, Mr. Owl. I can never teach those cowardly rabbits to be brave. (*Offstage barking is heard.*)

MR. OWL: If you take my advice, Peter, you'll follow their example. I hear a dog barking.

PETER: I won't! I won't run away!

MR. OWL: It's too bad you ever came to the Briar Patch, Peter. You've lived too long in the city. (*Offstage bang is heard.*) There go the guns! The hunting season has started.

PETER: Oh, dear! My poor little heart is going thumpity-thump!

MR. OWL: Run, Peter, run!

PETER: No! No! No!

MR. OWL:
   To-whit-to-whoo! This day you'll rue!
   They'll make of you a rabbit stew!
PETER: Don't say that, Mr. Owl! Oh, if I could only whistle!
MR. OWL: They're coming closer, Peter. Save yourself!
   Save yourself!
PETER (*His teeth chattering with fright*): I won't run, I
   tell you! I won't run!
MR. OWL: Then walk! Or hop! Or creep! Or crawl! But
   get over there under one of those bushes as fast as you
   can! Hurry! (PETER *scampers under a bush as* ROBBIE
   *enters wearing a red baseball cap. He has a lettuce leaf
   in his hand.*)
ROBBIE: Peter! Where are you? Mr. Owl, have you seen a
   little rabbit around here?
MR. OWL (*With an innocent stare*): Whooo . . . Whooo
   . . . Whooo!
ROBBIE: Peter! Peter! You must be here someplace! Come
   see what I have for you—a nice, fresh lettuce leaf.
PETER (*Poking his head around the edge of the bush*): It
   sounds like Robbie. It *is* Robbie! (*Dashing out and
   throwing himself into* ROBBIE's *arms*) Robbie!
ROBBIE: Peter! Why, your poor little heart is going like a
   trip hammer!
PETER: I saw your red cap and thought the hunters were
   coming.
ROBBIE: But you remember my old baseball cap.
PETER: And then I heard a ferocious dog barking.
ROBBIE: But that was only Skipper. He's your friend.
PETER: And then there was that terrible bang.
ROBBIE: We had a flat tire.
PETER: Oh, Robbie, I'm so ashamed.
ROBBIE: Ashamed? Why?

PETER: Ashamed of running away. You can never call me Peter the Great again!

ROBBIE: And why not?

PETER: Because I turned tail and ran, just like any other scared rabbit.

ROBBIE: Thank goodness you had that much sense! Mother was afraid you wouldn't be able to take care of yourself in the forest. That's why we came back for you.

PETER: Then you're not ashamed of me?

ROBBIE: Of course not! You're still the greatest rabbit in the world. My very own Peter the Great!

PETER: But that's the name of a king, and kings *never* run away.

ROBBIE: Is that so? When we get home, I'm going to give you some history lessons, Peter. Don't you know that some of the bravest kings in the world were defeated in battle and ran away?

PETER: They did?

ROBBIE: Sure they did. Remember the King of France? (*Singing*) "The King of France with forty thousand men, marched up the hill and then marched down again!"

PETER: But it doesn't say he *ran!*

ROBBIE: No, but I'll bet he and his men were marching on the double! You see, Peter, both kings and rabbits have to learn how to take care of themselves. There's a very wise saying: "He who fights and runs away, lives to fight another day!" Now come along. We've kept Mother and Daddy waiting long enough. (ROBBIE *and* PETER *exit.*)

MR. OWL:

Whooo! Whooo! Whooo!

Good for you! Good for you! Good for you!

You can't change the habits of scared little rabbits.

They'll do what they're fashioned to do!

(*Calling to rabbits*) You can come out now! The coast is clear! (MAMMA RABBIT *and her children run back on-stage.*)

ALL: Where's Peter?

FLOPPY: What happened to him?

MR. OWL: Don't worry about Peter. He went back home with Robbie where he'll be safe and sound. It's time you forgot about him and listened to what your mother has to tell you. (*Rabbits sit in a ring as* MAMMA RABBIT *sings.*)

MAMMA RABBIT (*Singing to tune of "Yankee Doodle"*):
Listen to your mamma's words,
And not to any stranger.
If you're afraid, you ought to turn
And run away from danger!
(*All join in and repeat verse, as the curtain falls.*)

THE END

The Tomboy and the Dragon

Characters

KING HORACE
QUEEN MIRANDA, *his wife*
PRINCESS GLORIA, *their daughter*
PRINCE MICHAEL
DRAGON
TWO GUARDS
TWO DRAGON KEEPERS
THREE PAGES

TIME: *Long ago.*
SETTING: *The kingdom of Glockenspiel. The stage is divided into three sections. The right stage area is the throne room of the palace; two chairs are at center. The center stage area contains a large "rock"; chains hang from either side of the rock. The left stage area contains a long couch or table.*
AT RISE: DRAGON *lies sleeping on couch at left, covered with a gray blanket.* THREE PAGES *stand before the three stage areas. As the curtains open, they walk center.*

PAGES (*Bowing to audience, and reciting together*):
We're here to bid you welcome

To our worthy play,
Of King and Queen and Princess,
Who grace our stage today.
(*They gesture, moving hands in arc.*)
Let your imagination
Create this royal scene:
(1ST PAGE *steps right and points to right stage area.*)
1ST PAGE:
There stands the royal palace
Where live the King and Queen.
2ND PAGE (*Indicating center stage area*):
Here is a rock so bleak and bare
That few will dare to venture there.
3RD PAGE (*Indicating left stage area*):
And in that cave, so dark and deep,
The fearsome dragon lies asleep.
(*Loud snoring is heard from cave.* PAGES *sit.* KING *enters at right, reading a newspaper.* NOTE: *If desired, appropriate stage area may be spotlighted as action takes place.*)
KING: Trouble, trouble. Nothing but trouble. I don't see why I read this paper. Nothing but bad news. (*Sits on throne*) And not a word on the front page about Gloria's birthday.
QUEEN (*Entering right, wringing her handkerchief*): Oh dear, oh dear! I'm so upset. Horace, how can you sit there reading the paper, when our daughter is about to be devoured by that hateful dragon?
KING (*Barely looking up from paper*): Calm yourself, Miranda. You know perfectly well that nothing will happen to Gloria. Prince Michael will overcome the dragon and rescue her.
QUEEN: How can you be sure? Something might go wrong.
KING: Nonsense! I overcame the dragon and rescued you, didn't I? Your father rescued your mother. My father

rescued my mother. Our grandparents rescued each other. So what is there to worry about?

QUEEN: Just the same, I hate this custom! What a way for a princess to celebrate her sixteenth birthday—chained to a rock, a dragon breathing in her face, just so that a prince can rescue her. I'll never forget how frightened I was, before you rescued me.

KING: Gloria isn't likely to be frightened. She's such a tomboy, it would take more than a dragon to scare her.

QUEEN (*Sitting*): That's another thing that worries me. It's not proper for a princess to be a tomboy—all that running and jumping and horseback riding and swimming. And those clothes she wears. Blue jeans, and Bermuda shorts, and slacks! Now, when I was a princess, that was not considered proper dress.

KING: That was a long time ago, my dear, and times have changed. (*Pointing to picture in paper*) Ah, here it is. I should have known a royal birthday would be written up on the society page. (*Reading*) "Tomboy Princess To Face Dragon on Sixteenth Birthday!" (*Showing paper to* QUEEN) And what a splendid picture. Look, my dear.

QUEEN (*Glancing at paper and speaking angrily*): Tomboy princess, indeed. And look at the disgraceful outfit she's wearing. She looks like a boy! (GLORIA *and* PRINCE MICHAEL *enter right, identically dressed in white, long-sleeved shirts, bright blue trousers, and blue satin shoulder capes.* GLORIA's *hair is covered with a blue beret trimmed with a white plume and a small gold crown.* MICHAEL *wears a similar beret.* GLORIA *carries a tennis racquet.*)

MICHAEL (*Bowing*): Good morning, Your Majesties.

GLORIA: Good morning, Mother and Father. Aren't you going to wish me a happy birthday?

KING (*Looking closely at* GLORIA): Is that you, Gloria? (*Looking at* MICHAEL) Or are you Gloria?

MICHAEL (*Taking off his beret*): I'm Prince Michael, Your Majesty. The Royal Seamstress made these outfits for us as a birthday surprise for Gloria.

GLORIA: Yes, aren't they lovely? I had my picture taken for the newspaper yesterday wearing these clothes.

QUEEN (*Angrily*): You've disgraced the Royal House of Glockenspiel.

GLORIA: But, Mother, what have I done?

QUEEN: Those dreadful clothes, and this awful picture of you wearing them. No daughter of mine is going to face a dragon looking like a tomboy. Michael, you go out and wait in the garden while Gloria goes upstairs and changes into her pink dress with the ruffles.

MICHAEL: All right, Your Majesty. I'll see you in the garden, Gloria. (*He puts on his beret, bows, and exits right.*)

GLORIA: But I don't want to change, Mother. (*Offstage gong is rung three times.*)

KING: Sorry, Miranda, there won't be time. She'll have to go as she is. That's the signal for the ceremonies to begin.

QUEEN (*Lying back limply on throne*): Oh dear! Oh dear! I think I'm going to faint!

KING: Now, Miranda, that's no way for a Queen to behave. We must give Gloria our blessing, and send her on her way. (*Descending from throne; to* GLORIA) Best of luck to you, daughter, and although I know your mother doesn't agree with me, I think that outfit is much better for rock climbing than any pink ruffles.

GLORIA: Oh, thank you, Father.

QUEEN (*Descending from throne*): Do try to be brave, Gloria, and remember . . . in spite of that disgraceful costume, I still love you.

GLORIA (*Hugging* QUEEN): Thank you, Mother. Don't worry about me. Michael will cut off that old dragon's head with a single blow, and we'll all live happily ever after. (*She starts to exit right.*)

QUEEN: Wait! Wait! (*Reaching in pocket of robe and bringing out a perfume atomizer*) I almost forgot to give you this!

GLORIA: A present? Thank you, Mother! (*Taking the atomizer; disappointedly*) Oh—perfume.

QUEEN: It's not just ordinary perfume, Gloria. It's made from a secret formula by the little men in the mountains. Every princess of Glockenspiel has used it on her sixteenth birthday. They say it helps to give you courage.

GLORIA: Thank you, Mother, but, really, I'm not one bit scared. So please don't worry. You have enough to do getting ready for the triumphant reception when Michael and I return. Bye! (GLORIA *exits right.*)

KING: She's a brave girl, Miranda. (*Offering* QUEEN *his arm*)

QUEEN: I know, but I can't help worrying. Suppose something does go wrong! (KING *and* QUEEN *exit right.*)

2ND PAGE (*Rising at center stage area*):
    Something has gone wrong, I fear,
    The Guards have brought Prince Michael here.
    (2ND PAGE *sits down as* TWO GUARDS *enter at center, dragging* PRINCE MICHAEL *between them.* MICHAEL *still wears his blue outfit, and struggles to free himself from the* GUARDS.)

1ST GUARD: Take it easy, Princess Gloria! We're only doing our duty.

MICHAEL: Unhand me, you villains! Can't you see I'm not the Princess?

2ND GUARD (*As* MICHAEL *pretends to kick him*): Ouch! I know you're a bit nervous, Your Highness, but don't worry. The Prince will rescue you from the dragon.

MICHAEL: But I *am* the Prince. Prince Michael of Albagania.

1ST GUARD: You can't fool us, Your Highness! I have your picture right here in the morning paper. (*Holding MICHAEL's arm with one hand, he pulls clipping from his pocket.*)

2ND GUARD: Now, come along like a good girl, and don't give us any trouble.

MICHAEL (*Sitting on floor and kicking*): Stop calling me a girl. I'm the Prince, I tell you. Let me go.

1ST GUARD (*Holding clipping in one hand, looking from clipping to MICHAEL*): This is your picture. You're even wearing the same blue outfit.

2ND GUARD (*Peering at clipping*): A good likeness of you, Your Highness.

MICHAEL (*As GUARDS pull him to his feet and drag him to rock*): Who will come to my rescue? Help!

1ST GUARD (*Reaching for chain and tying MICHAEL's wrist*): For shame, Your Highness. No other Princess of Glockenspiel has ever been so frightened.

2ND GUARD (*Tying other wrist, as MICHAEL struggles*): And no other Princess has ever been so strong.

1ST GUARD: No wonder they call her the Tomboy Princess. (*They finish tying MICHAEL to rock.*)

MICHAEL: Help! Help! Listen to me, you idiots. I am the Prince.

1ST GUARD (*Starting to exit center*): Come on, let's go, and leave her to her fate.

2ND GUARD (*Joining him*): It seems a cruel thing to do, but we know she is perfectly safe. Prince Michael is a brave lad, and he's very handy with a sword.

MICHAEL: I don't even have a sword. I was on my way to get it when you seized me in the palace garden.

1ST GUARD: What a little storyteller she's turned out to be. (*GUARDS exit center. MICHAEL stands quietly at rock during the next scene.*)

3RD PAGE (*Rising*):

Soon the Dragon will wake up,
Starved for meat on which to sup.
(3RD PAGE *sits down.* TWO DRAGON KEEPERS *enter left,
carrying spears.* 1ST KEEPER *also carries an alarm clock.*)
1ST KEEPER: Oh, dear! He's sleeping like a rock. (DRAGON
snores.) He'll never hear the alarm. (*Sets off alarm,
holding it close to* DRAGON, *who snores again.*)
2ND KEEPER (*Poking at* DRAGON *with spear*): Wake up!
Wake up, Dragon. It's time for action. (DRAGON *stirs
and snorts.*)
1ST KEEPER: I'll pull the covers off. That should wake him.
(*Pulls off gray blanket, disclosing* DRAGON.)
KEEPERS (*Poking*): Get up! Get up! (DRAGON *rolls over,
snorting several times.*)
1ST KEEPER: I never saw such a sleepyhead!
2ND KEEPER: You'd think he'd be hungry after sleeping for
twenty years.
1ST KEEPER (*Shaking* DRAGON): Come on, Dragon. Wake
up! You mustn't keep the Princess waiting.
DRAGON (*Yawning and swinging his tail over the edge of
the table*): Princess? What Princess?
1ST KEEPER: The Princess Gloria of Glockenspiel.
2ND KEEPER: As dainty a morsel as any dragon could wish
for!
DRAGON: Oh, dear. Don't tell me I have to go through that
again.
1ST KEEPER: But aren't you hungry?
DRAGON: Starved. But you know as well as I do that I'll
never get to eat her. Some prince will come along and
drive me away before I get a single bite.
2ND KEEPER: Maybe things will be different this year.
DRAGON: That's what you always say. But I know better.
One of these days I'll be killed.
1ST KEEPER: Now, now. We must look on the bright side.

2ND KEEPER: It's up to you to defend the honor of Dragon-dom.

DRAGON (*Crossly*): Oh, all right! If I must, I must.

1ST KEEPER: Do you want us to go with you?

DRAGON (*Snorting*): Certainly not! You'd be of no use whatsoever. I'll go by myself.

1ST KEEPER: But what if . . . what if something should happen?

DRAGON: Wait here. If I'm not back in ten minutes, you can come and look for what's left of me. (*Roaring fiercely*) Fee, fie, fo, fum! Look out, Princess, here I come. (DRAGON KEEPERS *exit left as* DRAGON *shuffles right to* MICHAEL) Ah, there you are, my little beauty.

MICHAEL: Look, Dragon, there's been a mistake. I am *not* the Princess. I am the Prince.

DRAGON: Well, that's a switch. I must say, you don't look very much like a princess. (*Approaching* MICHAEL *and sniffing*) And I don't smell any of that horrible perfume.

MICHAEL: Naturally not. Now, do be a good fellow and bite off my chains so I can get out of here.

DRAGON: I'll do nothing of the sort.

MICHAEL: But I'm not the Princess.

DRAGON: My stomach won't know the difference. For once in my life I can have a square meal without any prince coming to chop at my head! And without that terrible perfume to make me feel sick.

MICHAEL: You don't mean to say you'd . . .

DRAGON: Gobble you up? That's exactly what I mean to do. Yum, yum! What a breakfast you'll make.

MICHAEL (*As* DRAGON *approaches him with open jaws*): Help! Help! (GLORIA *runs in from center. She still carries the tennis racquet and atomizer.*)

GLORIA (*Calling*): Has anybody seen Michael? He's not in the garden . . . (*She sees* MICHAEL *and* DRAGON, *and runs to rock.*) Michael!

MICHAEL: Be careful, Gloria. He's dangerous.

GLORIA (*Brandishing her tennis racquet at* DRAGON): Get out of here! Shoo! Scat! Out! Out! (DRAGON *leaps and lunges at* GLORIA, *who sidesteps him and flails with her racquet. She swats at* DRAGON, *but he knocks the racquet out of her hand.*)

MICHAEL: Run, Gloria, run!

GLORIA (*Retreating*): I'll never leave you, Mike.

MICHAEL (*As* GLORIA *backs up against the rock beside him*): He'll kill both of us. Save yourself. Run!

DRAGON (*Gleefully*):
How your bones will snap and crunch.
One for breakfast. One for lunch.
(*He crouches ready to spring.*)

GLORIA: Maybe I can blind him with perfume. (*She squirts perfume at* DRAGON, *who falls back, staggering.* GLORIA *pursues him, still squirting perfume.*)

DRAGON: No! No! Not that! (*Staggers and is about to fall.* GLORIA *grabs her racquet and gives him a blow.* DRAGON *does an elaborate fall, with much writhing and twisting.*) I'm done for. Finished. (DRAGON *lies quietly on floor.*)

GLORIA (*Wiping her forehead*): Whew! Well, I guess that finished him off.

MICHAEL: Nice going, Gloria. Now, if you can only get me loose. . . .

GLORIA (*Running to him*): Oh, poor dear. Those nasty chains. Wait. (*Reaching in her pocket*) I think I have a nail file. (*She pretends to file chains, and frees* MICHAEL *after a moment.*)

MICHAEL (*Rubbing his wrists*): Thanks, Gloria, thanks a lot.

GLORIA: Thank heavens I arrived in time. Now we can go back to the palace and live happily ever after.

MICHAEL: I'm sorry, Gloria, but that is impossible . . . now.

GLORIA: Why? I slew the dragon and saved your life!

MICHAEL: That's just the trouble. *You* slew the dragon. *You* saved *me*. How do you think I feel—being rescued by a girl?

GLORIA: Michael! What a thing to say.

MICHAEL: A prince rescued by a princess? Everyone will laugh at me.

GLORIA: But I promise not to tell a soul! No one will ever know.

MICHAEL: It never would have happened, if you had dressed like a proper princess.

GLORIA (*Indignantly*): What do you mean?

MICHAEL: Well, I never said anything about it before, but I like a princess to *look* like a princess. Why do you always have to dress like a boy?

GLORIA: How can you talk like that, after what I did for you?

MICHAEL: I appreciate what you did, Gloria. You were ever so brave and strong, but . . . well . . . I guess that's part of it.

GLORIA: Part of what?

MICHAEL: Part of not wanting to live happily ever after. You see, it was *my* job to kill the dragon, not yours. Now I'm a failure as a prince.

GLORIA (*Furiously*): You're just jealous. That's what you are. And I hate you! I wish I had let that dragon grind you into bits. (*Sound of bells offstage*) Oh, dear. They're ringing the church bells. It's time for the triumphal procession. Listen to me, you ungrateful wretch. You can go back to Albagania and stay there for all I care. But if you don't show up for the procession and the grand ball, I'll get my father to throw you into his darkest dungeon forever. Understand?

MICHAEL: O.K., O.K. I'll be there. (*As* GLORIA *runs off center*) But I'm warning you, the minute that ball is over, I'm leaving for Albagania. (*Kicking at* Dragon) Some dragon you are. Letting a girl knock you dead with a tennis racquet.

Dragon (*Sitting up with a snort*): Who says I'm dead?

Michael (*Leaping back*): Gosh! He's alive.

Dragon: Of course, I'm alive. And don't look so scared. I'm not going to eat you. In fact, I won't be able to eat for days, not after that blast of perfume.

Michael: Perfume?

Dragon: Listen to me, young man. I heard every word of that stupid conversation you had with the Princess.

Michael: But I thought she killed you!

Dragon: Obviously, she didn't. But you're feeling sorry for yourself because you're not a hero. Well, let me tell you something. None of those other princes I've met were heroes, either.

Michael: But the prince *always* slays the dragon.

Dragon: You really do believe in fairy tales, don't you? The truth is, not one of those brave fellows ever so much as scratched me. It was always the *princess* who did me in.

Michael: How?

Dragon: That perfume! I can't stand it. Makes me sick as a dog. One whiff of it and I pass out of the picture. But I've been lucky so far. The prince has always been so eager to start living happily ever after with his princess that he's never bothered to see if I was dead!

Michael (*Wistfully*): Not me. I've lost my chances of living happily ever after.

Dragon: Oh, I wouldn't say that.

Michael: But Gloria will never forgive me. Not after what I said to her.

Dragon: Have you ever told her how beautiful she is?

Michael: I'd like to, but she's too much of a tomboy to think about her looks. She'd only laugh at me.

DRAGON: I've never seen a girl yet who was too much of a tomboy to want a compliment. Go try it and see.

MICHAEL: Thanks, Dragon! I believe I will. (*Turning, about to exit center*) Isn't there something I can do for you?

DRAGON (*Starting to crawl off left*): No, thanks, my boy! I'll just crawl back to my cave. Maybe my keepers will make me some tea and toast. That always settles my stomach. (DRAGON *crawls back to his rock, left, as* MICHAEL *runs off, center.*)

1ST PAGE (*Rising*):
The King and Queen think all is well,
And wait to hear the wedding bell. (*Sits*)

KING (*Entering right with* QUEEN): What did I tell you, my dear? Our little daughter is home again, all safe and sound.

QUEEN: But where is Prince Michael? We can't start the procession without him.

KING: He's probably cleaning up. Fighting a dragon, as I remember, is a pretty messy business.

GLORIA (*Entering right, wearing pink dress with ruffles*): Well, I'm ready. When do we start?

KING: Gloria! How beautiful you look!

QUEEN: You put on your pink dress.

GLORIA: Of course. You don't think I'd ride in the procession looking like a tomboy, do you?

QUEEN: Did you hear that, Horace? I do believe our Gloria is a proper princess, after all.

KING: Naturally, my dear, naturally.

GLORIA (*Impatiently*): Well, what are we waiting for?

QUEEN: For Prince Michael, of course.

GLORIA (*Contemptuously*): Oh, him!

KING: That's no way to speak of the Prince who just rescued you from a ferocious dragon.

MICHAEL (*Running in from right*): Gloria! Gloria! Can you ever forgive me?

GLORIA (*Turning her back on* MICHAEL): Don't even speak to me.

QUEEN: Gloria, I'm ashamed of you.

KING (*Shaking hands with* MICHAEL): Congratulations, son! You polished off that dragon in record time.

MICHAEL (*With a look at* GLORIA): It . . . it was really nothing, sire.

QUEEN (*Proudly*): Such a modest young man. Now, do come along, children. The golden coach is waiting.

MICHAEL: Just a minute, please. I have something to say to Gloria.

KING (*Offering his arm to* QUEEN *and leading her off right*): Come, Miranda. They wish to be alone. (KING *and* QUEEN *exit right.*)

GLORIA: There's nothing you can say that I want to hear.

MICHAEL: Please listen to me, Gloria. I'm sorry I was such a stupid idiot, and I can't go without telling you how beautiful you are.

GLORIA (*In surprise*): Me? Beautiful?

MICHAEL: Gorgeous! That dress is so becoming. It makes you look like a princess.

GLORIA: But I *am* a princess, silly.

MICHAEL: I know, but I've never told you that you're the most beautiful princess in the world.

GLORIA: You really mean it?

MICHAEL (*Kneeling*): I really mean it, Gloria, and, well . . . I've changed my mind. I want to live happily ever after.

GLORIA: Even with a tomboy?

MICHAEL: With the loveliest tomboy on earth. Please say yes.

GLORIA: Yes! Oh, Michael, I'm the happiest girl in the world.

MICHAEL (*Grabbing her hand*): Come on. I'll race you to the coach.

GLORIA (*Starting to run, then suddenly stopping*): Wait! We almost forgot. I am no longer a tomboy princess. I am the future Queen of Albagania. Please, sir, your arm. (MICHAEL *offers her his arm and they walk sedately off, right.*)

PAGES (*Together*): Long live Prince Michael and Princess Gloria! (*Quick curtain.*)

THE END

The Paper Bag Mystery

Characters

JUDY
NITA
CINDY
FLORRIE } *Girl Scouts*
PAM
DELLA
MISS ENDERS, *Girl Scout leader*
BRAINY
BRAWNY
FOXY (MR. FOX), *school janitor*
MR. DIEHL
TWO OFFICERS

SETTING: *A school office. At left is a safe with a combination lock.*

AT RISE: *Offstage pounding and banging is heard. After a short pause,* BRAINY *and* BRAWNY *enter.* BRAWNY *carries a large paper bag.* BRAINY *has two pairs of coveralls over his arm and carries a long-handled dust mop and a dustpan.* BRAINY *also carries large paper bag, concealed by the coveralls.*

BRAWNY: That old man is sure putting up a fuss!
BRAINY (*Putting mop and dustpan down*): Oh, let him

bang! Who can hear him? There's nothing more deserted than an empty school building.

BRAWNY: I still think we should have tied him up.

BRAINY: Since when do you do the thinking? I'm Brainy, remember? You're Brawny! I do the thinking, you do the heavy work.

BRAWNY: O.K., O.K. You're always right. But this place gives me the creeps.

BRAINY: That's because you *are* a creep. I tell you this old school building is deserted. They're tearing it down next month.

BRAWNY: Then why do they still have a janitor?

BRAINY: Good question! Maybe you do think after all. But Old Foxy has been here forever. Used to be janitor when I went to school here. I guess they're keeping him on till the last minute. Anyhow he's all nicely settled in the furnace room, and we have the place to ourselves. We can hide the jewels in the school safe and sack out here for the weekend.

BRAWNY: What about chow? I'm hungry.

BRAINY: It's in the bag, stupid!

BRAWNY: But I thought the jewels were in the bag.

BRAINY: There you go . . . thinking again! That bag you're carrying has our supplies.

BRAWNY (*Setting bag on nearest desk and looking inside*): Oh, boy, bananas! And ham sandwiches! Gee, I hope you remembered the mustard! Yep, here it is. But what about the loot?

BRAINY: Right here. (*He throws coveralls on a desk and produces second bag, the same size, which he was carrying under the coveralls.*)

BRAWNY: Let's have a look. (*Pulling out sparkling necklace*) Wow! What a string of ice!

BRAINY: Worth a fortune, that one. A single one of those stones will see us safely to Hong Kong.

JUDY (*Calling from offstage*): Mr. Fox, we're here! Mr. Fox, where are you?

BRAINY: Quick! Someone's coming!

BRAWNY (*Putting jewels back into bag*): The safe! Hurry! (*As* BRAINY *kneels in front of safe,* BRAWNY *puts the jewel bag on a chair.*)

BRAINY (*As he turns dial of combination lock*): A good thing I know the combination.

BRAWNY: Hurry up, can't you?

BRAINY: There's something wrong.

JUDY (*Calling again, louder, from offstage*): Mr. Fox! Yoo-hoo, Mr. Fox!

BRAINY: They're coming closer. Get into a pair of those coveralls, quick! (*As* BRAWNY *struggles to put on coveralls*) I'll need more time. This thing won't open.

BRAWNY (*With the coveralls half on, half off*): Let's make a run for it!

BRAINY (*Rising*): We'll duck into a classroom. Grab that mop and dustpan! Come on, this way! (*He snatches up second pair of coveralls and bag with lunch from top of desk. They dash off left,* BRAWNY *still struggling with the coveralls. Almost immediately* JUDY *appears at door. She carries a paper bag.*)

JUDY (*Entering*): It's all right, girls. The door's open. (NITA, FLORRIE, DELLA, CINDY, *and* PAM *enter, each one carrying a large paper bag.* CINDY *and* PAM, *entering last, carry a large cardboard carton between them. The girls all put their paper bags on a nearby desk.*)

NITA: Good old Foxy! He said he'd have everything ready for us.

FLORRIE: But where is he? He said he'd help us.

DELLA: Oh, he's around someplace. Don't worry. Old Foxy never misses a trick.

CINDY (*As she and* PAM *set box down on floor*): This box is heavy! I've never seen so much junk.

FLORRIE: Come on, Della, let's give them a hand with that. You and Pam take that side, Cindy, and we'll put it up on the desk.

JUDY: Wait a minute! Let's get these nose bags out of the way, so you have more room. There's plenty of space over there, Nita. (*She and* NITA *put all the lunch bags on another desk.*) There you are!

CINDY: Let's go, girls. One . . . two . . . three . . . heave! (*The girls lift the carton onto the desk.*)

JUDY: That's better. Now we can get at it.

PAM (*Noticing paper bag on chair*): Here's somebody's lunch. I'll put it with the others. (*Places jewel bag with other paper bags on second desk*)

JUDY (*Looking into box*): No wonder this thing's so heavy. (*Taking out a large pack of folded paper bags*) It looks as if we have enough to fill all these bags and more.

CINDY: I can get more bags if we need them, Judy. Mr. Burns at the grocery store said we may have as many as we need. He's one hundred percent for the Girl Scouts, and he thinks our Indoor Fair is a great idea. He even gave me some candy for the grab bags.

DELLA: I wish more people were like Mr. Burns. That nasty Mr. Diehl down at the jewelry store won't even let me put a poster in his window. He says Girl Scouting is for the birds.

FLORRIE: Mr. Diehl is the one who is giving Miss Enders such a hard time. He refuses to go along with the idea of leasing this old building to the Girl Scouts. (*Offstage banging and pounding is heard.*)

ALL: What was that?

NITA: It sounds like something down in the basement.

FLORRIE: Maybe we should investigate.

PAM: Not me! I wouldn't go down there for the world. It's bad enough to be in this building all by ourselves.

JUDY: For goodness' sake, Pam! How are you going to camp

overnight in the woods if you're afraid to spend a few hours in a school building in broad daylight?

NITA: Besides, we're not alone. Mr. Fox is here somewhere and Miss Enders should be arriving any minute.

DELLA: Anyhow I've heard that noise lots of times. It's nothing but the heat coming up in these old pipes.

PAM: Just the same I wish Mr. Fox would show up.

JUDY: Mr. Fox or no Mr. Fox, we must get to work if we're to fill these grab bags before lunch.

CINDY: Speaking of lunch . . . I'm hungry. Anybody mind if I eat a banana?

DELLA: Help yourself. The nose bags are all over there on that desk. (*As* CINDY *goes to lunch bags*) I'll set up these empty bags, and we'll dump all the stuff out on the desk. (DELLA *and* PAM *take various items from box.*)

FLORRIE (*Examining items*): A whole box of Life Savers, a pack of powder puffs, loads of ballpoint pens, crayons, nail polish, purse-size Kleenex, fancy pencils. . . .

DELLA: Beads, bracelets, pins. . . . We seem to have more jewelry than anything else.

CINDY (*Holding banana in one hand, jewel bag in the other*): And here's more jewelry, a whole bag full. I wonder how it got in with our nose bags.

PAM: That must be the one I picked up off the chair. I thought it was somebody's lunch.

JUDY: Just dump it in with the rest. (*As* CINDY *empties jewels from bag*) Oh, boy! This is much nicer than the rest of the costume jewelry.

FLORRIE (*Holding up necklace*): I'll say! Isn't this gorgeous?

JUDY: It looks almost real, doesn't it?

DELLA: Since all my experience with diamonds has been limited to the dime-store variety, I wouldn't know. But it *is* pretty.

NITA: How do we go about dividing all this junk?

JUDY: It really doesn't matter, just so each bag has a little of everything. We don't want anyone yelling about not getting her ten cents' worth. (*Girls begin to put various articles into bags.*)

FLORRIE (*Taking ball of string and scissors from carton and sitting at desk*): You girls fill the bags, and I'll tie them shut. (*Girls continue to talk as they fill bags and bring them to* FLORRIE'S *desk.*)

NITA: I still wonder who brought that necklace and all those pretty rings and bracelets.

CINDY: Probably Miss Enders. She said she was going to round up some stuff, so maybe she left it here earlier.

NITA: Then where is she?

DELLA: Probably in the gym. Mr. Fox put the booths up yesterday and I'll bet Miss Enders has some of the girls over there decorating.

JUDY: I guess that's why the doors happened to be open.

PAM: I still think it's funny about Foxy. Any other time he'd be right here checking on us. (MISS ENDERS *enters, also in Scout uniform, carrying several bags and packages.*)

MISS ENDERS: Sorry I'm late, girls, but there was a terrible traffic jam on Main Street. (*Puts packages on desk*) I see Mr. Fox had everything ready for you.

NITA: We haven't seen Mr. Fox, Miss Enders.

MISS ENDERS: Then how did you get in?

PAM: The building was open.

MISS ENDERS: The office, too? (*Girls nod their heads.*) Dear me, that isn't a bit like Mr. Fox. He's usually so particular about everything. That's why we're so anxious to keep him on here if the Girl Scouts take over the building officially.

JUDY: Maybe he's in one of the classrooms or went out on an errand.

MISS ENDERS: Just the same, I've never known him to leave the building open, to say nothing of the office.

DELLA: He should know by this time that Girl Scouts know how to take care of things.

MISS ENDERS: Well, I must say you've taken good care of things here. I see you've filled most of the grab bags. (*Looking inside one of the bags*) Who brought the lovely costume jewelry?

JUDY: Somebody brought it in early this morning.

CINDY: We thought you had brought it.

MISS ENDERS (*Opening one of her bags*): Oh, I brought a few pieces, but nothing as nice as those rings and pins. I wouldn't mind having some of those myself.

NITA: We'll have to fill a special bag just for you, Miss Enders. After all, you're the Number One VIP in Scouting.

MISS ENDERS: No VIP's today, Nita. I'll have to take my chances with the rest. Well, since you girls have everything under control, I think I'll run over to the gym. As soon as we decorate the booths, you can take the grab bags over there.

PAM: What about the baked goods and handicraft items?

MISS ENDERS: You didn't read your instructions, Pam. All that goes directly to the gym, and I do hope Mr. Fox has it unlocked. I suppose I really should make a tour of the building and track him down. (BRAINY *and* BRAWNY *enter, wearing coveralls and carrying mop and dustpan.*) I'll look for Mr. Fox now.

BRAINY: That won't be necessary, ma'am. Foxy won't be here today.

MISS ENDERS: Why not? And who are you?

BRAINY: I'm his nephew, ma'am, and this is my side-kick. Foxy asked us to work for him today. He's laid up with a bad back.

JUDY (*Amazed*): A bad back! Foxy?

MISS ENDERS: That's too bad, but thank fortune, you're here. I knew Mr. Fox would never let us down. What's wrong with his back?

BRAINY: Just the same old trouble, ma'am. Guess he strained a muscle.

JUDY: Strained a muscle!

MISS ENDERS: I do hope he didn't hurt himself on those booths.

BRAINY: Uncle Foxy's not as young as he used to be.

MISS ENDERS: We'll have to be more thoughtful of him in the future. Do you happen to know if the gym is unlocked, Mr. . . .

BRAINY: Just call me Joe, ma'am, and yes, yes, the gym doors are open.

BRAWNY: Yes, ma'am, that's where he was when we . . .

MISS ENDERS: You mean the poor man actually came to work this morning?

BRAINY (*With a dirty look at* BRAWNY): Well—yes—er—he came, but his back was so bad, he had to give up, so he called us from here. Brawny, I mean Barney, here, is supposed to do the cleaning.

MISS ENDERS: I'm so glad everything is under control. Now, if you girls have about finished, I can use you to help with the decorating.

CINDY: What about getting more bags from Mr. Burns?

MISS ENDERS: Maybe you'd better do that, Cindy. These grab bags always go like hot cakes.

JUDY: Do you think I should stay here and fill the few we have left?

MISS ENDERS: Oh, no, we have enough to start with, Judy, and perhaps Joe, or maybe. . . . (*To* BRAINY) What did you say his name was? (*Points to* BRAWNY.)

BRAINY: Barney, ma'am. And we'll be glad to look after things here.

MISS ENDERS: Oh, thank you. That would be a great help. (*To girls*) Come along, girls.

CINDY (*As she and others exit*): I'll run down and get more bags from Mr. Burns.

JUDY (*Exiting last*): Wait! Wait for me, Cindy. Wait a minute.

BRAINY (*As soon as girls are out of sight*): Now quick! Tell me where you left that bag, you goon!

BRAWNY (*Pointing to chair*): Right there on that chair.

BRAINY (*Looking*): Well, it's not here now! A fine mess you've made of things!

BRAWNY (*Looking at nose bags on desk*): Maybe it's over here with these. (*Opens one*) Nope . . . lunch! (*Examining the others*) More lunch! Gee, these girls must be big eaters.

BRAINY: Ye gods! It could be anywhere in this mess!

BRAWNY (*Still examining nose bags*): Hey, some of these lunches are great! Layer cake . . . cookies . . . oh, boy —grapes! Golly, there's nothing I like better than grapes. (*Pops one into his mouth*)

BRAINY (*Whacking BRAWNY's fingers*): Put those grapes back and help me look through these bags. This is all your fault, you stupid oaf!

BRAWNY: You're not so smart either! You said this building was deserted.

BRAINY: How did I know the place would be crawling with Girl Scouts? (*Pointing to grab bags*) Now untie these bags, look through them, and tie them shut again. We don't want these kids and that dame to get wise to us. (JUDY *enters with* CINDY *and* PAM.)

JUDY: Hey! What are you doing with those bags?

BRAINY: Nothing, miss. Er—this string just seemed to be a bit loose.

JUDY: Well, we'll fix it. Miss Enders wants both of you in the gym, right away.

BRAWNY: But we can't go now . . . we have some—er—work to do here.

BRAINY: Shut up, you! (*Taking him by the arm*) And come along. You heard what the young lady said. (*As* BRAINY *and* BRAWNY *exit, the offstage pounding resumes, this time in a definite Morse Code S.O.S. pattern—three dots, three dashes, three dots.*)

JUDY: Girls, there's something funny going on here.

CINDY: You mean that pounding?

PAM: It doesn't sound like radiators to me.

JUDY: Not only the pounding, but the whole thing—the unlocked building . . . these men. They're up to something.

CINDY: But what?

PAM: How do you know?

JUDY: Because that one who calls himself Joe is lying. Foxy never had a bad back in his life, and he couldn't have strained a muscle putting up those flimsy booths.

CINDY: That's right, Judy. Didn't Foxy take up weight lifting or something?

PAM: He's always bragging about how he can lift more than men half his age.

JUDY: And that's not all. He said Foxy called from here. How could he? The telephone has been disconnected for a week.

CINDY (*As pounding grows louder*): Listen. . . . Doesn't that sound familiar? (*Girls listen as pounding is heard again in S.O.S. pattern.*) That's the Morse Code for S.O.S. Somebody needs help!

PAM: Do you suppose it could be Foxy?

CINDY: The boiler room is right beneath us.

JUDY: Girls, I'll bet it *is* Foxy. I'll bet those men have him shut up in the boiler room!

PAM: I'm going to find out.

JUDY: But you said you wouldn't go down there for the world.

PAM: But I'd go for Foxy, if he were in trouble. (*Runs off left*)

JUDY: Cindy, I'm afraid. We need some help.

CINDY: I'll go get Miss Enders. (*As she starts to dash off right,* BRAWNY *enters and grabs her.*)

BRAWNY: Not so fast, little girl. Where do you think you're going?

JUDY: You let go of her. She's only going on an errand for Miss Enders.

BRAINY (*Entering*): What's the trouble?

BRAWNY: This one was trying to get away, and I stopped her.

JUDY: Don't be silly. She's only going for more paper bags, Joe. You heard Miss Enders tell her to get more.

BRAINY (*Sarcastically*): Oh, sure, that's what we need . . . more paper bags. (*To* BRAWNY) But let her go, you dope, let her go.

JUDY (*As* BRAWNY *releases* CINDY): Now listen to me, Cindy. I just thought of something. Instead of asking Mr. Burns for those paper bags, be sure to talk to his brother.

CINDY (*Puzzled*): His brother?

JUDY: Yes, his brother, Timothy. You tell him, and he'll send us exactly what we need. Understand?

CINDY (*Suddenly catching on*): Oh, now I get you . . . his brother! O.K., Judy, don't worry. I'll tell him.

JUDY: And hurry! We need those supplies plenty fast. (CINDY *exits.*)

BRAINY: You know I'm mighty curious about all these paper bags, miss. What's in them?

JUDY: Mostly junk, odds and ends the Girl Scouts collected.

BRAWNY: What are you going to do with the bags?

JUDY: Sell them, of course. Our troop has charge of the grab bags at the fair.

BRAINY (*Picking one up*): How much?

JUDY: Ten cents.

BRAWNY: Ten cents!

JUDY: Is that too much?

BRAINY: Not at all. In fact, I've just been thinking of offering to buy the whole lot.

JUDY: But that wouldn't be any fun.

BRAINY: Suppose I were to offer you fifteen cents, fifteen cents a bag for the lot? That way you'd make more money for your troop.

JUDY: I don't know. I don't know about that.

BRAINY: Suppose I make it twenty cents a bag, or even a quarter. . . .

JUDY: I—I'd have to ask Miss Enders. She wouldn't want us to charge that much.

BRAINY: Suppose I insist?

JUDY: What do you mean "insist"?

BRAWNY: Oh, for Pete's sake, Brainy, why don't you cut out all the double-talk and take the bags? (PAM *and* FOXY *enter, unnoticed by the others.* FOXY *carries a long-handled mop.*) There's nobody here to stop us!

FOXY: I'm not so sure about that. Nobody to stop you indeed!

JUDY: Foxy!

BRAWNY: The old coot got out of the furnace room! (*Snatches as many bags as he can carry*) Out of my way, old man, I'm coming through! (FOXY *flails about with his mop.*)

BRAINY (*Also snatching up bags*): We were too easy on you the first time. (*Gives* FOXY *a push that sends him sprawling.* BRAINY *and* BRAWNY *dash out right.*)

JUDY: Oh, Foxy, Foxy, are you hurt?

FOXY (*Picking himself up*): Only my pride! That's the second time today those thieves have bested me.

PAM: Thieves?

FOXY: Yes, thieves. They robbed Diehl's Jewelry Store this morning.

PAM: Judy, those rings and necklaces weren't costume jewelry after all. They were the real thing!

JUDY: And now the thieves have managed to get away! (*There is a scuffle at the doorway as* TWO OFFICERS *enter with* BRAINY *and* BRAWNY, *who are still clutching the paper bags.*)

1ST OFFICER: Put those bags on the desk. (BRAINY *and* BRAWNY *do so.*)

2ND OFFICER: Now hands up, both of you!

CINDY (*Rushing on breathlessly*): Oh, thank goodness the police arrived in time! Chief Burns called the cruiser right away. (MISS ENDERS *enters with* NITA, DELLA, *and* FLORRIE.)

MISS ENDERS: What in the world is going on here? (*Sees* FOXY) Mr. Fox, I thought you were ill!

FOXY: No such thing, Miss Enders, just tied up down in the boiler room till the girls caught on to my S.O.S. signal and came to the rescue.

FLORRIE: S.O.S.?

NITA: So that's what all the banging and pounding was about.

DELLA: We thought it was the radiators.

FOXY: I managed to bang on the pipes. When I remembered you girls were studying about signals in your Scouting manual, I decided to try Morse Code.

MISS ENDERS: But what has happened? Who are these men and how did the police get here?

1ST OFFICER: These two characters robbed Diehl's Jewelry Store early this morning.

2ND OFFICER: They were hiding out here, but one of your girls notified Chief Burns, and he called the squad car.

CINDY: It was Judy's idea. She told me to go to Mr. Burns's brother, and it finally dawned on me that Mr. Timothy Burns is the Chief of Police.

1ST OFFICER: Mighty quick thinking, young ladies. (MR. DIEHL *enters, wildly excited.*)

MR. DIEHL: Chief Burns just called me! Where are they? Let me get my hands on them!

2ND OFFICER: Now, now, Mr. Diehl. Everything is under control.

1ST OFFICER: We just want you to identify these men so we can take them down to Headquarters.

MR. DIEHL: Those are the two who robbed me all right. I'd know them anywhere. But the jewels, where are they?

JUDY: Right here, Mr. Diehl. (*Indicating bags*)

PAM: But I guess you'll have to look through the whole batch to find them.

DELLA: We didn't know they were real, so we tried to make a fair division . . . a few in each bag.

NITA: We thought they were costume jewelry.

MR. DIEHL: Costume jewelry! Young lady, these villains took the finest gems in my collection.

BRAWNY: Quick, Brainy, let's make a break for it! (*The two thieves break loose. There is a scuffle during which* FOXY *and* JUDY *manage to put two large paper bags over their heads.*)

FOXY: There! That ought to fix 'em. Take 'em away, men, before I really lose my temper!

1ST OFFICER: Come along, you two, and no more of your tricks!

2ND OFFICER (*As they steer* BRAINY *and* BRAWNY *off right*): Well, Mr. Diehl, it looks as if this case is really in the bag!

MR. DIEHL: I'll be right down to make a formal statement as soon as I recover the jewels. I want to thank Chief Burns personally for all he has done. Oh—and thank *you*, Officers. Thank you very much.

1ST OFFICER: Don't thank us, sir. Thank the Girl Scouts.

2ND OFFICER: If it hadn't been for them, these no-goods would have escaped. (OFFICERS *exit with* BRAINY *and* BRAWNY.)

MR. DIEHL: Just what did you Girl Scouts have to do with this?

FOXY: Plenty. Without their Scout training, they never would have recognized my S.O.S.

CINDY: And it was Judy who sent me to Chief Burns for help.

MR. DIEHL: Do you mean to say that a handful of little girls stopped those desperadoes in their tracks?

MISS ENDERS: But these are not ordinary little girls, Mr. Diehl. They are Girl Scouts living up to the Girl Scout Law, and a Girl Scout's duty is to be useful and to help others.

MR. DIEHL: Miss Enders, you and I have been on opposite sides of the fence for a long time, but from now on, I am one hundred percent on the side of the Girl Scouts. I can promise you my full support in acquiring this building for your headquarters. And what's more, the rental fees will come out of the reward money I have offered for the capture of the thieves and the return of my property.

GIRLS (*Ad lib*): Oh, boy! That's great! How marvelous! (*Etc.*)

MISS ENDERS: Thank, you, Mr. Diehl. I promise you you'll never regret it.

MR. DIEHL (*Extending his hand*): Let's shake on that, Miss Enders.

FLORRIE (*As* MISS ENDERS *extends her hand*): Give him the Girl Scout Handshake, Miss Enders. It's the best way to seal a friendship. (MISS ENDERS *gives* MR. DIEHL *the Girl Scout Handshake, which is repeated by the rest of the troop as the curtains close.*)

THE END

S.O.S. from Santa

Characters

SANTA	KING OF HEARTS
MRS. SANTA	QUEEN OF HEARTS
HOP ⎤	PETER COTTONTAIL
SKIP ⎬ *Santa's elves*	MRS. COTTONTAIL
JUMP ⎦	PILGRIM
SNIP ⎤ *Santa's tailors*	PILGRIM DAME
SNAP ⎦	UNCLE SAM
GHOST	APRIL FOOL

TIME: *Christmas Eve.*

SETTING: *Santa's sitting room.*

AT RISE: SANTA, *wearing high black boots and a bathrobe, is pacing up and down.* MRS. SANTA *follows, trying to calm him.*

SANTA: Donder and Blitzen! Here it is—Christmas Eve, and I have nothing to wear.

MRS. SANTA: Now, now, Santa. Remember your blood pressure.

SANTA: You should have thought of that when you sent my entire wardrobe to the cleaner.

MRS. SANTA: But everything was covered with soot.

SANTA: *Soot* doesn't bother me! It's my *suit!* I must have my suit!

Mrs. Santa (*Brightly*): There's always your summer seer-sucker.

Santa: Summer seersucker, bah! When it's cold enough to freeze the red light on Rudolph's nose, you talk to me about summer seersucker.

Mrs. Santa: But you'd be warm enough with your thermal underwear.

Santa: Thermal underwear, poppycock! What do you suppose the children would think to see me crawling out of a fireplace in a summer seersucker?

Mrs. Santa: The children will be fast asleep.

Santa: You don't know much about children on Christmas Eve. Half of them will be wide awake, peeping over the stair rail, or hiding behind the sofa to see me arrive.

Mrs. Santa: What about your gray flannel or your navy blue pin stripe?

Santa (*Turning on her*): For the last time, woman, I will hear no more about my summer seersucker, my gray flannel, my navy blue pin stripe, my Irish tweed, my Scotch plaid or my velvet smoking jacket. I cannot, I will not, I *dare* not stir out of this house without my red suit, my fur-trimmed cap, my heavy white gloves, my red muffler, and my thick woolen socks. Now where *are* they?

Mrs. Santa (*Wringing her hands*): Oh, dearie, dearie me! If only I knew. I don't remember whether I sent them to the Evergreen Cleaners, the Nevergreen Cleaners, or the Everclean Cleaners. But if you'll just be patient . . .

Santa: I don't have time to be patient. I should be dressed and ready to go right now.

Mrs. Santa: Hop, Skip and Jump are making the rounds of the cleaning establishments. They should be back any minute.

Santa: All the cleaning places are closed at this hour of the night.

MRS. SANTA: You can count on your elves to get in. After all, this is an emergency.

SANTA: That's the only thing you've said tonight that has my wholehearted approval.

MRS. SANTA (*As* HOP, SKIP *and* JUMP *enter left*): What did I tell you? Here they come now.

HOP: No luck, Santa. The man at Evergreen said he never saw your suit.

SKIP: Same story at the Nevergreen plant, Santa.

JUMP: The night watchman at Everclean went through the whole shop and there wasn't a trace of a Santa Claus suit.

SANTA: I'm done for! My whole career wiped out! My reputation ruined!

HOP: There's still a chance, sir. We stopped at HBN, the Holiday Broadcasting Network, and they're putting a special announcement on the air right away.

SKIP: An S.O.S. to everybody in Holiday Land.

JUMP: Surely someone will find your suit.

SANTA: No doubt! Along about Easter or the Fourth of July somebody will discover it. But I need help now, tonight, this very minute!

MRS. SANTA: What about Snip and Snap? With their new magic sewing machine they should be able to make you a whole new suit in a matter of minutes.

HOP: A great idea, Mrs. Santa. Let me ring for them. (*Rings a bell-pull made of sleigh bells*)

SKIP: Good thinking, Mrs. Santa. Snip and Snap will fix him up in no time.

JUMP: Your troubles are over, Santa. With Snip and Snap on the job you have nothing to worry about. (SNIP *and* SNAP *enter right.*)

SNIP: You rang for us, Santa?

SNAP: Snip and I were just about ready to go to bed, but we came as fast as we could.

SANTA: Sorry to disturb you after hours, but we have an emergency. How long would it take you to make me a new suit?

SNIP *and* SNAP: A new suit?

SANTA: From top to toe—coat, trousers, cap, everything.

SNIP: Well . . . we already have your measurements.

SNAP: And we can use the old pattern with just a few enlargements here and there. When do you need it?

SANTA: An hour ago! But if you can finish it in twenty minutes, I'll still have time.

SNIP: Twenty minutes!

SNAP: That's not very long.

SNIP: What do you think, Snap?

SNAP (*Shrugging his shoulders*): We can try.

HOP: This is a real S.O.S.

SNAP: We'll get to work at once.

SANTA: Splendid! (*Clapping them on the shoulder*) I knew I could count on you. (SNIP *and* SNAP *turn to exit, then stop and face* SANTA.)

SNIP: Oh dear! We *do* have one problem.

SANTA: What is it?

SNAP: It's the matter of color, Santa.

SNIP: What color would you like, sir?

SANTA: There's only one possible color for a Santa Claus suit . . . red!

SNIP *and* SNAP (*Nodding gravely to each other*): I was afraid of that.

MRS. SANTA: What do you mean?

SNIP: We don't have a single scrap of red material left in the workroom.

SNAP: We used the last bolt yesterday for the toy soldiers.

SNIP (*Brightly*): But we have yards and yards of a lovely green, Santa, and plenty of purple.

SNAP: And a beautiful bright blue that would just match your eyes.

SNIP: I'm not quite sure, but I think we have a few yards of brilliant orange.

SANTA (*Holding his head with both hands and groaning*): I can't bear it!

MRS. SANTA: Are you positively certain there's no more red?

SNAP: Absolutely, positively certain, one hundred percent sure!

SANTA (*Sinking into a chair*): Then you can't help me. Please go! Leave me to my misery.

SNIP: We're terribly sorry, Santa.

SNAP: We'd do anything we could.

MRS. SANTA: I know you would and we appreciate it. But there's just nothing you can do, so you might as well go to bed.

SNIP *and* SNAP (*As they exit right*): Good night, Mrs. Santa. Good night, Santa.

MRS. SANTA (*Starting to cry*): It's all my fault! If only I could remember where I sent that suit.

HOP: Maybe you didn't send it anywhere.

SKIP: Maybe it's right here in the house.

JUMP: Wrapped in mothballs or something.

MRS. SANTA: No, I know I sent it away to be cleaned. (*There is a pounding at the door.*)

SANTA: Don't let anyone in. I don't want to see a living soul. I'm a disgrace to Christmas.

MRS. SANTA: Don't say such a thing, Santa. (*Pounding grows louder and a deep groaning wail is heard from offstage.*)

HOP: Someone must be in trouble. (*Another offstage wail is heard.*)

SKIP: Maybe someone is lost or hurt.

JUMP: We'd better open the door.

MRS. SANTA: Yes! We couldn't turn anyone away on Christmas Eve! (*As she moves to open door left, she utters a shriek as* Ghost *enters wearing traditional ghost attire and carrying laundry bundle.*)

Hop, Skip *and* Jump: A ghost!

Santa: Who are you? What do you want?

Ghost (*Juggling laundry package so he can present a calling card to* Santa): My card, sir. I represent the Greater Ghosts and Goblins of Halloween Associates. We just heard your S.O.S. over the Holiday Broadcasting Network, and I've come to help.

Santa (*Making a grab for the laundry package*): You've found my suit!

Ghost: Sorry, Santa. That's my extra supply of pillowcases back from the laundry. I thought I might need them for toy packs when I take over.

Santa: When you take over!

Ghost: That's why I'm here, to make Santa's rounds tonight.

Mrs. Santa: But you're a ghost!

Hop: You'd scare the wits out of the children.

Skip: And think how you would look after just one trip down a chimney.

Ghost: May I remind you, friends, that I can make myself invisible whenever I wish, so I would not frighten anyone. Besides, I won't need to come down the chimneys. A ghost can go right through walls, doors, rooftops—anywhere he likes.

Santa: But you belong to Halloween, not to Christmas.

Ghost: I'm surprised at you, Santa. You should really spend more time in the public library. It just so happens that the most famous Christmas story in all the world is about ghosts.

Mrs. Santa: You must be talking about Dickens' *Christmas Carol*.

Ghost: Exactly, madam. There you will find the Ghost of

Jacob Marley as well as the Ghost of Christmas Past, the Ghost of Christmas Present and the Spirit of Christmas Yet to Come.

SANTA: I'm sorry, but somehow I just don't like the idea.

GHOST: It may seem a bit strange to you at first, Santa, but actually ghosts and witches and roving spirits have an honored place at Christmastime. All over the world children like to sit around the fire, listening to ghost stories on Christmas Eve.

JUMP: That would be fun.

GHOST: And besides, there are many superstitions about ghosts and witches who ride abroad at Christmastime.

SANTA: I hate to seem ungrateful, but, no, I really can't accept your offer. (*Knock at door is heard.*)

GHOST: If you don't mind, I'll just stay a while. Perhaps you'll change your mind. (*Sits*)

SKIP (*As knock sounds again*): I'll get it. Maybe someone has found the missing suit. (*He moves left and admits* PILGRIM *and* PILGRIM DAME, *who has a small basket on her arm.*)

PILGRIM: Good even. We beg your leave to enter.

MRS. SANTA: Do come in.

SANTA (*Greeting guests*): What a surprise! A pair of Pilgrims on Christmas Eve.

PILGRIM: My good dame and I have heard of your ill fortune, sir, and we have come to be of service.

PILGRIM DAME: When we heard your call for help, we set forth at once.

SANTA: Most good of you, but I am afraid there's nothing you can do.

PILGRIM: Be not so certain of that, my friend. I have come to drive your sleigh tonight.

HOP, SKIP *and* JUMP: Drive Santa's sleigh!

PILGRIM DAME: I know my husband has not had much experience with reindeer, but in England, he quite often drove a coach and four.

PILGRIM: The chimneys, of course, are out of the question. I would deliver the packages at the door.

SANTA: This is truly amazing. From what little I know of history, you Pilgrim folk did not exactly approve of Christmas celebrations.

PILGRIM: Quite so. But here in William Bradford's *Journal (Showing* SANTA *a small book which he carries under his arm)* is an account of Christmas Day at Plymouth Rock in the year sixteen hundred twenty. *(Showing page to* SANTA) You will note how when ye Governor called out men for work, most of the company excused themselves because it went against their conscience to work on ye Day.

PILGRIM DAME: And they spent their time at play, pitching ye bar, playing Stoole Ball and such like sports.

PILGRIM: Of course, we do not hold with gaming or reveling on ye streets, but times have changed, and what a man does in his own house is a matter of his own conscience.

MRS. SANTA: But you Pilgrims belong to Thanksgiving— not to Christmas.

PILGRIM: Every day should be a day of Thanksgiving, Mistress Claus, and what better day to give thanks than Christmas?

PILGRIM DAME: I am sure the children will be most grateful for the gifts they receive. In truth I could not bear to see the little ones deprived of their trinkets and their poppets.

SANTA: I never would have believed it, never! *(Knock on door is heard.)*

MRS. SANTA: More callers. See who it is, Skip.

GHOST *(As* SKIP *goes left to door)*: Good Pilgrims, if you

don't mind sitting next to a ghost, perhaps you will join
me on the sofa.

PILGRIMS (*Seating themselves*): Thank you, Master Spook.

SKIP (*Admitting* KING *and* QUEEN OF HEARTS): Wow! The
King and Queen of Hearts!

MRS. SANTA (*With a curtsy*): Welcome, your Majesties!

SANTA: We are indeed honored by this visit.

KING OF HEARTS:

> Your Christmas plea, your S.O.S.,
> The signal of your dire distress,
> Has touched our hearts, and so we've come,
> To help you make your Christmas run.

QUEEN OF HEARTS:

> My Lord and I would lend a hand
> And carry out your least command.
> To spare you sorrow and disgrace,
> The King of Hearts will take your place.

SANTA: Oh, thank you, but that's impossible. The children
would think it was Valentine's Day.

KING:

> But Christmas is a day of love,
> And joyful tidings from above.
> Because of all the day imparts,
> Who's better than the King of Hearts?

QUEEN:

> He'll fill each stocking to the brim;
> With *love* each Christmas tree he'll trim.
> And when the children see their toys,
> Our gift of love will swell their joys.

MRS. SANTA: They're right, Santa. Christmas wouldn't be
Christmas without love and kindness and happy hearts.

JUMP: I think it's a great idea, Santa.

SANTA: I couldn't allow it. I must go myself.

MRS. SANTA: Please, Santa, not in your bathrobe. (*Knock
at door is heard.*)

SANTA (*With a bow*): If your Majesties will wait a few minutes, we can discuss this further. (*Showing them to seats on either side of fireplace*)

SKIP (*Admitting* PETER *and* MRS. COTTONTAIL): Great jangling jingle bells! It's the Easter Bunny.

PETER COTTONTAIL (*Bowing*): Peter Cottontail, at your service, and Mrs. Cottontail, too. Now, Santa, if you will show me where things are, we will get Christmas on the road.

SANTA: Wait a minute! This is *Christmas*—not Easter!

PETER: And Christmas is a time for helping our friends and neighbors.

MRS. COTTONTAIL: The minute we heard your S.O.S. on the Holiday Network, we hopped right over.

SANTA: I thank you both from the bottom of my heart, but it just wouldn't do.

MRS. COTTONTAIL: Why not?

SANTA: For one thing, your clothing isn't suitable for chimney-hopping.

MRS. SANTA: And you're accustomed to filling nests . . . not stockings.

PETER: Nests or stockings, Easter eggs or Christmas gifts —what's the difference? You and I are in the same business, Santa—the business of making children happy.

MRS. COTTONTAIL: And every child loves the Easter Bunny.

SANTA: But it's the wrong time of year.

MRS. SANTA: We couldn't impose on you.

PETER: Nonsense! If Santa finds his suit by Eastertime, he can return the favor by delivering the Easter eggs.

SANTA: Me deliver Easter eggs? What is the world coming to? (*Knock at door is heard.*)

MRS. SANTA: Please, sit down. (*Showing them to chairs*) We've never had so many callers on Christmas Eve.

SANTA (*As* SKIP *admits* UNCLE SAM): Bless my buttons, if

it's not Uncle Sam! (*Shaking hands*) Come in. I think
you know all these good people.

UNCLE SAM (*Tipping his hat*): Of course. What a pleasure
to see our great holiday representatives gathered together.

MRS. SANTA: What can we do for you, Uncle Sam?

UNCLE SAM: It's what I can do for you! I've come in answer to Santa's S.O.S.

HOP: Don't tell me you want to play Santa Claus!

SKIP: Another applicant.

JUMP: If only Christmas came on the Fourth of July.

UNCLE SAM: Dates are not important, except in history
lessons, and as for playing Santa, I think I'd make a good
one. After all, America is the land of holidays . . . the
country where every man is free to celebrate the holidays
of his choice and observe the customs of his native land.
What do you say, Santa? Would you accept me as a substitute?

SANTA: It would be a great sight to see Uncle Sam driving
my reindeer through the skies, but I am afraid the children of other nations might not understand.

UNCLE SAM: You have a point there, Santa. We must think
of some way to help you.

MRS. SANTA: The best and only way would be to find his
suit.

UNCLE SAM: Since we haven't been able to do that, suppose
we do the next best thing.

ALL: What's that?

UNCLE SAM: Make do with what we have.

SANTA: But all I have is the boots!

UNCLE SAM: Splendid! We'll start with those and from
there on we'll invent, improvise, use the materials at
hand to build a complete outfit.

PILGRIM: Just as we did at our first Thanksgiving. Every
family in Plymouth contributed something.

PILGRIM DAME: Since Santa already has the boots, allow me to furnish the socks. (*Producing a pair from her basket*) I spun the yarn and knit them myself so I know they are good and warm.

SANTA: Thank you. Woolen socks are a must on Christmas Eve.

KING (*Standing*):
My trousers may be somewhat tight,
But then, at least, the color's right!

HOP: Hurry, Santa. Let's go to your dressing room and try them on.

SKIP: We'll help you, Santa.

JUMP: You'll be dressed in a jiffy. (SANTA, HOP, SKIP, JUMP, *and* KING *exit right.*)

MRS. SANTA: But can we find a coat that will fit him?

QUEEN:
My velvet coat is full and wide.
He just might squeeze himself inside.
(*Removes coat and hands it to* MRS. SANTA)

MRS. COTTONTAIL (*As* MRS. SANTA *is about to take coat off-stage*): A Santa Claus suit must be trimmed with fur, and I always carry an extra supply in case Peter catches himself on a briar bush. (*Searches in handbag and draws out a length of cotton batting*) I'm sure there's enough here for an edging.

MRS. SANTA: Splendid. Snip and Snap will be able to sew it on in a few seconds.

PILGRIM (*Unfastening his belt*): He'll need a good, broad belt to hold himself together. (*Handing belt to* MRS. SANTA) I hope it's big enough.

MRS. SANTA: Don't worry. Snip and Snap can always set a piece in the back where it won't show. (*Exits right*)

PETER (*Taking watch from pocket*): I'll give him my gold watch. It keeps perfect holiday time.

PILGRIM DAME: That tie of yours would make a fine muffler, Uncle Sam, if it's long enough.

UNCLE SAM (*Removing tie which is a long scarf wound around his neck*): An excellent idea. He'll need a warm scarf on a night like this.

GHOST (*Wailing*): But what about me? I'm all in one piece! I have nothing to give!

UNCLE SAM: Don't worry, friend. It's the spirit that counts.

MRS. COTTONTAIL (*Giggling*): I just happened to think, your Majesty, how will his Royal Highness manage without his trousers?

QUEEN:
> The King of Hearts will find a way!
> His velvet cloak will save the day!

(SANTA *appears right in doorway dressed in costume very much like his traditional suit, but with no hat.*)

SANTA: Here I am. How do I look?

ALL (*Ad lib*): Fine! Splendid! Perfect! Wonderful! (*Etc.*)
(SANTA *moves to center, followed by* SNIP *and* SNAP, MRS. SANTA, HOP, SKIP, JUMP, *and* KING, *who is clutching his cape about him.*)

UNCLE SAM: Just one more thing, Santa. (*Adjusting scarf around* SANTA'S *neck*) We can't have you catching cold. (*Removing white gloves*) Take my gloves. They're good and warm. (SANTA *takes gloves.*)

PETER (*Offering watch*): You'll need a timepiece, Santa. Allow me to offer you my watch.

SANTA: I'll take good care of it, Peter. And now, thanks to my good friends from Holiday Land, I'm ready to take off. Boys, you may harness my sleigh.

ELVES: It's ready and waiting, Santa.

SANTA: Good! Mrs. Santa, my pack, if you please.

MRS. SANTA (*Dumfounded*): Your pack! Oh my goodness sakes' alive!

SANTA: Don't tell me you don't know where it is.

GHOST: Never mind, Santa! (*Quickly undoing laundry bundle*) Take one of these. (*Holds up pillowcase*)

SANTA: But it's so small.

GHOST: There are plenty more. (*Hands bundle to* HOP) Fill them up as you please, Santa. It's my contribution.

SANTA: And I thank you, sir.

HOP: I've never seen you look better, Santa, only. . . .

SANTA: Only what, boy?

HOP: Well, sir, it's your cap.

SANTA (*Clapping hand to head*): My cap? What's wrong with my cap?

ALL: There isn't any!

UNCLE SAM: We'll soon fix that! (*Clapping his high hat on* SANTA) There! How's that?

ALL (*Laughing*): No!

SKIP: It looks great on you, Uncle Sam, but on Santa it's terrible.

KING: Since Santa is the King of Holidays, he should wear a crown. (*Offering his crown*)

SANTA: Oh, no! It wouldn't be proper. (*There is a loud knock at the door and* APRIL FOOL *rushes in. He is dressed in a red jester costume with a pointed red cap and carries a big red box tied with a green bow.*) The April Fool!

APRIL FOOL: Oh, Santa! Will you ever forgive me? (*Holding out box to* SANTA) Here is your suit.

SANTA: Where in the world did you find it?

APRIL FOOL (*Throwing himself on his knees in front of* SANTA): I can hardly bear to tell you. I had it all the time. I took it as a joke.

ALL: A joke!

APRIL FOOL: An April Fool prank. I thought it would be

funny to pretend I was Santa Claus and then shout *April Fool!*

QUEEN: You're worse than the Knave of Hearts who stole my tarts.

APRIL FOOL: I wasn't stealing. I meant to return it right away but somehow I forgot till just now when I heard Santa's S.O.S. on the radio.

PILGRIM: The wretch belongs in the stocks.

PETER: He's a disgrace to Holiday Land.

KING: He must be sent into exile . . . banished forever.

GHOST: My witches and goblins will make short work of him.

UNCLE SAM: Not without a trial. The Court of the Calendar must decide his fate. April Fool, I order your arrest.

SANTA: No, no, I forbid it.

HOP, SKIP *and* JUMP: But he's broken the law.

SANTA: And he has mended it by returning my property. I will bring no charges against him.

APRIL FOOL: Thank you, Santa. I'll never do such a foolish thing again . . . not even for fun.

SANTA: I'm sure you won't.

APRIL FOOL: I'd do anything to show you how sorry I am.

SANTA: Then give me your cap.

APRIL FOOL: My cap!

SANTA: It's just what I need to complete my outfit. If Mrs. Cottontail will put a ball of fur on the end, it will be perfect. (*Hands cap to* MRS. COTTONTAIL *who pins a bit of fur on the end*)

HOP: But you don't need a cap now.

SKIP: You have your very own suit.

JUMP: We'll help you put it on.

SANTA: No, thank you. I'd rather wear this one.

MRS. SANTA: But this one is made of bits and pieces. It really isn't a proper Santa suit at all.

SANTA: Oh, yes, it is, my dear. It's the best suit I ever had, because it's made of love and good wishes. (MRS. COTTONTAIL *returns cap which he puts on*) Thank you, Mrs. Cottontail. As for the other suit, Mrs. Santa, you can put it away in mothballs. From now on, I'm going to wear this one as a reminder that Christmas is every holiday rolled into one.

ALL: You're right, Santa!

KING *and* QUEEN: Christmas is a day of love and kindness,

PILGRIM *and* PILGRIM DAME: A day of faith and prayer,

PETER *and* MRS. COTTONTAIL: A day of joy and gladness,

APRIL FOOL: A day of fun and laughter,

GHOST: A day for remembering the past,

UNCLE SAM: A day of peace and goodwill to all mankind!

SANTA: So it's all aboard for the merriest Christmas ever! (*As he exits left*) You can tell the children I am on my way. (*All sing "Here Comes Santa Claus," as curtains close.*)

THE END

The Toy Scout Jamboree

Characters

SANTA CLAUS   SIX HOLLY BERRY SISTERS
BRITISH TOY SCOUT   HANS
DUTCH TOY SCOUT   KATRINKA
FRENCH TOY SCOUT   THREE FRENCH DOLLS
GERMAN TOY SCOUT   CHILD
ITALIAN TOY SCOUT   BETTINA
SWISS TOY SCOUT   TWO SWISS CHILDREN
CHINESE TOY SCOUT   CHINESE CHILDREN
AMERICAN TOY SCOUT

SETTING: *Club House of the Toy Scouts. There is a long table at center with a Christmas tree on it.*

AT RISE: TOY SCOUTS (*except for* AMERICAN TOY SCOUT) *are seated at table, with* SANTA CLAUS *presiding at the head.* SANTA *holds a golden gavel. Near* SWISS *and* CHINESE SCOUTS *are appropriate toys; as curtain rises, the* SCOUTS *are singing.*

SCOUTS (*Singing to the tune of "Jolly Old St. Nicholas"*):
Oh, we are Santa's Toy Scouts
On jolly jamboree,
And we are here to celebrate
The day that starts with "C".

So jingle-jangle-jingle,
And ding-a-ling-a-ling,
We're ready for Kriss Kringle,
So let the sleigh bells ring!

SANTA (*With three raps of the gavel*): The World-Wide Jamboree of Toy Scouts is now in session. (*Rising*) The Toy Scout Promise! (SCOUTS *rise.*)

ALL (*Saluting and facing Christmas tree, which lights up*):
On my honor, I will strive
To keep true Christmas joy alive;
In every country, every clime
To make this day a happy time.
(SCOUTS *take seats.*)

SANTA: Welcome to the Toy Scout Jamboree and congratulations on the fine work you have been doing. I could not get along without you loyal Toy Scouts working in every country to find new toys and games for Christmas. As you know, the Toy Scout who has made the most outstanding discovery of the year will be made a Reindeer Scout. And now, let us hear your reports, starting with our Scout from England.

BRITISH TOY SCOUT (*Rising*): The Toy Scouts of Great Britain are happy to report that the halls are all properly decked with holly, the plum puddings have been baked, and geese have been plucked, and the yule logs are ready and waiting.

SANTA: Excellent! But what about the toys? What new toy have you discovered this year?

BRITISH TOY SCOUT: Because of our misty-moisty climate, many English children find an umbrella under the tree on Christmas morning. Although these gifts are useful, they are not much fun. But this year, we have found a musical umbrella—an umbrella that sings its own happy little song. The Holly Berry Sisters will introduce it.

(*He sits as the* SIX HOLLY BERRY SISTERS *enter, each twirling a red umbrella and singing to the tune of "Deck the Halls."*)

HOLLY BERRY SISTERS (*Singing*):
Listen to our new umbrella,
Fa la la la la, etc.
For a British gal or fella,
Fa la la la la, etc.
Don we now our rain apparel,
Fa la la, la la la, etc.
Every raindrop sings a carol!
Fa la la la la, etc.
(*As all applaud,* SIX HOLLY BERRY SISTERS *exit. The last one leaves her umbrella underneath Christmas tree.*)

SANTA: And now our Toy Scout from the Land of Wooden Shoes. (DUTCH TOY SCOUT *rises.*)

DUTCH TOY SCOUT:
When jolly old St. Nicholas
Comes by the Zuider Zee,
He'll have a special new Dutch treat
To add to Christmas glee.
Hans and Katrinka will demonstrate the Windmill Toy!
(*He sits as* HANS *and* KATRINKA *enter, with red and green pinwheels.*)

HANS *and* KATRINKA (*Singing to tune of "Up on the Housetops"*):
Hans and Katrinka now will show
How the Holland windmills blow.
Give them a huff and a puff or two;
They'll do a whirly-gig just for you!
(*Chorus*)
Ho, ho, ho, see how they go!
Ho, ho, ho, see how they go!
Round and around they twirl and whirl,

All for a good little boy or girl!
(*With a final spin of the pinwheels,* HANS *and* KATRINKA
exit, placing the pinwheels under the tree.)
SANTA: Our next Toy Scout reports from La Belle France!
(FRENCH TOY SCOUT *rises.*)
FRENCH TOY SCOUT:
Bon jour! Bon jour!
Et Joyeux Noel!
My brief report
I'm glad to tell.
One day upon
A toyman's bench
I found three dollies,
Speaking French.
(THREE FRENCH DOLLS *enter with stiff, jerky steps and
halt in front of* FRENCH TOY SCOUT.)
Just wind them up—
I have the key—
And they will sing
For you and me.
(FRENCH SCOUT *"winds" them up.* FRENCH DOLLS *sing
"Frère Jacques" or "Alouette." At end of song* DOLLS
bow stiffly, the TOY SCOUT *rewinds them, and they take
their places by the tree.* FRENCH TOY SCOUT *sits.*)
SANTA: The Toy Scout from Germany will please step
forward. (GERMAN TOY SCOUT *does so.*)
GERMAN TOY SCOUT:
Deep in a German forest,
Beside a towering rock,
Within a little toyshop
I found a Cuckoo Clock.
The Cuckoo was so merry,
His song so bright and gay,
I knew a child would love him

To call out Christmas Day.

(Toy Scout *sits as* Child *enters carrying cardboard clock face. He sings to the tune of "I'm a Little Teapot."*)

Child (*Singing*):

I'm a little cuckoo, cuckoo clock,
Listen to my merry tick-tick-tock.
When the hour is striking, I pop out,
Now get ready to hear me shout . . .
(*Shouting loudly*) Cuckoo, cuckoo, cuckoo, cuckoo.
(Santa *pounds gavel as* Child *continues to sing.*)

Santa: Enough! Enough! Stop him! Stop him, I say.
(Child *stops singing and stands by Christmas tree.*) We must have time to hear from our Italian Toy Scout. (*He rises.*)

Italian Toy Scout:

In Italy I met a child,
A little girl—Bettina—
Who played a Christmas melody
Upon a concertina.
It looked so easy and such fun
To pull and push and squeeze,
I thought old Santa needed some
For under Christmas trees.
(*He sits, as* Bettina *enters and plays simple Christmas tune on accordion and then places it under the tree. She then exits.*)

Santa: From Italy we travel to Switzerland for a report from our Swiss Toy Scout. (*He rises.*)

Swiss Toy Scout:

In a little Swiss shop of watches and clocks
I found a tinkly music box,
With two little maids who waltzed to and fro,
Each making a bow and pointing a toe.
(Swiss Scout *plays music box as* Two Swiss Children

enter and dance. After dance, CHILDREN *exit.* SWISS
SCOUT *puts music box under tree and takes seat.*)
SANTA: Our next report comes from faraway China.
CHINESE TOY SCOUT (*Displaying kite as he rises and re-
cites*):
Chinese are clever people,
Their children, a delight,
And young and old all have such fun
With just a paper kite.

I'm sure when March winds whistle
To usher in the spring,
Some little boy will love to fly
This kite upon a string.
(CHINESE CHILDREN *enter and form a semicircle around
the* TOY SCOUT *with the kite. They sing to the tune of
"Put Your Little Foot"*)
CHINESE CHILDREN (*Singing*):
Fly your little kite, fly your little kite,
Fly your little kite up high,
Fly your little kite, fly your little kite,
Till it tosses in the sky.

Fly your little kite, fly your little kite,
When the balmy breezes blow.
Fly your little kite, fly your little kite,
See it caper to and fro!

Fly your little kite, fly your little kite,
Fly your little kite afar.
If it gets away, you may see it play
With a little twinkling star.
(CHILDREN *exit as* CHINESE SCOUT *places kite under the
tree and returns to seat.*)
SANTA: I am delighted with the toys you have discovered.

Now we will hear our final report from the Toy Scout representing the United States of America.

ALL (*Looking around*): He isn't here.

SANTA: Isn't here? But that is impossible. Where is he?

SCOUTS: We haven't seen him.

SANTA: But he *must* be here. No loyal Toy Scout ever misses a Christmas Jamboree.

BRITISH TOY SCOUT: He is breaking one of the Toy Scout laws.

SCOUTS: "A Toy Scout is always on time."

SANTA: I am afraid we will have to proceed without him. (AMERICAN TOY SCOUT *enters with empty green burlap bag slung over his shoulder. He carries letters in his pocket.*)

AMERICAN TOY SCOUT: I'm sorry I'm late, Mr. Santa. But I came as fast as I could.

SANTA: I hope you have a good excuse, young man. The Toy Scout representing the U.S.A. should be on time.

AMERICAN TOY SCOUT: I met so many children who wanted to talk to me about Christmas.

SANTA: Very well. You may make your report.

AMERICAN TOY SCOUT (*Looking around*): When I see all these fine toys the other Scouts have brought to the jamboree, I am afraid you will not want to hear my report.

SANTA: Of course we want to hear your report, and we are eager to see the new toys you have brought for us.

GERMAN TOY SCOUT: His toy bag does not seem to be very heavy.

AMERICAN TOY SCOUT: You are quite right, my friend. It is not in the least heavy, because (*Opening it*) it is entirely empty.

ALL: Empty!

SANTA: Do you mean to say that you did not find a single new toy?

AMERICAN TOY SCOUT: Oh, no, sir. I found plenty of toys
—wonderful toys—exciting toys—but—
SANTA: Then show them to us at once.
AMERICAN TOY SCOUT: I'm afraid I cannot do that, sir. You
see, it was like this:
A clown that walks,
A dog that talks,
A bird with flying wings,
A frog that hops,
Some magic tops,
And lots of other things . . .

All these I found,
But I'll be bound
I've not a one to show!
(*Kneeling*) Forgive me, please,
I'm on my knees,
I've let you down, I know.

I must confess
I've made a mess
Of my report today.
The girls and boys
So loved my toys,
I gave my gifts away.
ALL: You gave them away!
AMERICAN TOY SCOUT: Every single one.
FRENCH TOY SCOUT: But you knew that you would need to
show them at the jamboree!
SWISS TOY SCOUT: Don't you want to become a Reindeer
Scout?
AMERICAN TOY SCOUT: More than anything else in the
world. But as I told you, I met so many children . . .
CHINESE TOY SCOUT: What did the children have to do
with it?

AMERICAN TOY SCOUT: Everything. Toys are for children, aren't they?

SANTA: Of course they are.

SCOUTS (*Ad lib*): What does he mean? Toys are for children. What does that have to do with it? (*Etc.*)

SANTA (*Rapping with gavel*): Order! Order! We must hear this young man's story.

AMERICAN TOY SCOUT: Well, sir, I had my bag packed and jammed with toys when I happened to take a shortcut through one of the poorest streets in the city. You can imagine how I felt when some of the children told me they didn't believe in you.

ALL: Didn't believe in Santa Claus!

AMERICAN TOY SCOUT: Well, now, I couldn't have that, could I? So before I knew it I was handing out packages.

ALL: But it isn't even Christmas yet!

AMERICAN TOY SCOUT: Every child promised not to open his present until Christmas morning. I explained that the toys were really from Santa Claus, so they have written their thank-you notes to you, sir. Would you like to read them?

SANTA: Indeed I would. (*As* TOY SCOUT *hands him a note from his pocket,* SANTA *adjusts his spectacles and reads*)
"Our house is so crowded,
So poor and so small,
We never had Christmas—
No Christmas at all.

I guess poor dear Santa
Could not find our street,
But thank you this year
For a real Christmas treat!"
Bless my soul! I must make special note of this name and address. How did I ever happen to miss it?

AMERICAN TOY SCOUT: Then I passed a very splendid house, where a little girl stuck out her tongue at me and made all manner of fun of Santa Claus!

ALL: Made fun of Santa Claus!

GERMAN TOY SCOUT: I hope you didn't give any of the toys to *her*.

AMERICAN TOY SCOUT: Oh, but I did. You see, her parents were so rich and gave her so many gifts that she thought all children always got what they wanted for Christmas. She had never had the joy of giving, so I told her she might play Santa Claus with some of the toys in my pack. I think her letter shows she has caught the real Christmas spirit. (*Hands letter to* SANTA)

SANTA (*Reading*):
"I never believed in Santa Claus
But now I know it's true,
And I do want to help you
In everything you do.

This friendly little Toy Scout
Has pointed out the way
To find the happy secret
Of a merry Christmas Day."

Excellent! Excellent! I think I am beginning to enjoy your report. Do you have anything to add?

AMERICAN TOY SCOUT: Just one more thing, Santa. My way to the jamboree took me past a children's hospital where I stopped for a short visit.

SANTA: But I never forget to visit the hospitals on Christmas Eve. I always carry a special bag for children who are sick.

AMERICAN TOY SCOUT: Yes, I know, and the children know it, too. But they cannot go outside to do their Christmas shopping and so they miss all the fun of exchanging presents. When I left, there was a package tucked away under each little bed, and every child was bursting with a Christmas secret. (*Handing* Santa *a letter*) This letter is from the Head Nurse.

Santa (*Reading*):

"The children who are sick in bed
Have told me what to say:
'A special thank you from each one
For a happy holiday.' "

Splendid! Splendid! Do you have anything to add to your report?

American Toy Scout: Nothing more, Santa, except to tell you I will try to do better next year.

Santa (*Rapping with gavel*): You each have a slip of paper on which to write the name of the Toy Scout most worthy of being made a Reindeer Scout. After you fill out the slips, the American Scout can collect them in his bag. (Scouts *write.* American Scout *collects slips and hands bag to* Santa.) The British Toy Scout will count the votes. (Santa *hands bag to* British Scout.)

British Toy Scout (*As he counts votes*): One, two, three . . .

Dutch Toy Scout: Three votes for whom?

French Toy Scout: Hurry up, hurry up.

British Toy Scout: Four, five, six . . . I'm going as fast as I can. (*As he continues to count*) And it looks as though it's going to be unanimous. (*He counts rest of votes.*) It is! The winner is—the American Toy Scout!

Santa (*To* American Scout): Congratulations! You have received the honor of becoming my Reindeer Scout for the year.

Scouts: Hurrah! Hurrah! Hurrah!

American Toy Scout: There must be some mistake. I have not brought in a single discovery.

SANTA: Oh, yes, you have. You have made the best discovery of all. I am sure your fellow Toy Scouts can tell you what it is.

SCOUTS: "It is more blessed to give than to receive."

AMERICAN TOY SCOUT: Oh, thank you! Thank you! (SANTA *goes upstage and picks up Reindeer Scout emblem.*)

SANTA (*Hanging emblem around the* AMERICAN TOY SCOUT's *neck*): Now, may you wear this badge with honor and serve me faithfully as a true Reindeer Scout. Again my congratulations. (*They shake hands.*)

SCOUTS: Hip, hip, hooray! Hip, hip, hooray! Hooray for the American Toy Scout! (*All join in singing appropriate Christmas song. Curtain.*)

THE END

The Christmas Peppermints

Characters

DR. FIX	JACK-IN-THE-BOX	
NURSE MERRIEBELLE	RAGGEDY ANN DOLL	
SANTA CLAUS	DRUMMER BOY	
FIFI, *a French doll*	CLOWN DOLL	
DOLLY DIMPLES	JAPANESE DOLL	*carolers*
SCOTTY DOG	PINOCCHIO DOLL	
TOY SOLDIER	MICKEY MOUSE DOLL	

TIME: *The day before Christmas.*

SETTING: *Dr. Fix's consulting room at the New Hope Doll Hospital.*

AT RISE: DR. FIX *is removing a bandage from* FIFI's *head.* NURSE MERRIEBELLE *is assisting him.* FIFI *is seated.*

DR. FIX: Please sit still, Fifi. This won't take a minute.

FIFI: I am too excited to sit still, Dr. Fix.

DR. FIX: Scissors, please, nurse.

NURSE (*Handing him scissors*): You have been such a good patient, Fifi. (DR. FIX *cuts bandage.*)

FIFI: Thank you, Miss Merriebelle. Will there be a scar?

DR. FIX: I think not, my dear. But we will soon see. (*Unwinds the rest of bandage*) There!

NURSE: Beautiful! Beautiful!

FIFI: Let me see!

DR. FIX: The mirror, Miss Merriebelle. (NURSE *gives* FIFI *a hand mirror.*)

FIFI (*Looking in mirror*): Marvelous! Thank you! How do you say? I am as good as new.

NURSE: No sign of a scar.

DR. FIX: You be sure to tell that little girl who plays with you to be more careful. We don't want any more broken heads in this hospital.

FIFI: Will I be home for Christmas, doctor?

DR. FIX: Betty Sue is coming for you right after lunch.

NURSE: And I happen to know she's bringing you a beautiful new pink dress.

FIFI (*Clapping her hands*): My favorite color! (*Standing*) How can I ever thank you, Dr. Fix?

DR. FIX: By being more careful in the future. No more sitting on high shelves, or jumping off beds onto hardwood floors. You and Betty Sue must learn some safety rules.

FIFI: We'll be good, I promise. Goodbye, doctor. Goodbye, Miss Merriebelle. (*Singing as she exits*)
Jingle bells, jingle bells, I am on my way!
Oh, what fun it is to be at home on Christmas Day!

DR. FIX: That's what they all want. They expect me to perform miracles just so they can be home by Christmas. Now, how many cases do we have left for this morning?

NURSE: Only the patients in Ward X.

DR. FIX: Oh, dear! Must I see them again?

NURSE: I'm afraid so, doctor. They are so discouraged.

DR. FIX: And all begging to be home for Christmas, I suppose.

NURSE: No, sir. Not one of them has mentioned Christmas.

DR. FIX: That's good, because none of them will make it.

NURSE: Are you sure, doctor?

DR. FIX: How could they? I've tried everything in the book for that Toy Soldier with the creaking joints, and his leg still squeaks like a rusty hinge. I can't cure the Scotty Dog's cough. I've done all I can do for Dolly Dimples, who has a "pain in her sawdust," and the Jack-in-the-Box who lost his voice still can't talk above a whisper. It's the same story with the rest of them. Nothing does any good.

NURSE: If you don't mind, sir, I have a suggestion. What would you say to a consultation?

DR. FIX: With another toy specialist?

NURSE: I was thinking of a certain old gentleman I know. He's not a doctor really, but—

DR. FIX: Not a doctor? That settles it.

NURSE: But this old gentleman knows all there is to know about dolls and toy soldiers and Scotty dogs. He's an international authority.

DR. FIX: Good gravy, nurse! You don't mean that old fossil up at the North Pole, do you?

NURSE: He's not an old fossil, Dr. Fix. Just ask anybody. Surely it wouldn't do any harm to let him look at the patients in Ward X.

DR. FIX: Maybe not. But how could we get in touch with him? The North Pole isn't Paris or London.

NURSE: I happen to know he's right here in town. In fact, he called this morning to ask about visiting hours.

DR. FIX: Oh, he did, did he? Meddlesome old busybody!

NURSE: He's nothing of the sort. He's just a kindly old man who can't bear to see children or toys or even grownups feel lonely and forgotten at Christmastime. Oh, please, sir, won't you talk with him?

DR. FIX: Talk with him? You mean on the telephone?

NURSE: Oh, no, sir. He's out in the waiting room this very minute. Won't you let me show him in?

DR. FIX (*Sternly*): Nurse Merriebelle, what have you been up to?

NURSE: I'm sorry, sir, but you said yourself nothing we do seems to help those poor little toys in Ward X.

DR. FIX (*Crossly*): Oh, very well. Show him in. But I'm warning you—I want no monkeyshines.

NURSE: Oh, thank you, Dr. Fix. I'll get him right away. (*She exits.*)

DR. FIX: Oh, me! Running a doll hospital is no joke. Santa Claus! He wouldn't know a compound fracture from a compound fraction! (NURSE *enters with* SANTA CLAUS.)

NURSE: Dr. Fix, this is Mr. Santa Claus.

SANTA (*Holding out his hand*): This is a great pleasure, Dr. Fix. It is an honor to meet the greatest toy specialist in the United States.

DR. FIX (*Shaking hands*). Thank you, sir.

SANTA: Fine hospital you have here, doctor. You are performing miracles every day.

DR. FIX: Not miracles, Mr. Santa Claus, just repair work. I understand Nurse Merriebelle has told you about our problems in Ward X. She suggested a consultation.

SANTA: I'll be glad to do anything I can, sir, but, as you know, I am not a doctor. However, I will be glad to see the patients.

DR. FIX: Please bring them down, nurse, one at a time.

NURSE: Right away, doctor. (*Exits*)

DR. FIX (*Handing* SANTA *a clipboard holding many papers*): Maybe you would like to see their case histories and charts before you talk to them.

SANTA (*Adjusting glasses, then looking through papers*): Thank you. Hm-m. I see! Hm-m. Quite so! Yes, I think I understand. Dr. Fix, I have one little favor to ask of you. I would like to see these patients alone. Would you mind?

DR. FIX: But I am their doctor. This was to be a consultation.

SANTA: I know. But you see, it embarrasses me to speak in front of a qualified physician. I am just a simple old man with no training in medicine or surgery—

DR. FIX: I understand. Very well, sir. Make yourself at home. I will take this time to make my rounds.

SANTA: Thank you very much.

DR. FIX: Nurse Merriebelle will give you any help you need. (*He exits.*)

SANTA (*Sitting in* DR. FIX's *chair and laughing*):
Something tells me, Dr. Fix,
That you and I will never mix,
Until you learn some Christmas tricks!
And I do believe I'm just the one to teach you. (NURSE *enters with* DOLLY DIMPLES, *who is moaning and holding her stomach.*)

SANTA: Well, bless my soul, if it isn't Dolly Dimples. Merry Christmas, Dolly.

DOLLY (*Between groans*): How did you know my name?

SANTA: Because I named you myself. The first time I saw you smiling in my workshop and caught sight of those dimples flashing in and out, I said to myself, "This is little Miss Dolly Dimples."

DOLLY: But I can't smile any more, Santa. My dimples are all gone.

SANTA: Nonsense! I never made a doll who couldn't smile.

DOLLY: But I have a terrible pain in my sawdust.

SANTA: A pain in your sawdust, indeed! That's impossible!

DOLLY: I think I need an operation.

SANTA: Poppycock! In the first place, you don't have any sawdust, so how could you have a pain in it? You are a modern plastic doll, and plastic dolls don't get pains in their sawdust.

DOLLY (*Amazed*): They *don't?*

SANTA: Of course not. (*Takes a striped bag of candy from his pocket and offers it to* DOLLY) Here, have a peppermint.

DOLLY (*Taking one*): Thank you. (*Eats it*)

SANTA (*Offering bag to* NURSE): You have one, too, nurse.

NURSE (*Taking one*): Thank you, Santa. (*Eats it*) I love peppermints. Now I will go for the next patient. (*Exits*)

DOLLY: I love peppermints, too, but I've been afraid to eat any.

SANTA: Everybody eats peppermint candy at Christmastime.

DOLLY (*Crying*): Oh, dear! It's Christmas again.

SANTA: Stop that boohooing! Christmas is the happiest time of the year.

DOLLY: Not for me!

SANTA: Why not?

DOLLY: Because (*Starting to cry again*)—because Mary Ann will get a new doll, and she won't ever play with me again.

SANTA: Stuff and nonsense! You don't know Mary Ann very well, do you?

DOLLY: I know her better than anyone else in the world.

SANTA: You only think you know her. Now, I could tell you something about Mary Ann that will really make you open your eyes.

DOLLY: What?

SANTA: It's a secret. A Christmas secret.

DOLLY: Oh, please tell me. I love secrets.

SANTA: I can't. It's something only Mary Ann and I know.

DOLLY: Can't you whisper it in my ear?

SANTA: Maybe I could, if you promise not to tell.

DOLLY: I promise. (SANTA *whispers in her ear.*) Not really, Santa, not really and truly?

SANTA: Really and truly!

DOLLY (*Jumping up and down*): Oh, goody, goody! I'm the happiest doll in the world.

SANTA: How could you ever think Mary Ann would want a new doll for Christmas when she already has you?

DOLLY: And did she really order a new set of doll clothes just for me?

SANTA: She did! And a tea table and a set of dishes for your very own parties.

DOLLY: Oh, hurry, Santa. Please call Dr. Fix and tell him I *must* be home for Christmas.

SANTA: What about that pain?

DOLLY: What pain?

SANTA: The pain in your middle.

DOLLY: I don't have it any more. I guess that peppermint cured it.

SANTA: It wasn't the peppermint, Dolly. It was your Christmas spirit.

DOLLY: My Christmas spirit?

SANTA: Yes. It happens all the time. People and toys lose their Christmas spirit and they get a sad, lonely ache in their middles. When the Christmas spirit comes back, there's no room for the pain, and so it goes away.

DOLLY: Oh, thank you, Santa. I feel wonderful. (NURSE *enters with* SCOTTY DOG, *who is coughing and sneezing.*) Nurse Merriebelle, please take me to Dr. Fix so he can see how well I am and send me home.

NURSE: That's the best news I've heard this week. I knew Santa Claus could help you, and I've been telling this fellow that Santa can do the same for him. Santa Claus, this is our problem Scotty Dog. (*As* SCOTTY *coughs and sneezes*) He has a cold on his chest. (*Singing to tune of "John Brown's Body"*)
Poor old Scotty has a cold upon his chest,

Poor old Scotty has a cold upon his chest,
Poor old Scotty has a cold upon his chest,
And they rubbed it with camphorated oil!

SANTA: Camphorated oil! A lot of good that will do. Come over here, young fellow, and let me have a look at you.

DOLLY (*As she begins to exit with* NURSE): Good luck, Scotty. I know you'll have a merry Christmas after you talk with Santa Claus. (*Exits with* NURSE)

SCOTTY (*Speaking as if he has a bad cold*): No more Christmas for me. I'm done for. (*Sneezes*)

SANTA (*Pulling a red and green handkerchief from his pocket*): Here—blow! (SCOTTY *blows his nose, and then starts to cough.* SANTA *offers him the peppermints.*) Here, have a peppermint. It will stop that cough. (*As* SCOTTY *takes a peppermint and eats it*) There, that's better. We'll have you home for Christmas in no time.

SCOTTY: I don't want to go home for Christmas.

SANTA: What's that? I don't think I understood you.

SCOTTY: I don't want to go home for Christmas.

SANTA: That's what I thought you said, but I couldn't believe my ears.

SCOTTY: My folks moved away and left me. They said Bobby was too old for me, and so they put me in the trash box.

SANTA: Yes, I know all about that.

SCOTTY: You do?

SANTA: It's all here (*Indicating clipboard*) in your records. But I know something you don't know, Mr. Scotty Dog.

SCOTTY: What's that?

SANTA (*Reaching in his pocket and taking out a letter*): I received this letter yesterday. It's from a little boy in a real hospital. His name is Jackie. I'll read it to you. (*Adjusting glasses and reading*) "Dear Santa: I am six years old. I am in the hospital, and I won't be home for Christmas. All the nurses and doctors are very kind to me and say I am brave. But I get lonely at night. Could you please bring me a toy Scotty for Christmas to tell my troubles to? Please, Santa, don't forget. A toy Scotty for Jackie Jones, City Hospital."

SCOTTY (*Talking normally*): You mean you would take me to Jackie, and I would have a little boy all my own?

SANTA: I was thinking about it, but I wouldn't want Jackie to catch your cold.

SCOTTY: What cold? I don't have any cold.

SANTA: All that coughing and sneezing would never do in a children's hospital.

SCOTTY: But I'm not coughing or sneezing any more. Oh, Santa, please tell Dr. Fix I must leave at once so I can be with Jackie on Christmas morning.

SANTA: O.K., I will, if you really think you're cured.

SCOTTY: Of course I'm cured. It was that peppermint. You tell Dr. Fix he should give them to all of his patients. Gee, I wish—no, it wouldn't work.

SANTA: What wouldn't work?

SCOTTY: I was wishing you could cure the Toy Soldier the way you cured me, but I guess peppermints wouldn't help a creaky leg. (TOY SOLDIER *marches in stiff-leggedly, leaning on* NURSE)

TOY SOLDIER: Hello, Scotty. How are you?

SCOTTY: I'm great. I'm going home. And I'll bet Santa Claus will cure you, too.

TOY SOLDIER: Nobody can cure me. I'm a hopeless case.

NURSE: Nonsense. Where did you get such an idea?

TOY SOLDIER: I heard Dr. Fix talking to the nurses.

SANTA: You never hear anything good by listening to things you're not supposed to hear. Now, walk over here and let me have a look at that leg while Nurse Merriebelle helps Scotty pack his bag.

SCOTTY: Goodbye, old friend. Merry Christmas. (SCOTTY *and* NURSE *exit*.)

TOY SOLDIER: I wish they'd stop wishing me a merry Christmas. I don't feel the least bit merry.

SANTA: Why not?

TOY SOLDIER: Would you feel merry if your legs creaked and groaned at every step?

SANTA: That would depend on where I was going.

TOY SOLDIER: I'm not going anywhere.

SANTA: I have news for you, young man. You're going home.

TOY SOLDIER: Ha! I don't have a home—only a shelf in the damp basement of old McGregor's toystore. I've been down there for years. That's where I got these rusty joints.

SANTA: So you're the Toy Soldier I delivered to McGregor's toystore on special order for Mrs. Higgins. Now I remember.

TOY SOLDIER: Then you're the only one who remembers. Mr. McGregor has forgotten all about me. He never even puts me on the shelf in the toyshop.

SANTA: That was a sorry mix-up, I must admit. Tommy Higgins wanted a toy soldier. His mother told me about it, and so I took you to Mr. McGregor. In the meantime his Uncle Dan gave Tommy a whole set of toy soldiers for his birthday.

TOY SOLDIER: So that's why nobody ever came for me.

SANTA (*Offering peppermints*): Here, have a peppermint, son! (TOY SOLDIER *takes peppermint and eats it*.) I must look over my mail. (*Takes a few letters from his pocket and scans them*) Ah! Here it is. It's from a Mr. Joshua Jennings. He's seventy-five years old.

TOY SOLDIER: Seventy-five years old and still writing letters to Santa Claus?

SANTA: Certainly. What's wrong with that? Mr. Jennings runs a toy museum in a place called Oregon City. He has a collection of toy soldiers from all over the world, but to make it complete, he needs one from your regiment. How would you like to go there?

TOY SOLDIER (*Distastefully*): To live in a museum?

SANTA: In a big sunny room, with thousands of other toy soldiers all together in a big glass case where there are never any drafts!

TOY SOLDIER: That sounds great! But what about children? I've always wanted to be with lots of little boys.

SANTA: That's the best part. Mr. Jennings invites all the children in the schools to come and look at the soldiers, and every Christmas he has open house. The children come in and take the soldiers out of the cases and play with them to their hearts' content.

TOY SOLDIER: Oh, boy! This is for me. When can I go?

SANTA: Do you think you can make it in time for Christmas?

TOY SOLDIER: Sure. (*Strutting up and down*) I could even walk there myself if I had to. Imagine spending every Christmas with real boys and girls.

SANTA: What about your leg?

TOY SOLDIER (*Laughing*): Oh, that! (*Swings his leg forward and backward*) I forgot all about my leg. Anyhow it's limbered up. Please tell Dr. Fix to sign my papers so I can be on my way.

SANTA: I'll do that, soldier.

TOY SOLDIER: And thanks for the peppermint. I do wish you could give some of them to poor old Jack-in-the-Box.

SANTA: He's on my list, and I think he's coming now. (NURSE, DOLLY, *and* SCOTTY *enter, pulling a small hand cart which contains a large box with* JACK-IN-THE-BOX *inside.* TOY SOLDIER *runs to help.*)

NURSE: Here's our last patient, Santa, the Jack-in-the-Box who has lost his voice.

SANTA (*Lifting lid*): Hello there, fellow! Merry Christmas. (JACK *pops up, waving his arms limply, and mouths the word "boo."*)

DOLLY: Poor Jack can't talk, Mr. Santa. He's trying to say "boo."

SANTA: That's a funny greeting from a Jack-in-the-Box.

NURSE: Have you read his case history, Santa?

SANTA (*Consulting clipboard*): First Christmas in the Harper family. Scared the Harper baby, and so they gave him to the Smiths. Scared the Smith baby half to death, and so they passed him along to the Kents. Kent baby also afraid of him, and so he was given to the Children's Home, where he lost his voice entirely.

TOYS: Poor old Jack! He's had a bad time.

SANTA: And no wonder—if all he can say is "boo." I'll have to treat his vocabulary as well as his voice. (*Offering peppermints*) Here, boy, have a peppermint. (*As* JACK *takes one and sucks on it*) Now, listen to me. Try to say "Merry Christmas." (JACK *tries, but makes no sound.*) Try it again.

JACK (*Whispering*): Merry Christmas.

SANTA: That's better. Come on, the rest of you, try to help him.

TOYS (*Shouting*): Merry Christmas! Merry Christmas! Merry Christmas!

JACK (*Whispering, louder*): Merry Christmas.

SANTA: You're doing better. If you can say it real loudly, I'll give you a surprise.

TOY SOLDIER: Another peppermint?

SANTA: Something much better. I know a Spanish family spending their first Christmas in America. They would like to wish their neighbors a merry Christmas, but they can only say, "Feliz Navidad." Now, with a smart Jack-in-the-Box to help them, they could learn in no time.

JACK (*Shouting*): Merry Christmas! Merry Christmas! (*As he is shouting,* DR. FIX *enters.*)

DR. FIX: What's this I hear?

JACK: Merry Christmas, Dr. Fix! I can talk!

ALL: Hurrah! Hurrah!

DR. FIX: This is amazing. You have cured every patient in Ward X. What in the world did you do?

JACK: He gave us peppermints.

DR. FIX: Peppermints!

SANTA: I'm afraid there was more to it than peppermints, Dr. Fix.

NURSE: Dear me, doctor. You don't look a bit well. (*Feeling his head*) Your head is like fire (*Taking his hand*), and your hands like ice. I'm afraid you're coming down with a cold.

DR. FIX: Nonsense! I'm just a bit tired. Christmas always takes it out of me.

SANTA (*Offering peppermints*): Do have a peppermint.

DR. FIX: I seldom eat between meals, but peppermints are my favorite candy. (*Helps himself, and eats one*)

DOLLY: It's time for our surprise. (*Running to door*) Come in, everybody. (*Carolers enter, carrying brightly wrapped Christmas packages and singing.* DRUMMER BOY, *who enters first, also carries a small Christmas tree, which he puts on* DR. FIX's *desk at the end of the song.*)

CAROLERS:
We wish you a merry Christmas,
We wish you a merry Christmas,
We wish you a merry Christmas,
And a happy New Year!

ALL (*Shouting*): Merry Christmas, Dr. Fix! Merry Christmas, nurse!

DR. FIX: What's all this?

RAGGEDY ANN: It's a Christmas party for you, doctor. All
of us toys want you to know how much we appreciate
what you have done for us. (*Handing* DR. FIX *a package.*
SANTA *sits at* DR. FIX's *desk.*)
For mending the hole
In my raggedy head,
I give you these slippers
To wear in your bed!

DRUMMER BOY (*Giving package*):
For mending my arm
That was aching and numb,
I want you to have
This cooky jar drum!
And it's filled with cookies, too!

CLOWN DOLL (*Giving package*):
For fixing the kink
And the pain in my side,
Here's a necktie for you.
May you wear it with pride.

JAPANESE DOLL (*Giving package*):
For fixing the scratches
On poor Yanki-San,
A present for you,
Mister Medicine Man!

PINOCCHIO DOLL (*Giving package*):
For healing the cut
On my poor wooden nose,
Some hankies for you,
And a new pair of hose!

MICKEY MOUSE DOLL (*Giving package*):
For mending my whiskers,
I hope you will please
Accept as your present

This package of cheese.

(DR. FIX *puts packages next to tree.*)

ALL: Merry Christmas! Merry Christmas!

DR. FIX: Thank you! Nurse Merriebelle, I feel a song coming on. How do you feel about a good old-fashioned carol sing with hot chocolate and cookies afterward?

ALL: Hooray!

NURSE: But you have a cold, doctor, and you are so very tired.

DR. FIX: Who, me? I've never felt better in my life. Santa Claus, I must have the formula for those peppermints. They work wonders.

SANTA: Ah, yes, the peppermints! I tell you what, Dr. Fix. You look in the toe of your stocking on Christmas morning, and you'll find a list of my secret ingredients. Meanwhile, I think I'll sample a few myself. (SANTA *props his feet on desk, leans back in the chair, and eats a peppermint. All sing a Christmas carol as curtain falls.*)

THE END

Santa Calls a Conference

Characters

REDDIE ⎫
GREENIE ⎪
TING ⎪
LING ⎬ *Santa's elves*
JINGLE ⎪
JANGLE ⎭
MRS. SANTA
SANTA CLAUS
ST. NICHOLAS
KRISS KRINGLE
PELZNICKLE
JULENISSE
ST. LUCIA
LA BEFANA
BABOUSHKA
SNOW MAIDEN
GRANDFATHER FROST
FATHER CHRISTMAS
PÈRE NOEL
DONNA POINSETTIA
CHILDREN OF THE WORLD, *9 boys and 9 girls*

SETTING: *Christmas Convention Hall at the North Pole. At center are a long conference table and chairs. Two armchairs are at either end of table.*

AT RISE: GREENIE *is arranging place cards about the table as* REDDIE *looks on in disapproval.*

REDDIE *(Shaking his head)*: This will never do, Greenie! Never! Never! Never!

GREENIE: Why not? What's the matter?

REDDIE: You can't put Santa Claus at the head of the table today because he sat there yesterday.

GREENIE: So what? This is Santa's house, and this is his table. Besides, he's the chairman of the whole Christmas Convention.

REDDIE: But we must show every delegate equal respect and courtesy. Do you want to insult our good friends from France by seating their Père Noel at the foot of the table?

GREENIE: But someone must sit there. What do you suggest?

REDDIE: Perhaps a round table would be better.

GREENIE: That's a great idea! No head! No foot! I'll go get one.

REDDIE *(Stopping him)*: There isn't time.

GREENIE *(Tossing all the cards on the table)*: Then let them sit where they like. I give up!

REDDIE: Take it easy, pal. This is no time for a tantrum.

GREENIE: I don't care! I'm sick of the whole business. Nineteen days of discussion and what have they settled?

REDDIE: Patience! Every country must defend its own customs and traditions. The Convention will sift them out and select the very best for a universal celebration. This means decisions, decisions, decisions. (TING *and* LING *enter, carrying stacks of red and green folders.* JINGLE *and* JANGLE *follow, carrying pencils and scratch pads.*)

TING: Well, boys, here's the agenda for today, and believe

me, it's a long one. I hope Jingle and Jangle have brought plenty of pencils and pads.

JINGLE (*As they place materials around table*): I think we have enough.

REDDIE: How many items for today's discussion, Ting?

TING: I really haven't counted. Ling drew up the list.

LING: It's my guess we'll be here till midnight. (*Showing folders*) Look!

GREENIE (*Examining one of the folders*): Hm-m-m. I see we've hit the S's. (*Reading*) "Saints, sayings, seals, and seasons. . . ."

REDDIE (*Reading from another folder*): "Sledges, sleds, sleep, sleighs, and sleighbells." Now, I ask you, what does *sleep* have to do with Christmas?

TING: Oh, that's a big issue. Some of the delegates, like our own Santa Claus, demand that all children be fast asleep when they arrive. But Pelznickle and some of the others want the children to be wide awake. There are plenty of arguments on both sides.

LING (*Reading*): What about "Snow, snowballs, and snow-men"? The southern Gift-Bearers are opposed to snow in any form.

JINGLE (*Reading*): "Soldiers, songs, and sounds."

JANGLE: I thought *songs* came under the heading of *Carols*.

LING: But these are popular songs of Christmas. I heard that Mrs. Santa objects to the one entitled, "I Saw Mommy Kissing Santa Claus."

REDDIE (*Reading*): "Spirit, spooks, sprites, and spruce."

GREENIE: St. Nicholas has prepared a special report on the Spirit of Christmas.

TING: There's sure to be a debate over the spruce tree. Some feel that only the balsam and pine should be used as Christmas trees, while others want to include all ever-greens and the palm tree as well.

JINGLE (*Reading*): "Stockings, stores, and stories. . . ."
What's the point of all this? What difference does it make
whether the toys are put into the children's shoes or into
their stockings?

JANGLE: St. Nicholas is strongly in favor of the Christmas
stocking. It seems he invented it.

REDDIE: And Santa Claus is getting tired of all those personal appearances in the department stores.

GREENIE: This list goes on forever! (*Reading*) "Sugar and
spice! Sugar cakes, sugar candy, sugar canes, and sugar
plums"!

TING (*Reading*): "Sweets and switches"—now there's an
odd combination. (MRS. SANTA *enters, much disturbed.*)

MRS. SANTA: Oh, dear. Oh, dear, oh, dear! How much
longer will this go on?

GREENIE: Good morning, Mrs. Santa. You seem upset.

MRS. SANTA: And with good reason! Santa didn't sleep a
wink last night, worrying about poor Rudolph.

REDDIE: We were sorry to hear the Convention voted to
drop him, red nose and all, just because he wasn't one
of the original reindeer!

JINGLE: I'm afraid there's more trouble ahead.

JANGLE: Tomorrow they take up the T's.

LING: Teddy bears, tinsel, toys, trains, trees, and turkey!

REDDIE: *Uniforms* will come under U. Suppose they make
Santa give up his red suit?

GREENIE: And then there's the rest of the Christmas alphabet. V—vehicles, verses, and vocabulary!

JINGLE: W—waits, walnuts, wassail, weather, Wenceslaus,
whiskers. . . .

JANGLE: The lady delegates are sure to vote against whiskers!

LING: That would be going too far!

MRS. SANTA: In my opinion this Convention has already

gone too far. All this hullabaloo over our favorite holiday! We must put a stop to it!

REDDIE: But there's so much unfinished business.

MRS. SANTA: The business of Christmas is never finished. That's the beauty of it. It goes on from year to year. And Christmas is everybody's business. It's high time we sent these delegates home where they belong, so they can prepare for the holidays, each in his own fashion.

ALL: But how? What can we do?

MRS. SANTA: We'll think of something!

GREENIE: Nobody is happy with so many changes.

JINGLE: The Italian Gift-Giver, La Befana, was weeping because they want her to give up her broom.

JANGLE: Pelznickle is angry because Santa Claus disapproves of scaring the children!

TING: Saint Lucia from Sweden refuses to give up the candles on her headdress.

LING: Father Christmas is cross because St. Nicholas disapproves of mistletoe.

GREENIE: All these debates and arguments!

TING: It just isn't proper!

REDDIE: The children won't like it!

MRS. SANTA: That's it! That's it! The children! The children will help us! Reddie! Greenie! How soon can you harness the reindeer?

REDDIE and GREENIE: Right away, Mrs. Santa.

MRS. SANTA: Good! Ting and Ling can take turns driving.

TING: But I've never driven without Santa to show me the way.

LING: And I don't have my reindeer license.

MRS. SANTA: Your learner's permit will do. This is an emergency. Jingle and Jangle will do the map work and serve as messengers. Now come along! (*Moves left*)

JINGLE: But where are we to go?

JANGLE: What do you want us to do?

MRS. SANTA (*Steering them off left*): I'll explain on our way to the stables. Now here is my plan. . . . (*She exits left with* JINGLE, JANGLE, TING, LING, REDDIE, *and* GREENIE. SANTA *enters from right with* ST. NICHOLAS *and* KRISS KRINGLE.)

SANTA (*Wearily*): Ho-hum! Another morning, another meeting.

ST. NICHOLAS (*Patting him on the shoulder*): Bear up, old friend. The Christmas spirit will see us through.

KRISS KRINGLE: Well-spoken, St. Nicholas! Well-spoken!

SANTA: Sometimes I'm not so sure if this convention was such a good idea, Kriss Kringle.

KRISS KRINGLE: Nonsense, Santa. It's a wonderful idea! Only a few more days and we will have settled all our differences. Christmas will be Christmas all over the world. Everything the same from Aden to Zanzibar! (PÈRE NOEL *enters, followed by* FATHER CHRISTMAS *and* GRANDFATHER FROST.)

PÈRE NOEL: Ah, *bon jour, bon jour!*

SANTA: And *bon jour* to you, Père Noel. (*Greeting others*) Good morning, Father Christmas. Good day to you, Grandfather Frost. Did you sleep well?

FATHER CHRISTMAS: Like a top!

GRANDFATHER FROST: I was out early this morning feeding the reindeer.

ST. NICHOLAS (*Picking up a folder*): It looks as if we have a long day ahead. Shall we begin, gentlemen?

PÈRE NOEL: Not without the ladies! (*The* JULENISSE, *a gnome, capers in, followed by* ST. LUCIA, LA BEFANA, BABOUSHKA, *and the* SNOW MAIDEN.)

JULENISSE: Make way for youth and beauty! Right this way, ladies. Permit me to escort you to your places. (*He leads them to the table.*)

ALL: Good morning, ladies.

JULENISSE (*At table*): But where are we to sit? Where are the place cards?

KRISS KRINGLE (*Indicating pile of cards*): Altogether they are! In one great pile!

SANTA: Dear me! Something must be amiss! It is not like my elves to be so careless. But come, my friends, make yourselves at home. (*Taking center seat facing audience*) I will sit here with La Befana and Madame Baboushka on my right and left.

LA BEFANA and BABOUSHKA: Thank you, Santa. (*They sit.*)

ST. NICHOLAS: I suggest that St. Lucia and the Snow Maiden grace the head and foot of our table.

ST. LUCIA and SNOW MAIDEN (*Taking places*): Thank you, St. Nicholas.

JULENISSE: My stool! My stool! I must have my stool!

ST. LUCIA: It's right here beside me, Julenisse. (JULENISSE *climbs on stool beside* ST. LUCIA. *The others find seats, leaving two vacant chairs.*)

KRISS KRINGLE: I like this informality.

SANTA (*Rising and reciting*):
Good friends, we now begin our meeting
With roll call and a hearty greeting—
Merry Christmas!
(*All applaud.*) I first call the name of our good friend and co-worker, Father Christmas.

FATHER CHRISTMAS (*Rising*):
As spokesman for the British Crown,
Good health and cheer from London town!
(*Applause*)

SANTA: St. Lucia and her jolly companion, the Julenisse!

ST. LUCIA and JULENISSE (*Rising*):
From Norway, Sweden, Denmark, too,
We wish the same to all of you—

God Jul!
(*Applause*)
SANTA: Père Noel!
PÈRE NOEL (*Rising*):
From France, good cheer! We wish you well!
Joyeux Noel! Joyeux Noel!
(*Applause*)
SANTA: La Befana.
LA BEFANA (*Rising*):
From Venice, Rome, and Napoli,
From Padua to Sicily—
Buon Natale!
(*Applause*)
SANTA: Kriss Kringle!
KRISS KRINGLE (*Rising*):
From those who speak my native tongue,
Wherever German words are sung—
Fröhliche Weinachten!
(*Applause*)
SANTA: St. Nicholas!
ST. NICHOLAS (*Rising*):
So many lands I represent,
So many greetings I have sent,
I hardly know which one to choose!
But from the land of wooden shoes—
Prettig Kerstmis!
(*Applause*)
SANTA: The Snow Maiden!
SNOW MAIDEN (*Rising with* BABOUSHKA *and* GRANDFATHER
FROST):
Grandfather Frost, Baboushka, and I
To Santa's roll call make reply.
Since Russian words of Christmas cheer
May somewhat strangely strike your ear,
We bring a greeting none can miss—

To one and all . . . a Christmas kiss!
(*The three delegates throw kisses as others applaud. All resume seats.*)

SANTA: Pelznickle! (*No answer*) Pelznickle!

ALL (*To each other*): Pelznickle! Where is he?

SANTA: Does anyone know what has become of Pelznickle?

KRISS KRINGLE: I am sorry to tell you, Santa, that Pelznickle will not attend our session this morning.

SANTA: And why not? Is he ill?

KRISS KRINGLE: No, not exactly ill, but he is suffering from a bad case of hurt feelings.

SANTA: Oh, dear! He is angry with me because I disapprove of those ugly faces he wears to scare the children.

KRISS KRINGLE: And the switches! He told me he will resign unless he may continue to carry his bundle of switches for the bad children.

SANTA: But there are no bad children at Christmastime.

PÈRE NOEL: But what about the other three hundred and sixty-four days of the year? Even in France where children are usually obedient and well-mannered, I find it necessary for Père Fouettard to accompany me on my rounds.

SANTA: Père Fouettard? Who is he?

PÈRE NOEL: A most important gentleman, Santa. "Père Fouettard" means Father Spanker, and he sees to it there's a good supply of switches in every French home!

SANTA: I wouldn't have believed it of you, Père Noel!

KRISS KRINGLE: I must admit, Santa, that I, too, leave a bundle of rods where they are requested.

SANTA: Kriss Kringle! I am surprised at you!

FATHER CHRISTMAS: Spare the rod and spoil the child!

SANTA: How do you feel about this, St. Nicholas?

ST. NICHOLAS: I fear we cannot abandon this custom without dire consequences.

SANTA (*Looking around the table*): And the rest of you?

(*They solemnly nod their heads.*) Very well, I agree! But only on condition that we prohibit their use on December 25th. No slapping, no spanking, no switching, not even any scolding on Christmas Day! Agreed?

ALL: Agreed!

SANTA: Kriss Kringle, will you please inform your countryman of our decision?

KRISS KRINGLE: I am sure you will not regret it, Santa. Pelznickle is a great favorite, not only in Germany, but also in many of the Pennsylvania German communities in your own United States. (*He exits.*)

SANTA: Is there any old business?

LA BEFANA: Mr. Chairman, I wish to bring up the matter of the Three Kings.

BABOUSHKA: We have been hoping they would attend our Christmas convention.

SANTA: Alas, we will not be honored by these wise and holy men whose offerings of gold, frankincense, and myrrh were the first Christmas gifts in all the world. But we do have a request for the admission of a delegate who will speak for them and the Spanish countries they serve . . . a certain Donna Poinsettia.

ALL: Donna Poinsettia!

JULENISSE: Never heard of her!

FATHER CHRISTMAS: Is she listed in the *Santa Claus Who's Who*?

PÈRE NOEL: Is she an authorized Gift-Bearer?

SANTA: No, gentlemen. She is only a substitute. But her credentials are in order and she comes here on the recommendation of the Three Kings.

LA BEFANA: Then let us admit her by all means.

SANTA (*Rising*): Ladies and gentlemen of the yuletide, may I present the unofficial representative of Spain, Portugal, and our Latin American neighbors, Donna Poinsettia. (DONNA POINSETTIA *enters as all rise.*)

DONNA POINSETTIA:
Felices Navidades, amigos,
From all Spanish lands near and far
Where Santa's replaced by the Magi,
The Wise Men who followed the star.
ALL: Welcome, Donna Poinsettia.
LA BEFANA: Please take my place next to Santa, Donna
Poinsettia.
DONNA POINSETTIA (*As she sits down*): *Gracias!* It is most
kind of you to permit me to attend your convention.
(KRISS KRINGLE *enters with* PELZNICKLE.)
PELZNICKLE: My apologies to you, Santa, and to all of the
delegates for delaying your proceedings.
SANTA: You are duty-bound to defend your convictions,
Pelznickle. May I present our new delegate, Donna
Poinsettia. Donna Poinsettia, our two German repre-
sentatives, Kriss Kringle and Pelznickle. (DONNA POIN-
SETTIA *curtsies as* KRISS KRINGLE *and* PELZNICKLE *bow*.)
And now, we are ready to open our discussion of the
Christmas season. When is it to begin? When is it to
close?
SNOW MAIDEN: Mr. Chairman, I move that December 6th,
the Feast Day of our beloved St. Nicholas, be adopted as
our opening date.
PÈRE NOEL: I second the motion.
SANTA: All those in favor of December 6th as the opening
of the Christmas season, please say Aye.
ALL: Aye!
SANTA: Opposed, No! (*No one speaks.*) The Ayes have it.
Henceforth the Christmas season or yuletide officially
opens on December 6th.
ST. LUCIA: This pleases me because my own Feast Day is
December 13th.
JULENISSE: And what a happy day it is for Sweden! The

youngest daughter in every household awakens her parents and brothers and sisters by serving them Lucia buns and cakes while they are still in bed. I propose we make this a worldwide custom.

SANTA: It would indeed be a delightful custom, Julenisse, but I am afraid there would be serious objection in America because of the fire laws.   ·

ALL: Fire laws!

KRISS KRINGLE: What do fire laws have to do with it?

SANTA: It's that headdress! Those lighted candles! In the United States we take every precaution against holiday accidents. Candles are not allowed. Not even on Christmas trees.

KRISS KRINGLE (*Horrified*): No candles on the Christmas trees!

SANTA: Only electric lights are permitted, and even so, we must exercise great care. Now if St. Lucia would change her headdress. . . .

ST. LUCIA: No! No! Never! Never!

SANTA: Then I fear we must drop the subject and proceed with the selection of our closing date. (*Producing paper*) I have a note here from Father Time suggesting that all festivities cease with the arrival of the Baby New Year on January first.

DONNA POINSETTIA: Objection! Our yuletide season must extend through Twelfth Night.

PELZNICKLE: Twelfth Night? What is Twelfth Night?

DONNA POINSETTIA: Twelfth Night, or Epiphany, is the sixth of January. It is the night when the Three Kings distribute gifts throughout Mexico, South America, and all Spanish speaking countries.

PÈRE NOEL: The people of France also observe Twelfth Night.

LA BEFANA: Oh, please, please, let us do nothing to offend the Three Kings. I have spent my whole life in sorrow because I was too busy sweeping my cottage to join them in their journey to Bethlehem.

BABOUSHKA: And it was I, Baboushka, who misdirected these holy men when they asked me the way. I agree with La Befana that the Festival of the Three Kings must always be part of the Christmas season.

JULENISSE: The longer the merrier!

SANTA: Is everyone agreed on January 6th as our closing date?

ALL: Agreed!

SANTA (*Rapping gavel*): It is so ordered! (*Consulting agenda*) Now let me see . . . oh yes, the matter of sleighs and sleighbells!

ST. NICHOLAS: If I agree to sleighs and sleighbells, we must also include ships.

ALL: Ships!

ST. NICHOLAS: But, of course. There is Christmas on the sea as well as on the land. And I always arrive in Holland by boat.

KRISS KRINGLE: But what about your white horse? When we were arguing about the reindeer, you insisted on keeping your horse. Now you want a boat! It doesn't make sense.

ST. NICHOLAS: It makes sense to my friends in Holland who are always on the dock to welcome me.

ST. LUCIA: Mr. Chairman, I suggest we postpone this discussion until we reach the subject of Christmas vehicles.

SANTA: An excellent suggestion, St. Lucia. We have so much business today. Now what is your pleasure in the matter of Christmas stockings?

ST. NICHOLAS: As the inventor of the Christmas stocking, I am in favor of keeping it as a worldwide Christmas custom. But we must also include shoes. I have been using both for years.

PÈRE NOEL: The French *sabots* must never go empty.

JULENISSE: I don't see why we have to have either one. In Norway and Denmark I toss my gifts in at the open door.

KRISS KRINGLE: We can always hang them on the Christmas tree.

DONNA POINSETTIA: More countries should adopt the custom of the *piñata,* the earthen bowl which contains all Mexican presents.

GRANDFATHER FROST: The Snow Maiden helps me fill the plates which are placed on the windowsills.

BABOUSHKA: But the plates aren't big enough for the toys I carry. They're really only suitable for sweets.

SANTA: And there's another big problem—sweets! Parents are complaining about too many sweets at Christmas.

FATHER CHRISTMAS: Bad for the teeth! Bad for the teeth!

PÈRE NOEL: But we can't veto cake and candy for the holidays!

KRISS KRINGLE: What would we do without Christmas cookies and the gingerbread men?

ST. LUCIA: And my sweet buns and coffee cake?

FATHER CHRISTMAS: To say nothing of the English plum pudding.

JULENISSE: Oh, no, we could never give up sweets. Every Scandinavian family fills a special plate for me, the Julenisse, who is hidden away in the attic.

SANTA: Ladies! Gentlemen! Please! We will never get anywhere at this rate. We must each sacrifice something if we are to make our Christmas customs the same all over the world. (*Sound of sleighbells is heard.*)

KRISS KRINGLE: What's that?

BABOUSHKA: It sounds like sleighbells!

SANTA (*Jumping up*): It *is* sleighbells! Someone is using my sleigh!

TING (*From offstage*): Whoa there, Dancer! Whoa, Prancer! Easy, Comet! Whoa, Cupid and Vixen!

SANTA: It's those elves! They've been driving my sleigh! Excuse me. (*He goes toward right.*) I must see about this at once. (MRS. SANTA *enters.*)

MRS. SANTA (*Blocking his exit*): Now, wait a minute, Santa! There's no need for you to go outside. The children will be here in a minute.

ALL: Children! What children?

MRS. SANTA: The children you have almost forgotten in your mighty discussions. The children who should have the final say about any and all Christmas changes.

SANTA: But children are not allowed to attend the Convention.

MRS. SANTA: And who has a better right to be here? If Christmas is for children, they must be consulted. Come in, boys and girls! (CHILDREN OF THE WORLD, *dressed in appropriate national costumes, march in to the music of "Jingle Bells."*)

CHILDREN (*Singing to the tune of "Jingle Bells"*):
Please come home, please come home,
Please come right away!
Do not make a single change
To spoil our Christmas Day!

Please come home, please come home,
Listen to our plea!
Christmas Day must stay the same
For all eternity!
(CHILDREN, *in pairs, run to appropriate delegates.*)

AMERICAN BOY AND GIRL:
We want our Santa just the same,
And we want Rudolph, too!
Without the reindeer and the sleigh
What would we ever do?

FRENCH BOY AND GIRL:

Oh, Père Noel, dear Père Noel,
The children of "Paree"
Are begging you to stay the same—
On this they all agree!

ENGLISH BOY AND GIRL:

Dear Father Christmas, please come home,
And keep our Christmas jolly.
We want our yuletide gay and bright
With mistletoe and holly.

SCANDINAVIAN BOY:

Julenisse, Julenisse, our jolly wee gnome,
Please hurry and scurry and scamper back home!
Stay snug in your attic room all through the year,
But come down at Christmas with holiday cheer!

SCANDINAVIAN GIRL:

St. Lucia, dear lady, with halo of light,
We need you to help us keep merry and bright.
In the long, northern night you're a true shining star,
So promise, St. Lucy, to stay as you are!

RUSSIAN BOY AND GIRL:

Our country is so very large, as big as it can be,
One Santa Claus is not enough and so we need all three!
Baboushka and the Snow Maid and Grandpa Frost so
dear,
Please promise you will visit us each and every year.

ITALIAN BOY AND GIRL:

Befana, Befana, go on with your sweeping,
And bring us surprises when we are all sleeping!
In every small cottage there always is room
For you, La Befana, and your Christmas broom!

MEXICAN BOY AND GIRL (*To* DONNA POINSETTIA):

We want our *piñata,* no stockings for us!
No Santas, no sleighbells, no Christmas tree fuss!
We want our Three Kings and the presents they bring,
We want our fiesta when all churchbells ring!

GERMAN GIRL (*To* KRISS KRINGLE):
Don't change a single whisker,
Don't change a single hair!
A change in our Kriss Kringle
Is more than we could bear!

GERMAN BOY (*To* PELZNICKLE):
And Pelznickle, too, though you stomp and you shout,
You're part of our Christmas we can't do without!
We shiver and shake, but we only pretend!
We're not scared a bit, for we know you're our friend!

DUTCH BOY AND GIRL:
The best of the lot is our jolly St. Nick!
On horseback or shipboard, so lively and quick!
Come by sleigh or on foot, any way that you choose,
But bring us the goodies for our wooden shoes!
(REDDIE, GREENIE, TING, LING, JINGLE *and* JANGLE *run in.*)

ELVES:
Merry Christmas, Santa! And all of you take note!
You've heard the children tell you the way you ought to
    vote!
No changes, please, no changes! No change in Christmas
    Day!
But let all people celebrate in their own special way!
(CHLDREN *jump up and down, clapping hands.*)

SANTA: Dear me! I hardly know what to think.

MRS. SANTA: Then don't! The children have made all of
your decisions, so why not put an end to this holiday
hubbub before you do any real damage?

ST. NICHOLAS: I think you're right, Mrs. Santa. The children have a point. It's not *how* we celebrate Christmas
that is important. It's the spirit that really counts.

MRS. SANTA: And the children have the true Christmas
spirit after all.

ALL: Agreed!

FATHER CHRISTMAS: Mr. Chairman, I move that we abide by the wishes of the children we serve and agree to make no changes at all in any Christmas customs anywhere in the world.

ALL: Agreed!

SANTA: I hereby declare the meeting adjourned. (*Cheers and applause*)

ST. NICHOLAS: But before we take our departure, I propose a vote of thanks to Mrs. Santa, the elves, and the children of the world for bringing us to our senses. (*All delegates rise.*)

ALL (*Singing*):
We wish you a merry Christmas!
We wish you a merry Christmas!
We wish you a merry Christmas!
And a happy New Year!
(*Curtain*)

THE END

The Gentle Giant-Killer

Characters

MISS BLANK ⎱
MISS BURTON ⎰ *owners of the Busy Bee*
MISS BROWN ⎰ *Employment Agency*

JACK
MISS GOODE, *a teacher*
MR. MASON, *a janitor*

MARY ⎫
HENRY
SALLY
FREDDIE
SARA
JILL ⎬ *children in Miss Goode's class*
BETTY
JOHNNY
JANE
JOSEPH
WILLIE ⎭

SCENE 1

SETTING: *The Busy Bee Employment Agency. Two chairs and a desk with telephone and index-card file are placed at one side of stage, in front of curtain.* MISS BLANK *enters, sits at desk, and begins filling out an application;*

JACK, *carrying attaché case, enters and sits in front of desk.*

MISS BLANK: Name, please.
JACK: My name is Jack. (*Places attaché case on floor beside him*)
MISS BLANK: Last name?
JACK: Blank.
MISS BLANK: What did you say?
JACK: Blank! Leave that blank.
MISS BLANK (*Angrily*): Young man, are you poking fun at me?
JACK: Of course not! What ever made you think such a thing?
MISS BLANK: Because my name is Blank. Bertha Blank.
JACK (*Rising*): How do you do, Miss Blank? Please believe me—I was not making fun of you. I merely asked you to leave a blank space for my last name, because I don't have one.
MISS BLANK: Nonsense! Everybody has a last name.
JACK (*Sitting*): Everybody but me!
MISS BLANK: But I must put down something.
JACK: Fine! Put down "Something." Jack Something. I like that.
MISS BLANK: This is most irregular.
JACK: But then, I'm not a regular guy!
MISS BLANK: Now look here, Mr.—er—Mr. Something, if you really want the Busy Bee Employment Agency to find a job for you, you must cooperate!
JACK: I'll try.
MISS BLANK: Now what experience have you had?
JACK (*Blankly*): Experience?
MISS BLANK (*With exaggerated patience*): Job experience. What is your line of work?

JACK: Killing giants! I'm a giant-killer.

MISS BLANK (*Rising*): I'm warning you, sir, I will not put up with your bad jokes any longer.

JACK: But I'm not joking. I am a professional giant-killer.

MISS BLANK (*Reaching for phone*): I'm going to call the police.

JACK: Don't bother. They already know about me.

MISS BLANK: They do?

JACK: Certainly. I've already offered my services to the police, but they don't need a giant-killer.

MISS BLANK (*Nervously*): I—I think you'll have to excuse me. I—that is—there's something I must attend to in the other office.

JACK: Oh, dear! You're afraid of me! Please don't run away! I wouldn't hurt a fly!

MISS BLANK: But you're a giant-killer!

JACK: An ex-giant-killer! I haven't slain a giant for centuries! Not since the days of King Arthur.

MISS BLANK: King Arthur! Now I know you're out of your mind! I'm getting out of here!

JACK (*Blocking her way*): Please, please, Miss Blank! Let me explain!

MISS BLANK: Don't try to stop me! Help! Help! (MISS BURTON *and* MISS BROWN *enter*.)

MISS BURTON: What's the matter, Bertha?

MISS BLANK: This—this man! He's a madman! A killer!

JACK: Please, ladies, I can explain everything!

MISS BLANK: Get him out of here! Run for your lives!

MISS BROWN: Now, now, Bertha, don't get hysterical. He looks like a harmless fellow.

MISS BURTON: Who are you, young man? What are you doing here?

JACK: I'm trying to get a job, and your agency was recommended.

MISS BURTON: What is your name?

JACK: Promise you won't panic if I tell you.

MISS BURTON: Miss Brown and I are not the panic type.

JACK: Very well, then. Here goes. I am Jack the Giant-Killer.

MISS BROWN (*Laughing*): I'll bet you are! (*She laughs again.*)

MISS BURTON: Don't be silly! Jack the Giant-Killer, indeed!

MISS BROWN: What are you trying to do? Tell us a bedtime story?

MISS BLANK: He means it, girls. He's a dangerous character.

JACK: I'm nothing of the sort! Even when I was at the peak of my career, I always shied away from violence. Usually I arranged matters so that the monsters would destroy themselves.

MISS BURTON: Sit down, young man. You're beginning to interest me.

JACK (*As he and* MISS BURTON *sit down*): Thank you, Miss —er—Miss—

MISS BURTON: Miss Burton. I am the president of the employment agency. My partner, Miss Brown, is the first vice-president, and my other partner, Miss Blank, whom you have already met, is the second vice-president.

MISS BROWN: That's why we call our agency the Busy Bees —Burton, Brown, and Blank!

JACK: How clever! And I'm sure you can help me find a job, if you will only listen to me.

MISS BROWN: We've never had any calls for a giant-killer.

JACK: That's why I'm out of work. There just aren't any more giants! At least not the kind they had in the days of King Arthur.

MISS BURTON (*Thoughtfully*): Well, there's that giant they're always putting into new washing machines.

MISS BROWN: And that other one, the jolly green fellow who raises vegetables.

MISS BLANK: But they are all friendly giants! You couldn't kill them!

JACK: You still don't understand! Actually I never liked giant-killing. I went into the business only as a public service.

ALL: A public service!

JACK: Take my first giant—(*Rising*) Cormoran, his name was. I had to get rid of him because he was devouring all the crops and cattle for miles around. Had he lived much longer, all the farmers in our area would have been ruined.

MISS BURTON: I hope they were properly grateful.

JACK: Oh, yes. They're the folks who named me Jack the Giant-Killer, and I still have the magic sword they gave me. Then the next giant, old Blunderbore, had a whole castle filled with prisoners, mostly women and children. So I did away with him, and released the victims.

MISS BURTON: A real rescue mission!

JACK: Right! And that's what I like best, rescue work. Don't you have anyone in your files who needs to be rescued?

MISS BURTON: Look through the card index, Bertha, and see what you can find. (MISS BLANK *starts to look through file.*)

MISS BROWN: Basically every "Help Wanted" notice is a plea for rescue. Tired mothers want to be rescued from too much housework—

JACK: Count me out on housework! I want a man's job. (*Sits*)

MISS BURTON: Perhaps something in the technical field. Bertha, look under the T's.

MISS BLANK (*Flipping through the cards*): T . . . Tailor

. . . Taxi driver . . . Taxidermist . . . Teacher . . .
Wait a minute! What about that teacher who was in here
yesterday? What was her name?

MISS BROWN: Miss Goode! Look under the G's.

MISS BURTON: I remember her! She was a damsel in dis-
tress, if I ever saw one.

JACK: What was her trouble?

MISS BURTON: The children! All twenty-three of them.
(NOTE: *Use number of children in participating class.*)

MISS BLANK: But you wouldn't want that job!

JACK: Why not? I love children.

MISS BLANK (*Taking card from file*): Not these children!
Listen to this: (*Reads*) "Wanted: Assistant English
teacher to instruct children who are absentminded,
bored, careless, disorderly, exasperating, forgetful, gig-
gly, headstrong, impolite, jittery, know-nothing, lazy,
mischievous, naughty, outrageous, pesky, quarrelsome,
rude, slangy, tantalizing, ungrammatical, vague, wiggly,
yawning, and zany!

JACK (*Leaping to his feet*): A giant! A giant is loose in that
schoolroom!

MISS BURTON: What are you talking about?

MISS BROWN: We agreed there aren't any more giants.

JACK: But there must be! Only a giant could weave such a
spell over innocent children! I must rescue them at once.

MISS BURTON: This is not the age of knighthood, Jack.

JACK: Nevertheless, I smell a giant!
Fee, Fie, Fo, Fum!
I smell the blood of a giant, by gum!
And, furthermore, I think I know who it is! (*Unpack-
ing attaché case*)

MISS BLANK: What are you doing?

JACK (*Taking out a pointed cap, a sword, a cloak and a pair
of fancy bedroom slippers*): Getting my equipment
ready.

MISS BROWN: But you don't even know where the school is!

JACK (*Putting on cap*): I do now! This is my Know-It-All cap—I captured it from a two-headed giant in Wales. (*Listening*) Aha! I was right! Ladies, my cap has not only given me the location of the school, but it has also confirmed my suspicions! The giant who holds those children in his power is a frightful monster called Blunderbore!

MISS BROWN: But I thought you had slain all the giants.

JACK: There's always one who gets away. This is Blunderbore the Second, son of Blunderbore the First! He was only a baby when I came to his father's castle, so I spared his life. I might have known he'd cause trouble. (*He changes his shoes for the bedroom slippers.*)

MISS BURTON: Why are you changing your shoes?

JACK: These are my magic slippers. They will take me anywhere I want to go, as swiftly as the wind. (*Buckling on his sword*) And with this magic sword I will slay that wicked Blunderbore and set those children free! (*Drawing sword and striking a pose*)

I swear before this day is dead,

I'll grind his bones to make my bread!

(*All exit*)

*   *   *

SCENE 2

SETTING: *Miss Goode's classroom. At one side of room is a large screen with names of parts of speech on the front. A pile of straw is hidden behind it.*

AT RISE: *All the children are seated at their desks, wiggling, giggling, stretching, yawning, and some even sleeping. MISS GOODE, seated at her desk, is trying to get their attention.*

MISS GOODE: Now, please, children, let me have your attention.

WILLIE: We don't have any! We gave you our attention yesterday, and you never gave it back!

MISS GOODE: Willie Jones, you are an impudent little boy! Sara, sit up! Johnny, sit still! Henry, wake up! Freddie, it's impolite to be yawning all the time.

FREDDIE: But we're so bored! (*Yawning*) Ho-hum!

MISS GOODE (*Sternly*): Boys and girls, I will not put up with such talk! Now we are going to review the parts of speech.

SARA: What parts of speech?

MISS GOODE: You know perfectly well what parts of speech, Sara. Jane, what is a noun?

JANE: I'm sorry, Miss Goode, but I've forgotten.

MISS GOODE: Forgotten! How could you forget when we've been going over these definitions all week? Now get out your notebooks, children, and we'll go over them once more.

JOSEPH (*As children look in desks for notebooks*): I can't find mine, Miss Goode.

MISS GOODE: Joseph Jennings, don't tell me you left your notebook at home again!

JOSEPH: I don't know where I left it—honest! I must have lost it.

MISS GOODE: Carelessness! Carelessness! Carelessness! (*There is a knock at the door right, and* JACK *looks in.*)

JACK: Excuse me, Miss Goode. May I come in?

MISS GOODE: I'm sorry, but this is not a visiting day.

JACK (*Entering*): But I am not a visitor. I am the assistant you requested. The Busy Bee Employment Agency sent me.

MISS GOODE: Oh, do come in, sir, and let me introduce you to the children. Boys and girls, this is Mr.—Mr.—

JACK: Mr. Jack.

ALL: Good morning, Mr. Jack.

JACK: And good morning to you! My, oh, my! What a bright, handsome, intelligent, lively group of children!

ALL (*Straightening up and smiling*): Thank you, Mr. Jack.

JACK: And so polite, too!

MISS GOODE: I'm glad you find them so cooperative, Mr. Jack.

JACK: But naturally. I expect them to be cooperative . . . also alert, busy, careful. . . .

HENRY: But we're really not like that at all, sir. Usually we are . . .

ALL: Careless, disorderly, exasperating, forgetful. . . .

JACK: So I've heard. But I know it can't be true.

JOHNNY: Oh, but it is!

MARY: We don't really want to be lazy, mischievous, naughty, or outrageous.

SALLY: We try not to be pesky, quarrelsome, rude, or slangy. . . .

FREDDIE: But no matter how hard we try, we always end up being terribly tantalizing and ungrammatical!

JACK: That's your whole trouble. You're ungrammatical, so the wrong words come out of your mouths, and you appear to be much worse than you really are.

MISS GOODE: I've tried and tried to teach them good grammar, but they haven't learned a thing!

MARY (*Sadly*):
Our subjects and verbs! Oh, they never agree!
We *know* "It is I," but we *say* "It is me"!

HENRY:
"He don't" is all wrong, and "He *doesn't*" is right,
But we never remember from morning till night!

SALLY:
And verbs are so dreadful! We're ready to scream

With *take, took,* and *taken,* and *see, saw,* and *seen!*

WILLIE:
And when to say *lie* and when to say *lay,*

SARA:
And when to say *can* and when to say *may!*

FREDDIE:
And when to say *let* and when to say *leave,*

BETTY:
Does "i" follow "e" when you're spelling *receive?*

JOHNNY:
You speak of a *house,* and two of them—*houses;*
You speak of a *mouse,* but two are not *mouses!*

JANE:
More than one *goose* turns out to be *geese,*
But more than one *moose* is not ever *meese!*

JOSEPH:
Oh, grammar is dreadful! It doesn't make sense!
All mixed up with clauses and pronouns and tense!

JILL:
If you open your mouth, you're breaking a rule!

ALL:
And that is why grammar should not be in school!

MISS GOODE: You see, Mr. Jack, that teaching grammar is a hopeless task.

JACK: The children are not to blame, Miss Goode, and neither are you. It's old Blunderbore who has you in his power!

BETTY: Blunderbore? Who's he?

JACK: Sh! Not so loud! He might hear you! (*Looks about suspiciously*)
Old Blunderbore is a terrible fellow
With two big heads and a horrible bellow!
And once he has you in his grip,
He makes you stumble, he makes you slip!

He makes you blunder, and what is more,
He makes your lessons a terrible bore!

He takes all the fun out of study and learning.
He makes you feel that your books are for burning!
He makes you look stupid and lazy, too,
You make mistakes in whatever you do.
You can put it down as a general rule,
When children hate to go to school,
And mumble and grumble and moan and howl,
Old Blunderbore is on the prowl!

SARA (*A little frightened*): Oh, dear, Mr. Jack, do you think he's here now?

JACK: I'm positive.

WILLIE: But where is he?

JACK: He could be anywhere. (*Drawing his sword and pointing*) Maybe he's up there in the light fixture.

JOHNNY (*As all look up*): I thought you said he was a giant! A giant couldn't get into a light fixture!

JACK: Blunderbore could. He's an adjustable giant!

MARY: But I don't see him.

JACK: No doubt he's wearing his invisible cloak.

FREDDIE: I don't believe he's up there.

JACK: Maybe he's behind the bookcase. (*Looks behind bookcase*) No! Not there! (*A loud offstage roaring and banging is heard.*) Hear that? He's coming! Quick! Duck down behind your desks! (*As children duck*) You, too, Miss Goode. Get behind your desk. (*As noise increases*) Now don't be afraid! I won't let him hurt you!

MISS GOODE: Nonsense! We often hear that noise. It's the heat coming on in the radiators.

JACK: That's what you think, Miss Goode, but I know better. It's Blunderbore himself, and he's coming this way! Now do as I tell you! Get behind that desk and stay there till I sound the all-clear. Hurry! Here he comes, heading right for the grammar display. (JACK *goes behind screen; grunts and groans and other sounds of thrashing and fighting are heard.*) Aha, you wretch! This time you have *me* to reckon with! Take that! (*A swishing sound and more grunts are heard.*) And that! (*A swish and a groan are heard.*) And that! And that! And that! And that! (*The shouts and groans fade into silence.* JACK, *still standing behind screen, calls to children.*) All clear, boys and girls. Old Blunderbore is dead! (*Children remove screen and reveal* JACK, *standing with his sword held aloft and his foot firmly planted on a pile of straw.*)

ALL (*Ad lib*): Where is he? Where's the giant? (*Etc.*)

JACK (*Pointing with sword to pile of straw*): Right there in front of you! At least all that's left of him!

FREDDIE: But there's only a pile of straw.

JACK: Naturally. What did you expect?

JOHNNY: I'd say you really knocked the stuffing out of him!

SARA: But if he was made only of straw, we could have destroyed him ourselves.

JACK: Oh, no! Not while you were under his wicked spell. From now on, though, you are free.

MISS GOODE: Oh, thank you, thank you, Mr. Jack. How can we ever repay you?

JACK: By making the most of your freedom and learning those parts of speech the easy way.

MARY: Is there an easy way?

JACK: There's an easy way to do most everything, young lady, if you take the trouble to find the formula.

MISS GOODE: Formula? What formula?

JACK (*Looking around*): It should be here someplace. (MR. MASON *enters carrying a long-handled mop.*)

MR. MASON: What's going on here? All that crashing and

banging! And what's this dirty straw doing on my nice, clean floor?

HENRY: That's a giant!

MR. MASON: A giant! It looks more like one of those silly projects to me! Sorry, Miss Goode, I don't mean to criticize, but sometimes those projects are pretty messy.

MISS GOODE: It's hard to explain, Mr. Mason, but I can assure you it won't happen again. Perhaps some of the boys can help you clean it up.

MR. MASON: No, thank you. It's really no trouble. My dust cart's right outside, so I'll just sweep it into the hall, if you're sure you've finished with it.

MISS GOODE (*As* MR. MASON *sweeps*): Quite sure, Mr. Mason, and thank you. (JACK *leans over and picks up a thick envelope from under the straw.*)

JACK: Oho! Here it is! I knew it must be here somewhere.

MISS GOODE (*As* JACK *hands her the envelope*): What is it?

JACK: The formula for learning those parts of speech the easy way.

SALLY: Open it! Open it!

JACK (*Holding up his hand*): Not till after I've gone.

MISS GOODE: Oh dear! Must you be going? Can't you stay with us for a while?

JACK: Sorry, but I have work to do. Now that I'm back in the business of giant-killing, I must keep right on the job.

JANE: Are there more giants?

JACK: I'm afraid so. Blunderbore had plenty of relatives. There was his twin brother, Bungle-Brain, and I think he had a cousin called the Mix-Up Monster. I also seem to remember some other relatives, Muddle-Mind and Knuckle-Head. I'd better go back to the Busy Bee Agency and see if they've had any more calls from distressed teachers.

MISS GOODE: Just the other day our math teacher, Miss Minus, was complaining about her boys and girls.

JACK: A sure sign that another giant is on the loose. Well, goodbye, Miss Goode. It's been a pleasure to serve you. Goodbye, boys and girls.

ALL: Goodbye, Mr. Jack. (*He exits.*)

JILL: Aren't you going to open the envelope, Miss Goode?

MISS GOODE: Right this minute, Jill. (*She opens envelope, which contains a sheaf of song sheets and a note.*)

JOSEPH: What's in it?

MISS GOODE: Some song sheets and a note. I'll read it to you. It's headed THE MAGIC FORMULA. (*Reading*) "When study is hard and learning is slow, Here is a secret it pays you to know: Just fit the subject to a song And sing the verses loud and long. And when you know the words and tune, You'll learn your lessons very soon."

BETTY: It sounds like fun.

WILLIE: Let's try it.

MISS GOODE (*As she distributes the song sheets*): Here are the words and the tune is one that we all know—from the song, *Do, Re, Mi.* (MISS GOODE *leads class in the song.*)

ALL (*Singing*):
Go—a *Verb,* an action verb,
Noun—a person, place or thing,
Me—a *Pronoun* for my name,
Prepositions phrases bring!
Adjectives can all describe,
Adverbs tell how, where and when,
And and *But* connect the tribe
Of words we sing again.
Oh, oh, oh—

(*Children repeat song, with* Miss Goode *giving the command before each line.*)

Miss Goode: Verbs!

Children (*Singing*):
  Go and come or walk and run!

Miss Goode: Nouns!

Children (*Singing*):
  Town and country, land and air!

Miss Goode: Adjectives!

Children (*Singing*):
  Big and small or short and tall!

Miss Goode: Adverbs!

Children (*Singing*):
  Now and then and here and there!

Miss Goode: Prepositions!

Children (*Singing*):
  In and out and by and for!

Miss Goode: Pronouns!

Children (*Singing*):
  You and I and everyone!

Miss Goode: Conjunctions!

Children (*Singing*):
  And and but and either, or!
  The Parts of Speech are fun!
  (*Curtain*)

THE END

Cupid in Command

Characters

EDNA	CHARLES
CINDY	PATRICK
HENRY	MARIE
JOHN	JEFF
DOROTHY	DAN
DELLA	

SETTING: *At center stage is a long work table covered with materials for making valentine cards. A large valentine box is at center of table.*

AT RISE: *All but* DAN *are present, cutting and pasting, and as each child finishes a valentine, he drops it into the box.*

EDNA: I love to make valentines.

CINDY: So do I. But my mother says it's so messy.

HENRY (*Dropping one into the box*): There goes number six. (*To* JOHN) Hurry up, slowpoke. You're still working on your first one.

JOHN: This paper keeps sticking to my fingers.

DOROTHY: What will rhyme with YOU besides TOO?

DELLA: View, through, Sue . . .

DOROTHY: That's good, SUE. Now I can send this one to Sue Boyd.

DELLA: I thought you didn't like Sue. You never walk home from school with her any more.

DOROTHY: What difference does that make? I don't have to like her to send her a valentine. I always send one to everybody in our room.

CHARLES: So do I. I just go right down the alphabet.

PATRICK: I need some more of those little red hearts.

MARIE (*Pushing paper hearts toward him*): You may have some of these.

JEFF (*Leaning back in his chair and rubbing his hand*): My fingers are stiff. I haven't written this much in ages.

HENRY (*Dropping another valentine into the box*): Number seven! (*Shakes box*) This box is getting pretty full.

JOHN: I don't see how you do them so fast.

HENRY: I have a system. I make them all alike.

DELLA: I like to make mine different.

HENRY: I have an idea to speed things up. John could cut all the paper, Marie could do the folding, Cindy could paste, Della could help us write the rhymes, and we'd finish in half the time, with half the work.

PATRICK: That's not a bad idea. That's the way they work in my father's shop. (*A knock is heard at door.*)

EDNA: I'll see who it is. (*Goes to door, opens it.*) Oh, hello. What can I do for you?

DAN (*As he steps into room*): My name is Dan. I live in the neighborhood, and I heard you were making valentines. May I help you?

EDNA: I don't believe I've seen you before, but—

DAN: I haven't been here very long, but I love valentines.

EDNA: Then come in and join us. These are all my friends —Cindy, Henry, John, Dorothy, Della, Charles, Patrick, Jeff, and Marie. My name is Edna.

DAN: And my name is Dan.

ALL (*Ad lib*): Hi, Dan. Come in. Sit down. (*Etc.*)

EDNA: Just make yourself at home. Let me take your coat.

DAN (*Wrapping coat more closely about him*): No, thank you. I'd rather keep it on. (*Points to table*) You all seem to be working hard.

JEFF: Oh, this isn't work. This is fun.

JOHN: Henry holds the record for speed. He's already made seven cards.

HENRY (*Dropping another valentine into the box*): That's my eighth one.

DAN: How do you do it? Do you follow any special directions? What materials do you use?

GIRLS (*In chorus*):
Scissors and paste, scissors and paste!

BOYS (*Together*):
Folding and cutting and snipping in haste.

GIRLS (*Together*):
Draw a red heart and an arrow for fun.

BOYS (*Together*):
Add a short verse, and presto! It's done.

CINDY: There's really not very much to it.

DAN: So I see. (*Examining box*) What a pretty box! Who made it?

MARIE: Nobody made it. We bought it.

CHARLES: It takes too much time to make a box.

PATRICK: It's too hard.

DAN (*Lifting box and shaking it*): But the box is very full —you must have a great many friends. May I look at some of the cards?

EDNA: Oh, sure, help yourself.

DAN (*Pulling an envelope out of box*): Sally Walker. Who is she?

DOROTHY: Oh, she's a girl I know. I really don't like her very well, but she always sends me a valentine, so I send her one.

DAN (*Selecting another valentine from box*): And this one is for Max Higgins.

CINDY: That's from me. Max is a pest, but I always send him a valentine.

DAN (*Selecting another*): Polly Porter.

PATRICK: Polly Porter? My mother knows her mother so she says I have to send her a valentine.

HENRY: Let's not waste any more time. What do you say we try my new system?

DAN: What system is that?

JOHN: It's Henry's new system for saving time. One of us will cut, another will fold, another will paste, and the rest will write the verses.

DAN (*Suddenly pounding on the table*): Stop it! Stop it! I won't have it!

EDNA: You won't have what?

JOHN: What's the matter with you?

DAN: I won't have it, I tell you. This is no way to make valentines!

HENRY: Maybe you know a better way.

DAN: I certainly do.

JOHN: If it will save time and work, let's hear it.

DAN: No, it won't save any time, and it won't save any work. In fact, it will take more time and more work.

PATRICK: Then we don't want to hear about it.

DAN: But you *must* hear about it. You *must* listen to me. You can't make valentines with scraps of paper and dabs of paste and a few little hearts and expect them to mean anything.

EDNA: Of course not. The valentines don't mean anything without the verses.

DAN: And what sort of verses did you write?

DOROTHY: Some pretty good ones.

"I'm sending this red heart to you,

Because there's no one like our Sue."

DELLA: But you said you don't like Sue.

DOROTHY: Maybe I don't, but it's a good rhyme just the same.

DAN: It is not a good rhyme, and it's not a good valentine. It's not a valentine at all.

PATRICK: Say, Edna, who is this fellow?

CHARLES: Why did you let him in here?

HENRY: He doesn't like the way we do things.

DAN (*Pounding table*): I certainly don't, and I'm going to stop it.

BOYS: How?

DELLA: What right do you have to tell us how to make valentines?

EDNA: Who are you anyway?

DAN (*Leaping on top of table*): I'll show you who I am. (*Starts to unbutton his coat*) And I'll prove to you that I have a perfect right to tell you how to make valentines. (*Takes off coat and reveals a red and white costume with a baldric labeled* DAN CUPID. *He also wears a cord over one shoulder, to which is attached a quiver of arrows. Fastened to his belt is a golden bow.*) I'm Dan Cupid, that's who I am, and I say you have broken every valentine law there is this afternoon!

ALL: Dan Cupid!

EDNA: Are you really Dan Cupid?

PATRICK: There is no such person.

HENRY: Pay no attention! He's only fooling.

DAN: I'll show you if I'm fooling. (*Takes bow from belt, selects arrow from quiver*)

JOHN: Scram! He really means it. (*All duck under the table.*)

EDNA: You put that away, you wicked boy. I'm going to call my mother!

DAN: Your mother isn't here. I passed her down at the

corner near the market. And she can't help you when you're breaking the law!

DELLA: What law are we breaking?

DAN: You are breaking my law and the law of St. Valentine.

MARIE: I never knew there was such a thing.

DAN: The first law of St. Valentine's Day is the law of love. A valentine is not a valentine unless it expresses love, affection and friendship. You boys and girls don't even care about your valentines. Your idea is to finish as soon as possible.

HENRY: What's wrong with that? We have other things to do.

DAN: Then go do them, but stop making these silly verses and paper hearts that don't mean a thing.

EDNA: I think maybe I understand.

DAN: I hope so. By the time I'm finished with you, you will all understand that a valentine is worth only as much as the love that goes into it.

JOHN: I took a lot of time with mine.

HENRY: That's only because the paste stuck to your fingers.

DAN: And what about those children you said you didn't even like?

DOROTHY: Oh, I don't *dislike* Sue Boyd, but she's not a close friend.

DAN: Maybe if you'd try being nicer to her, she'd end up being a better friend. And the same thing is true of Max and Polly and Sally.

DOROTHY: Sally often asks me to play with her, but I never ask her to play with me.

CINDY: Maybe Max wouldn't be such a pest, if I didn't tease him.

PATRICK: Polly Porter really isn't so bad. I think I'll help her with her arithmetic tomorrow.

DAN: Maybe there's some hope for you after all. (*Putting*

his bow and arrow aside) You don't need to hide from me. I won't hurt you. (*Children resume places.*)

EDNA: If you will come down off that table, Dan, you could help us sort out the valentines and make better ones.

DAN: All right, I will, but first, I want you to remember this:

St. Valentine and Cupid, too,
Declare a special day
For showing love and friendship
In every sort of way.

So do your very best to make
Each valentine you send
A message warm that's from the heart,
A greeting from a friend.

And when the great day passes,
And Cupid must depart,
Let every day remind you
To have a loving heart.
(*The curtain falls.*)

THE END

The Trial of Mother Goose

Characters

OLD KING COLE
QUEEN
COOK
MARY, *the maid*
PETER, *the pipe-maker*
FELIX ⎫
FREDDY ⎬ *King Cole's fiddlers*
FRITZ ⎭
MOTHER GOOSE
MISTRESS MARY
LITTLE BOY BLUE
MISS MUFFET
JENNY
TOM, THE PIPER'S SON
THE OLD WOMAN IN THE SHOE
TWO SOLDIERS
HERALD
TWELVE CHILDREN
PRINCE GEORGE

SETTING: *The kitchen of King Cole's palace. A long table covered with a cloth is at center, with benches on either side and a high-backed chair at the head.*

AT RISE: COOK *is stirring an iron pot at fireplace up right.* MARY *is at the worktable at left, polishing a silver bowl, and* PETER *is sitting on fireplace stool, cleaning and rubbing a new pipe.*

MARY (*Holding up bowl*): There! It's as bright as I can make it.

COOK: Why are you working so hard, Mary? King Cole hasn't called for his bowl in weeks.

MARY: I want to have it ready for him, just in case.

PETER: That's why I'm making this new pipe. He must be tired of his old ones. Never sends for them any more!

COOK (*Shaking her head*): There's something wrong here. I smell trouble. (FELIX, FREDDY *and* FRITZ *enter left with their fiddles.*)

FELIX: Ummm! Something smells good. (*Approaching* COOK) May I have a taste? (*Reaches for pot*)

COOK (*Slapping his hand*): Out of my way, Felix. This is no place for three lazy fiddlers.

FRITZ: But we're not lazy, not lazy at all. It's not our fault the King hasn't called for us in a month of Sundays.

FREDDY: We came to help. Isn't there something we can do?

FELIX: Freddy and I could fill the wood box and Fritz could help with the dishes.

FRITZ: Or set the table, or shell the peas!

FELIX: I'd even peel potatoes just for something to do.

PETER: Why don't you go practice your scales or write a new tune?

FREDDY: What's the use? King Cole wouldn't even let us play it.

COOK: The King is not himself these days. Nothing pleases him any more.

ALL (*Reciting sadly and slowly*):

Old King Cole is a grumpy old soul,
And a grumpy old soul is he.
He *won't* have his pipe,
And he *won't* have his bowl,
And he *won't* have his fiddlers three!
(QUEEN *enters right during last lines, wiping her eyes with a flowing handkerchief.*)

QUEEN: And he won't even talk to me!

ALL (*Bowing and curtsying*): Your Majesty!

FELIX: Pray forgive us!

FREDDY: We were not making fun of His Majesty.

FRITZ: But the King really is grumpy.

COOK: There's no pleasing him.

MARY: The truth is, we're worried about him.

QUEEN: So am I! Cole was always such a dear, merry soul. And now he hardly ever laughs or smiles. (*Weeps into handkerchief*)

COOK (*Helping her to chair at head of table*): There, there, Your Majesty! Do let me make you a cup of tea. (*Busies herself filling a cup at fireplace*)

FRITZ: Let us play a tune for you. Perhaps it would cheer you up.

QUEEN: No thank you, Fritz. I couldn't bear it.

PETER: The King has everything to make him happy.

MARY: Not an enemy in the world!

QUEEN: But that's just the trouble. He claims he *does* have an enemy! An enemy who must be hunted down and brought to him in chains before he ever smiles again.

ALL: Who is it?

QUEEN: I have no idea!

MARY: Every man, woman and child in the Kingdom is devoted to Old King Cole.

QUEEN: If only he would believe that, my child. (*Sound of knocking on door left is heard.*)

MOTHER GOOSE (*Calling from off left*): Let me in! Help! Let me in!

COOK: Quick! Open the door! (PETER *runs left to open door and* MOTHER GOOSE *rushes in, looking over her shoulder in fear.*)

MOTHER GOOSE: Oh, please, hide me! Hide me! They're after me! They're right on my heels!

QUEEN: Hush, my good woman. Do not be afraid. You are among friends. (*Rising and helping* MOTHER GOOSE *to a bench*) Now, sit down and calm yourself. Tell us who you are and who is hunting for you.

MOTHER GOOSE: The soldiers are after me! The King's men!

FELIX: What have you done?

MOTHER GOOSE: I swear I have done nothing to harm a soul. I am only a poor, old woman, helpless and alone.

QUEEN: What is your name?

MOTHER GOOSE: My name is Mother Goose, and all my life I have written verses for children. Oh, please, take pity on me and protect me from the soldiers. (*Loud pounding is heard from off left.*)

1ST SOLDIER (*Shouting from off left*): Open in the King's name!

MOTHER GOOSE: The soldiers! Please hide me!

QUEEN: Quick! Under the table! (MOTHER GOOSE *ducks under the table as* QUEEN *and* MARY *pull the tablecloth over the edge to hide her.* TWO SOLDIERS *burst in left.*)

1ST SOLDIER: Where is she?

2ND SOLDIER: We saw her come in here!

1ST SOLDIER: Hand her over!

2ND SOLDIER: By order of the King!

QUEEN: Gentlemen, you forget yourselves. You are in the presence of your Queen.

SOLDIERS (*Dropping on one knee*): Pardon, Your Gracious Majesty, pardon.

QUEEN: Now what is the meaning of this? (*They rise.*)

1ST SOLDIER: We were on the trail of an enemy of the King, Your Majesty.

2ND SOLDIER: He ordered us to bring her in—dead or alive.

QUEEN: You must be mistaken. Such a poor, harmless, old woman! (*Claps her hand over her mouth*)

1ST SOLDIER: Your Majesty has seen her.

2ND SOLDIER: Then she *did* come in here.

FELIX: Shall we throw them out, Your Majesty? We're six against two! (*COOK raises a saucepan aloft, MARY raises her bowl, PETER brandishes his wooden pipe, and the fiddlers lift their violins in a threatening manner.*)

PETER: Just say the word, Your Majesty! (*KING COLE suddenly rushes in right, followed by his HERALD, who carries scroll and pen.*)

KING COLE: What is the meaning of this? What goes on here?

1ST SOLDIER: We trailed the old woman through the palace grounds, sire.

2ND SOLDIER: She must be hiding in this very room.

KING COLE: Then find her! What are you waiting for? (*HERALD and SOLDIERS search.*)

QUEEN: Sire, I will not stand by and see a harmless old woman hunted down by these ruffians. (*The table shakes and moves a little.*)

HERALD (*Pointing*): Look! Look, Your Majesty! The table! (*All watch the table. Again it shakes and moves noticeably.*)

KING COLE: Aha! (*He pulls off the tablecloth and bends over to look at MOTHER GOOSE, who is kneeling under the table.*) So there you are!

QUEEN: Please, sire, let her go!

MOTHER GOOSE (*Coming out*): It's no use, ma'am!

KING COLE: Guard the prisoner, men. (*Seats himself in chair; HERALD stands beside him. SOLDIERS hold MOTHER*

GOOSE *between them at foot of table.*) Herald, read the charges against this woman.

HERALD (*Reading from scroll*): The prisoner is charged with writing silly, stupid and insulting verses about His Majesty, King Cole, members of the Royal Family, and many important citizens.

KING COLE: You have heard the charges, Mother Goose. How do you plead? Guilty or innocent?

MOTHER GOOSE: I admit writing many verses, Your Majesty, but I deny that they are silly, stupid or insulting.

KING COLE: Make a note, Herald. (*As* HERALD *writes*) She admits writing the verses. We will now take up that ridiculous rhyme she wrote about me.

QUEEN: Everyone knows that, sire.
"Old King Cole was a merry old soul,
And a merry old soul was he . . .

PETER: "He called for his pipe . . .

MARY: "He called for his bowl . . .

FIDDLERS: "And he called for his fiddlers three!"

QUEEN: Now what is so silly or insulting about that?

KING COLE: It makes me look foolish. Wasting my time eating, drinking, and listening to music. I want the world to know about my great deeds—the damsels I've rescued, the laws I've made, the battles I've won. Besides, I am not old. I'm only thirty-nine!

MOTHER GOOSE: But, Your Majesty . . .

KING COLE: Quiet! The Herald will now read what she wrote about our son, Prince George.

HERALD (*Reading*):
"Georgie Porgie, pudding and pie,
Kissed the girls and made them cry!"

KING COLE (*As all laugh*): Silence! I will not allow you to laugh at our son.

QUEEN: But you know Georgie is always kissing the girls.

KING COLE: I also know they don't cry. At least, not many of them. Herald, it's time for the witnesses. You may show them in. (HERALD *moves right, announces names in loud voice. As each name is called, the witness enters right and stands behind the table, facing the audience.*)

HERALD: Mistress Mary! Little Boy Blue! Little Miss Muffet! Jenny! Tom, the Piper's Son! The Old Woman in the Shoe!

KING: Mistress Mary, what is your complaint against Mother Goose?

MISTRESS MARY (*Pointing at* MOTHER GOOSE): It's *her* fault everybody calls me "Contrary Mary." All because of that silly rhyme she wrote:
"Mistress Mary, quite contrary,
How does your garden grow?"

KING COLE: Little Boy Blue, what is your complaint?

LITTLE BOY BLUE (*Pointing*): It's *her* fault I can't get a job. No one will hire me to mind the sheep because *she* said I was under a haycock fast asleep.

KING COLE: Little Miss Muffet will state her case.

MISS MUFFET (*Pointing*): It's *her* fault folks think I'm a fraidy-cat because *she* said I ran away from a spider.

KING COLE: Jenny, what is your charge against this woman?

JENNY (*Pointing*): It's *her* fault I can earn only a penny a day, because she said I can't work any faster.

KING COLE: Tom, the Piper's Son, is our next witness.

TOM (*Pointing*): It's *her* fault I was beaten for stealing one little old pig.

KING COLE: Our final witness is the Old Woman Who Lived in a Shoe.

OLD WOMAN (*Pointing*): It's *her* fault that people think I'm cruel to my children. She wrote that I gave them some broth, without any bread, and whipped them all 'round and sent them to bed.

KING COLE: You have heard the complaints against you, Mother Goose. What do you have to say for yourself?

MOTHER GOOSE: Nothing, Your Majesty. I only wrote the truth.

KING COLE: In that case, the trial is ended. You stand guilty as accused.

QUEEN, MARY, PETER *and* FIDDLERS: No, no, Your Majesty! Have mercy!

KING COLE: I repeat! The court finds you guilty, but because I am a just and kindly man, I will give you one more chance.

QUEEN: Thank you, thank you, sire.

KING COLE: I have asked each one of our witnesses, before coming into court, to prepare his own version of his case. If you will sign these new rhymes which I have written down here (*Takes out papers*), and agree to have them printed in every Mother Goose book from now on, we will set you free. Do you agree?

MOTHER GOOSE: Before I decide, I must hear the rhymes.

KING COLE: Very well. We will start with Mistress Mary.

MISTRESS MARY:

Mistress Mary, light and airy,
How does your garden grow?
With cockle shells and silver bells,
And pretty maids all in a row.

LITTLE BOY BLUE:

Little Boy Blue is blowing his horn
To keep the animals out of the corn.
He is the one to look after your sheep,
Always alert, and never asleep!

MISS MUFFET:

Little Miss Muffet, she sat on a tuffet,
Eating of curds and whey.
There came a great spider, who sat down beside her,
But bravely, Miss Muffet did stay!

JENNY:

   See-saw, Margery Daw,

   Jenny shall have a new master;

   She must earn more than a penny a day,

   Because she works faster and faster!

TOM:

   Tom, Tom, the piper's son,

   Stole a pig and away he run!

   If you would know what happened then—

   Tune in next week on Channel Ten!

OLD WOMAN:

   There was a good woman who lived in a shoe;

   For children she always knew just what to do.

   She fed them their supper and put them to bed,

   Giving each little darling a pat on the head!

KING COLE: In the absence of Prince George, I have written the following: (*Reading from papers*)

   The young Prince George had a charming way

   Of kissing the girls to make them gay!

   And as for myself, I have composed what I think you will agree is a masterpiece:

   Great King Cole was a mighty fine soul,

   And a mighty fine soul was he!

   He called for his sword,

   And he called for his gun,

   And he marched off to victory!

(*Gives papers to* HERALD)

HERALD (*Bringing papers to* MOTHER GOOSE): Just sign here, my good woman.

MOTHER GOOSE: Never! Never! Never! I would rather be put in the dungeon forever than sign such a pack of lies and falsehoods.

KING COLE (*Angrily*): Then go to the dungeon! You have had your chance. To the dungeon with her!

QUEEN *and* SERVANTS: No! No! No! No!

CHILDREN (*Chanting from off left*): No! No! No! No! (*If desired,* CHILDREN *may be seated in audience and come up on stage at* KING COLE's *command.*)

KING COLE: What is this shouting? Where is it coming from?

QUEEN (*Moving left*): Out there, Your Majesty.

PETER *and* MARY (*Peering left*): Out there in the darkness.

KING (*Joining them*): Where? I can't see anyone.

FIDDLERS (*Pointing*): Way out there in the distance.

KING COLE (*Calling*): Who are you out there?

1ST CHILD: We are the children of the world.

2ND CHILD: We demand to be heard.

KING COLE: Come here where I can see you. (PRINCE GEORGE, *disguised as a peasant, enters left, followed by* TWELVE CHILDREN. KING COLE *sits in chair.*) Who are you who dare defy me? What do you want?

3RD CHILD: We want justice!

PRINCE GEORGE: Mother Goose belongs to the children of the world, and we are here to defend her.

TOM: We only want a few changes in her rhymes.

1ST CHILD:
The world is changing, so they say!

2ND CHILD:
The world is changing every day!

3RD CHILD:
Yes, Mr. Change is on the loose!

CHILDREN:
But we'll have no change in Mother Goose!

MISTRESS MARY: But our new rhymes are ever so much better than the old ones.

PRINCE GEORGE: That's because you're too contrary to see the difference.

MISTRESS MARY (*Stamping her foot*): I am not! I am not contrary!

CHILDREN: Yes, you are!

4TH CHILD: That's why we love you.

5TH CHILD: That's why you're famous.

MISTRESS MARY (*In amazement*): Me? Famous?

PRINCE GEORGE: Of course. Mother Goose has made every one of you famous all over the world.

6TH CHILD:
From Zanzibar to Isles Canary,
The children love Contrary Mary!

7TH CHILD:
In China, India, and Peru,
The children sing about Boy Blue!

LITTLE BOY BLUE: And don't they mind that I fell asleep?

8TH CHILD: They wouldn't like you half so much if you had stayed awake.

MISS MUFFET: And what about me? Do they make fun of me because I ran away from a spider?

9TH CHILD: Lots of little girls are afraid of spiders.

10TH CHILD:
In civilized places and lands where they rough it,
The children know and love Miss Muffet.

TOM: I'll bet they don't like me because I stole that pig.

CHILDREN: Oh, yes, they do!

PRINCE GEORGE:
Many children make mistakes,
Some little, and some big.
And we are sure you never stole
Another little pig!

TOM: You're so right! I learned my lesson.

11TH CHILD:
And as for Jenny standing here,
Although we went right past her,

We like her just the way she is!
We wouldn't want her faster!

OLD WOMAN: How about me? Do children know I really love them?

12TH CHILD:
Our mothers love us very much,
On that we're always banking.
But also every now and then,
I guess we do need spanking.

OLD WOMAN: If this is what the children of the world think of us, Your Majesty, I move that all charges against Mother Goose be dismissed.

WITNESSES: Agreed!

KING COLE: But what about me? And what about my son, Prince George?

PRINCE GEORGE: For goodness' sake, Father, don't you know me?

KING COLE: Never saw you before. Who are you?

PRINCE GEORGE (*Taking off hat and putting on crown*): I'm Georgie—Georgie Porgie, pudding and pie!

KING COLE *and* QUEEN: Son!

KING COLE: What are you doing in those clothes?

PRINCE GEORGE: I believe that a prince should go out and mingle with the people. Get to know them. So I have been traveling around the land, talking to all the boys and girls.

KING COLE: And do you mean to say you let them call you by that horrible name?

PRINCE GEORGE: Georgie Porgie, pudding and pie? I like it! And I like the rhyme Mother Goose wrote about me.

KING COLE: Even the part about making the girls cry when you kiss them?

PRINCE GEORGE (*Laughing*): I don't think you know very much about little girls, Father. (*Softly*) They only *pretend* to cry. Inside they're really full of giggles.

KING COLE: It's all very well for the rest of you to withdraw your charges against Mother Goose. But I am the King, and I demand to be treated with respect.

PRINCE GEORGE: But, Father, they love you best of all.

1ST CHILD: We read about lots of kings who have won great battles, but half the time, we can't even remember their names.

PRINCE GEORGE: In my travels, I've seen your statue in children's gardens and public parks.

2ND CHILD: There are always plenty of warlike kings around, but it's hard to find a jolly one, like you.

KING COLE (*Chuckling*): I'm beginning to feel a bit merry in spite of myself.

ALL: Three cheers for Old King Cole! (*All cheer*)

KING COLE (*Rising*): Mother Goose, I apologize, and grant you a full pardon. (*More cheers*) Herald, I wish to make a proclamation. (HERALD *takes notes as* KING COLE *proclaims*)

Hear ye! Hear ye! From this day,
Mother Goose shall hold full sway.
Honor her when she appears,
Greet her with resounding cheers!
Ring the bells from spire and steeple,
Teach her verses to the people.
Never once forget the name
Of Mother Goose, who brought us fame!

MOTHER GOOSE (*Rising and curtsying to him*): Thank you, King Cole!

PRINCE GEORGE: Thank you, Father. When I grow up to be a king, I'm going to be just like you.
I'll try to be a merry old soul,
A merry old soul I'll be!
I'll call for my pipe (*Beckons*)
And I'll call for my bowl (*Beckons*)
And I'll call for my fiddlers three! (*Beckons*)

KING COLE: That's fine, son. But right now, I'll give my own orders. (*Claps his hands once*) Peter, my pipe! (PETER *brings him the pipe. He pretends to puff and returns it to* PETER. *Claps his hands twice*) Mary, my bowl! (*As she hands it to him*) Mother Goose, here's to your health. (*Drains bowl and returns it to* MARY. *Claps hands three times*) And now, for my fiddlers three! (*As they step forward and bow*) I order you to play the merriest tune that you know, as we choose our partners for the Mother Goose Hop. (*With a bow to* MOTHER GOOSE) Madam, will you do me the honor? (PRINCE GEORGE *bows to* QUEEN, *as all choose partners and dance as violin music is played, pantomimed by fiddlers. Curtain.*)

THE END

The Mount Vernon Cricket

Characters

LAUREL BAILEY
SHIRLEY ⎤
DRINA ⎥
DEAN ⎬ *her friends*
ARTHUR ⎥
JACK ⎦
MR. BAILEY ⎤ *her parents*
MRS. BAILEY ⎦
MR. HARVEY, *a real estate agent*
MRS. SIMPSON, *a neighbor*

TIME: *February.*
SETTING: *The living room of the Bailey home.*
AT RISE: LAUREL, SHIRLEY, DRINA, ARTHUR, *and* DEAN,
   wearing outdoor clothing, enter left.

SHIRLEY: Well, here we are. Now let's see it.
DRINA: I still don't believe it.
ARTHUR: Neither do I.
DEAN: Who ever heard of a cricket in *February?*
LAUREL: I told you, it's not a real cricket. It's a little stool
   —a footstool.
DEAN: Does it have six legs?

LAUREL: Of course not!

DEAN: Then it's not a cricket. A cricket is an insect and insects have six legs.

LAUREL: But this is *not* an insect! It's a piece of furniture.

ARTHUR: Then why is it called a *cricket?*

LAUREL: How should I know? *Cricket* is just an old-fashioned word for an old-fashioned stool. If you'll stop asking questions and take off your coats, I'll run up to my room and get it. (*They remove coats and fling them on sofa.* LAUREL *exits right.*)

SHIRLEY: Do you really believe Laurel has a footstool from Mount Vernon?

DRINA: Of course not, Shirley. She's making it up.

DEAN: But what if the footstool really did belong to George Washington?

ARTHUR: Are you kidding, Dean? You know Laurel and her imagination.

DEAN: Sh! Here she comes. (LAUREL *enters right carrying an old-fashioned stool.*)

LAUREL: Well, here it is. Mother is letting me keep it in my room, but when we move into our new house, it will go by the fireplace.

ARTHUR: What new house?

LAUREL: It isn't really a new house, Arthur. It's the old Martin place.

ARTHUR: That house is a wreck! My dad says it's coming apart at the seams!

LAUREL: It is not! Mr. Harvey says there's not a crack in the walls and the foundation is solid as a rock.

SHIRLEY: Why are we talking about old houses? It's an old cricket we came to see.

LAUREL (*Placing stool on floor*): Mother says it's solid cherry.

DEAN (*With sarcasm*): No doubt made from the famous Washington cherry tree!

LAUREL: Don't be funny, Dean. Look. (*Turns stool upside down*) Here are his initials.

DEAN (*Examining it*): You're right. "G.W.", plain as day.

ARTHUR (*Looking*): And there are some numbers—not very plain, but I can make out a one and a seven. That would be seventeen hundred and something.

SHIRLEY: Golly! George Washington was born in 1732.

DRINA: Maybe it did belong to George Washington, after all. (*There is an offstage bang as* JACK *rushes in left*)

JACK: Oh boy! Am I glad your front door was open!

ALL: What's the matter?

JACK: I just cut through old Mrs. Simpson's backyard, and that rickety gate of hers came right off its hinges!

DEAN: That spells trouble, Jack. Do you think she saw you?

JACK: She couldn't miss! She was standing at her kitchen window. But I was going so fast she'll never recognize me.

ARTHUR: Let's hope not. With "No Trespassing" signs all over the place, you can't say you weren't warned.

LAUREL: What possessed you, Jack? You know how she hates to have anyone on her property . . . especially boys.

JACK: I only hope she doesn't catch up with me and tell Dad. Do you mind if I stay here awhile, Laurel? I don't want her to see me heading for home.

LAUREL: Of course not. Take off your coat and join us. (JACK *adds his coat to pile on sofa*)

DEAN: And take a look at Laurel's latest antique.

LAUREL: It's not mine. It's Mother's. She found it.

JACK: What is it?

DEAN: Nothing less than a footstool that came from Mount Vernon!

JACK: You're kidding!

DRINA: It even has George Washington's initials on it.

JACK: Let me see it. (*Examines stool*) Wow! This ought to be in a museum.

SHIRLEY: We don't have any antiques in our house. My dad says they break if you look at them.

JACK: I'll bet this one wouldn't. It's solid as a rock. (*Sits on it*) See. It doesn't even wiggle. (*Doorbell rings.*)

LAUREL: Excuse me. (*Exits left*)

JACK: I never thought I'd be sitting on a George Washington footstool or a George Washington anything.

MRS. SIMPSON (*Offstage*): I know he's in here. I saw him run up on your porch!

SHIRLEY: Good grief! It's Mrs. Simpson.

DRINA: You'd better scoot out the back door, Jack. She's coming in.

DEAN: No! Just sit tight. She'll never be able to pick you out. (MRS. SIMPSON *rushes in, followed by* LAUREL. JACK *remains on stool.*)

LAUREL: Really, Mrs. Simpson, Mother's not here.

MRS. SIMPSON: I'm not here to see your mother. I'm here to collar the boy who broke my gate and snapped the limb off my lilac bush. (*Seeing boys*) Aha! There you are. Now speak up. Which one of you did it?

SHIRLEY: Are you sure it was one of us, Mrs. Simpson?

MRS. SIMPSON: Not you girls. It was a *boy*. Vandalism. That's what it was. Sheer vandalism.

LAUREL: Oh, no, Mrs. Simpson. It was an accident.

MRS. SIMPSON: So! You know all about it.

LAUREL: Well, I know what you've just told me, but I'm sure no one would have damaged your property on purpose.

MRS. SIMPSON: That's a matter for the police to decide.

ALL: The police!

MRS. SIMPSON: As soon as I discover the guilty party, I'm going straight to the police. Trespassing is no accident. Now! Who did it?

JACK: I did, Mrs. Simpson, and I'm sorry. My father has told me a hundred times not to cut through your yard, but I really didn't mean to break your gate. (*He rises.*)

MRS. SIMPSON: I might have known it was you, Jack Roberts.

JACK: I'll be glad to fix it for you, or I can pay to have it repaired out of my allowance.

MRS. SIMPSON: You won't get out of it that easily, young man. I'm going straight home and report this. (*As she turns to go, she stumbles.*)

LAUREL (*Grabbing her arm*): Look out, Mrs. Simpson. Your shoelace is untied. Sit down here and I'll tie it for you. (*Seats* MRS. SIMPSON *on stool*)

MRS. SIMPSON: Is this a new stool? I don't remember seeing it before.

LAUREL: It's Mother's latest find, Mrs. Simpson. It came from Mount Vernon.

DRINA: And it has George Washington's initials carved on the bottom.

MRS. SIMPSON: Do tell!

LAUREL: There! Your shoelace is good and tight. It won't trip you again.

MRS. SIMPSON: Thank you. I think I'll just sit here a minute and catch my breath. I'm not as young as I used to be, and all that excitement over my gate and lilac bush . . .

JACK: Honest, Mrs. Simpson, I admit breaking your gate, but I swear I never touched that lilac bush!

MRS. SIMPSON: Of course you didn't. That limb snapped off with the heavy snow we had last week.

ARTHUR: But you just blamed Jack for it!

MRS. SIMPSON (*Rubbing her forehead*): Then I was mistaken. It was the snow. And as for that gate, the hinge has been loose for a month. It almost came off for the milkman yesterday morning.

JACK: Then I really wasn't to blame?

MRS. SIMPSON: Well, you shouldn't have cut through my yard, but as for the gate, it would have come off sooner or later. (*Rising*) Oops! I feel a mite dizzy.

ARTHUR: Here, take my arm.

MRS. SIMPSON: Thank you, young man.

JACK: I'll still be glad to fix your gate, Mrs. Simpson.

DEAN: My dad has a pair of hinges he's not using.

MRS. SIMPSON: I just might accept your offer. And about that trespassing. . . . Oh, well, I guess boys will be boys!

SHIRLEY: Even George Washington chopped down that cherry tree, you know.

MRS. SIMPSON: Pure legend, my dear, but a legend we like to believe because it points out the value of telling the truth. Since Jack has been so truthful, I guess I can afford to overlook the trespassing.

JACK: Thanks, Mrs. Simpson. You can count on us to come over and fix that gate this afternoon.

MRS. SIMPSON: Fine. I'll have a piece of fresh cherry pie for each of you. Tell your mother, Laurel, that's a very remarkable stool she has there. If she should ever want to sell it, let me know.

LAUREL: Oh, she'd never sell it, Mrs. Simpson. You know how Mother is about antiques.

MRS. SIMPSON: I expect she could get a handsome price for it. Just imagine—a footstool from Mount Vernon. (*Exits left*)

ARTHUR: What got into you, Jack?

JACK: What do you mean?

DEAN: Why did you suddenly own up to breaking her gate when you ducked in here to avoid getting caught?

JACK: I don't know exactly. It's a funny thing, but the truth popped out almost before I knew it.

DRINA: And Mrs. Simpson—I thought wild horses couldn't get her to admit she was in the wrong.

SHIRLEY (*Staring at stool*): Do you suppose . . . ? No, no, it couldn't be possible!

LAUREL: What couldn't be possible, Shirley?

SHIRLEY: I was just thinking that both Jack and Mrs. Simpson were sitting on the George Washington cricket when they blurted out the truth.

ARTHUR: So what?

DEAN: That's what you call a coincidence.

DRINA: But it happened twice.

ARTHUR (*Sitting on stool*): Well, I'll bet it won't happen the third time. Not while I'm sitting here.

JACK: After what happened to me on that stool, I wouldn't be surprised at anything.

ARTHUR: Go ahead and try me.

LAUREL: But you're naturally a truthful person, Arthur.

SHIRLEY: Arthur does exaggerate every now and then.

ARTHUR: What do you mean—exaggerate?

DEAN: You know what she means, Art. Take for instance that picture of Mickey Mantle you're always showing to anybody who will look.

ARTHUR (*Drawing picture from pocket*): You mean this one?

DEAN: The one with the autograph—"Best regards from Mickey Mantle."

ARTHUR: That's what it says all right. I got it from my uncle.

JACK: Who is buddy-buddy with Mickey.

ARTHUR: I never said that!

JACK: Just close friends.

ARTHUR: Well, no, not exactly. They don't live next door to each other or anything like that.

DEAN: But you always said . . .

ARTHUR: I don't care what I said. My uncle went to see the Yankees play and after the game they were selling these autographs and he bought one for me.

DEAN: So that's how it *really* happened.

ARTHUR: Sure, that's how.

JACK (*With a mock bow*): Footstool, I salute you. You finally got the truth out of him.

ARTHUR (*Jumping up*): Now, look here. Do you mean to say I haven't been telling the truth about that picture?

DEAN: About the picture, yes—but not about your uncle. You had us all believing he and the great Mickey Mantle were pals.

ARTHUR: But I never said that.

JACK: Maybe not in so many words, but that's the impression you gave us.

DRINA: And you certainly never told us your uncle *bought* the picture.

ARTHUR: Well, no. I never thought the details were important. I guess everybody stretches the truth once in a while.

LAUREL: Not when he's sitting on the Mount Vernon cricket!

DEAN: I'm beginning to think there *is* something queer about that stool.

LAUREL: Wait till Mother hears about this. (MR. *and* MRS. BAILEY *enter left, each carrying a large, ugly vase.*)

MRS. BAILEY: Wait till Mother hears about what, Laurel? Hello, everyone. I see you brought down the old footstool.

LAUREL: And wait till you hear what's happened, Mother.

MRS. BAILEY: Wait till you see what I've just bought. Do be careful, Jim. Set it here on the table. (*She puts her vase on table.*)

MR. BAILEY (*Placing vase on table and removing his coat*): Your mother can't pass an antique shop without buying something. (*Phone rings.*)

MRS. BAILEY: I'll get it. (*Takes off her coat and hands it to* MR. BAILEY *as she picks up receiver*) Hello. . . . Oh, yes, Mr. Harvey. . . . Well, yes, as far as I know. (*Puts hand over mouthpiece*) It's Mr. Harvey, Jim. He has the final papers for the Martin house. Wants to know if he can stop by in a few minutes.

MR. BAILEY: Fine. Tell him to come ahead. I'll get everything we need out of my desk. (MR. BAILEY *exits right.*)

MRS. BAILEY (*On phone*): That will be fine, Mr. Harvey. We'll expect you. Goodbye. (*Hangs up*) Marvelous! He wants to close the deal this afternoon. I think I'll make some coffee. It's such a bitter cold day. (*Exits right*)

DRINA: If your parents want to talk business, we'd better go. Come along, Shirley. (*Girls put on coats.*)

JACK: What do you say we do that job for Mrs. Simpson right away? You guys promised to help.

DEAN: I could use a piece of that cherry pie. (*Boys put on coats.*)

ARTHUR: Me, too. So long, Laurel. And don't forget what I told you about that house. Don't let your Dad be talked into a quick deal. Mr. Harvey probably stretches the truth as much as I do!

LAUREL: They're not likely to ask my advice, Arthur. But I just might give Mr. Harvey the cricket test. Bye, everybody. See you later. (*They exit left as* MRS. BAILEY *enters right.*)

MRS. BAILEY: We have a few minutes to straighten up a bit before Mr. Harvey arrives.

LAUREL: Mother, there's something I'd like to ask you.

MRS. BAILEY: Not now, dear. Better take this stool upstairs and put it away.

LAUREL: But it's the stool I want to ask you about.

MRS. BAILEY: I said not now, dear. Please get this stool out of the way. It doesn't belong here.

LAUREL: Can't it just stay down here till after Mr. Harvey leaves?

MRS. BAILEY: I don't know what has come over you, Laurel.

That's the whole point. I want the room to look nice
when Mr. Harvey comes. (*Doorbell rings*) Oh dear!
There he is now. You answer the door while I get the
coffee. (*She exits right.*)

LAUREL: Saved by the bell! (*She exits left and returns with*
MR. HARVEY, *who wears an overcoat and carries a briefcase.*) Come in, Mr. Harvey. Let me take your coat.

MR. HARVEY: Thank you, Laurel. (*Removes coat, changing briefcase from hand to hand as he does so*) Brr! It's
cold outside. Nice and warm in here.

LAUREL: Won't you sit down? My parents will be here in
a minute.

MR. HARVEY (*Seating himself in chair and holding briefcase on lap*): Your parents are lucky people, Laurel. The
old Martin place is the best buy in town.

LAUREL: Let me take your briefcase, Mr. Harvey. (*She
removes it from his lap and places it on the footstool
which she moves beside his chair.*) I'll put it right here
on the Mount Vernon cricket.

MR. HARVEY: The what?

LAUREL (*Laughing*): On our footstool from Mount Vernon, Mr. Harvey. It has George Washington's initials
on the bottom. (*Shows initials to* MR. HARVEY, *then replaces stool and briefcase*)

MR. HARVEY: Well, what do you know! George Washington, who never told a lie. (MR. *and* MRS. BAILEY *enter,
the latter with a coffee tray.*)

MR. BAILEY: Hello, Harvey. Good to see you. (*Holding up
papers he is carrying*) I think I have all the papers we'll
need.

MRS. BAILEY (*Setting tray on table*): Good afternoon, Mr.
Harvey. I'm so excited, I can hardly wait to sign the
agreement.

MR. HARVEY: I'm ready and waiting, folks.

MRS. BAILEY: Let me give you a cup of coffee.

MR. HARVEY: Thank you, Mrs. Bailey. I'll drink to the new owners of the Martin place.

MRS. BAILEY (*Placing a cup of coffee on table beside his chair*): Cream or sugar?

MR. HARVEY: No, thank you. I take it black. (*Leaning over to unzip briefcase*) The blacker the day, the blacker the deed, I always say.

MR. BAILEY: What an odd remark. Let's hope there's nothing black about this deed, Harvey.

MR. HARVEY: Oh—er—certainly not. (*Fumbling in case*) Now let me see, where is that original deed? I know it was right here.

LAUREL (*Picking up stool with briefcase and putting it on his lap*): Let me help you, Mr. Harvey.

MRS. BAILEY: Laurel, Mr. Harvey doesn't want that stool on his lap.

MR. HARVEY: Oh, yes, yes, indeed. I'm quite honored as a matter of fact. Here it is. Of course, you people realize that the one wing of the house was built after the great fire.

MRS. BAILEY: Fire! I never knew there was a fire at the Martin place.

MR. HARVEY: Quite a bad one, back in the 1880's. Lightning did a lot of damage, too, but the walls have been reinforced.

MR. BAILEY: What's this about lightning and reinforced walls?

MR. HARVEY: Surely we mentioned that when we were talking about the foundation.

MRS. BAILEY: Good grief! What's wrong with the foundation?

MR. HARVEY: Well, as the house settled after the flood of '92 . . .

MRS. BAILEY: Fire and flood!

MR. BAILEY: Next thing you'll tell us there was an earthquake!

MR. HARVEY: Oh, no! Never an earthquake, although the chimneys were weakened by the hurricane a few years ago.

MR. BAILEY: Harvey, what are you trying to tell us?

MR. HARVEY: Actually, I don't know. But you and your wife are such nice people, and, well, to be quite honest about it, that Martin house is a real wreck. We've been trying to get rid of it for years.

MR. *and* MRS. BAILEY: But you said . . .

MR. HARVEY: I know, I know. I said a lot of things. But take my word for it—that place isn't worth half the price we're asking for it. Now the Collins house is something else again.

MR. BAILEY: You know we could never afford that, Harvey.

MRS. BAILEY: It's just been done over. I'd adore it, but the price is out of sight.

MR. HARVEY: You're right. But right here and now I'm offering you the Collins house at the Martin place figure.

MR. BAILEY: Do you really mean it?

MR. HARVEY: That's the least I can do for you after misrepresenting the other place. And besides, the price is really fair and square.

MRS. BAILEY: Oh, Jim! When can we look at it, Mr. Harvey?

MR. HARVEY: First thing in the morning. (*Packing up his papers*) And now, if you will excuse me, I must be going. I—I guess I'm tired or it's too hot in here or something. I don't quite feel like myself.

LAUREL: Let me take that stool away, Mr. Harvey. (*She does so.*)

MR. HARVEY (*Looking at it*): A most remarkable piece of

furniture, if you don't mind my saying so, Mrs. Bailey.

MRS. BAILEY: Thank you, Mr. Harvey. I didn't know you liked antiques.

MR. HARVEY: I never did, especially. But I have real respect for that one. (*Slipping into coat which* LAUREL *holds for him*) Thanks for the coffee, Mrs. Bailey, and I'll pick you two up at nine-thirty tomorrow morning.

MR. *and* MRS. BAILEY: Goodbye.

LAUREL: I'll see you to the door, Mr. Harvey. (MR. HARVEY *and* LAUREL *exit left.*)

MRS. BAILEY: Well! That was the most amazing experience I've ever had in all my life.

MR. BAILEY: I don't get it. Old Harvey handing us a line about that Martin place and then coming clean at the last minute. I just don't understand it.

LAUREL (*Re-entering*): I do, Dad. It was the stool.

MR. *and* MRS. BAILEY: The what?

LAUREL (*Picking up stool and almost hugging it*): I just knew he'd have to tell the truth when I showed him George Washington's initials.

MRS. BAILEY: George Washington's initials? What are you talking about?

LAUREL: You should know, Mother. You're the one who brought it from Mount Vernon.

MRS. BAILEY: Of course, I did . . . Mount Vernon, New York. The G.W. on the bottom stands for George Williams, a distant cousin of ours. He made it when he was seventeen years old!

LAUREL: You mean this stool has nothing to do with George Washington?

MRS. BAILEY: Absolutely nothing! Whatever gave you such an idea?

LAUREL: But it works, Mother. You saw yourself how it made Mr. Harvey tell the truth.

MR. BAILEY: Ridiculous!

LAUREL: It's not ridiculous, Dad. The minute I told Mr. Harvey about George Washington and showed him the initials, he began to change.

MR. BAILEY: You actually told Harvey the cricket belonged to George Washington?

LAUREL: I told everybody.

MRS. BAILEY: But, Laurel, how could you?

LAUREL: But I believed it, Mother, and so did they—Jack and Arthur and Mrs. Simpson—they all came out with the truth when they were in contact with the stool.

MRS. BAILEY: Then you'll have to correct your statement, dear. This cricket was never any closer to Washington's Mount Vernon than the distance between New York and Virginia.

LAUREL: Then why did it bring out the truth that everyone was trying to hide?

MR. BAILEY: Perhaps the power of truth as exemplified by George Washington is pretty hard to resist, even today. In Harvey's case, I simply think his better nature took over.

MRS. BAILEY: You planted the George Washington idea in their minds, and they acted accordingly—the power of suggestion.

LAUREL: I guess I'll have to call the gang and tell them I made a mistake. But I still think that stool has some mysterious power.

MRS. BAILEY (*Holding stool*): Honey, when will you grow up? You should have stopped believing in magic long ago. Now take the stool up to your room.

MR. BAILEY: No, wait a minute, Laurel. I want to ask your mother a question. Betty, just how much did you really pay for those vases?

MRS. BAILEY (*Floundering*): Why—er—didn't I tell you,

dear? They were seventeen . . . er . . . I mean seventy-five dollars.

MR. BAILEY (*Frowning*): Hmm! I thought I heard you mention a much lower figure. (*Smiling*) But I really don't care if they cost seven hundred and fifty dollars. With this wonderful bargain on the Collins house, you can buy every antique in town. Just so long as you give the Mount Vernon cricket a place of honor.

MRS. BAILEY: We'll put it right in front of the living-room fireplace. What a conversation piece.

LAUREL: That will be perfect, Mother. Just what every household needs—a cricket by the hearth! (*Curtain*)

THE END

The Birthday Pie

Characters

GEORGE WASHINGTON SMITH

MRS. SMITH, *his mother*

BETTY SMITH, *his sister*

TRUDY

ANNE

BILLY

HARRY

FRED

NANCY

BOB

BETSY

STEVE

TIME: *The afternoon of George's birthday—February 22.*

SETTING: *The Smith living room.*

AT RISE: GEORGE *is slumped in a chair, unhappily twiddling with a small radio.* BETTY *is putting red, white and blue napkins at places set for a birthday party. The centerpiece is a hatchet with flags around it.*

BETTY: You'd better hurry up and dress, George.

GEORGE: I don't feel like dressing.

BETTY: But it's almost time for your birthday party. The guests will soon be here.

GEORGE: I don't feel like having a birthday party.

BETTY: What's the matter with you? Are you sick?

GEORGE: I think I have the birthday blues.

BETTY: You'd better not let Mother hear you say that. She's worked very hard on your party.

GEORGE: Who said I ever wanted a party?

BETTY: But it wouldn't be a birthday without a party.

GEORGE: I don't even want a birthday.

BETTY: George Washington Smith! I never heard such silly talk.

GEORGE: And I never heard such a silly name! George Washington Smith! Phooey!

BETTY: George Washington is a very famous name. It's a great name for any American.

GEORGE: But not for a Smith. It just doesn't go with Smith. Oh, why did I have to be born on the twenty-second of February?

BETTY: Well, you were, so stop fussing and go get dressed. (MRS. SMITH enters.)

MRS. SMITH: The table looks lovely, Betty. Dear me, George! You aren't dressed for the party. Now, go upstairs right away and put on your good suit.

GEORGE: All right, Mother. (From door) Are we having cherry pie again this year?

MRS. SMITH: Of course, dear.

GEORGE: I might have known! (Exits)

MRS. SMITH: Now what did he mean by that?

BETTY: Pay no attention to George, Mother. He's just annoyed about everything—mostly his name.

MRS. SMITH: I think George is a fine name for a boy.

BETTY: He doesn't mind the George by itself. It's the Washington he doesn't like—George Washington Smith!

MRS. SMITH: But my name was Washington before I was married. I never minded being called Martha Washington when I was a child. (Suddenly) Oh, dear, I hope those pies cool in time for the party. I have them on the back porch.

BETTY: Your pies are wonderful, Mother. Hot or cold, they're delicious. (Doorbell rings.)

MRS. SMITH (*Calling*): George, hurry up. Your guests are arriving.

BETTY: I'll answer the door, Mother. (*Exits and admits* TRUDY, ANNE, *and* BILLY, *each with a present*)

TRUDY: Good afternoon, Mrs. Smith.

ANNE: The table looks pretty, Mrs. Smith.

BILLY: George is lucky to have a birthday on a school holiday.

MRS. SMITH: Let me take your coats and hats. (*Children give them to* MRS. SMITH.)

BILLY: Do you want to take our presents now, Mrs. Smith, and bring them in later as a surprise?

MRS. SMITH: Thank you, Billy. That's a wonderful idea. (*Doorbell rings.*) Trudy, would you and Anne please take the others around to the sun porch. They can put their gifts and wraps in there. (*Exits*)

BETTY (*Ushering in* HARRY *and* FRED): Make yourselves at home. George will be down soon.

TRUDY: Hello, everybody. Anne and I will take your coats. (*They exit and return*)

HARRY: Hi, Billy.

BILLY: Hi, Harry. Hello, Fred. Don't you wish we could go to a birthday party every day instead of to school?

HARRY *and* FRED: You bet.

BETTY: I wonder what's keeping George. I'll run upstairs and see. (*Exits right. Doorbell rings*)

BILLY: I'll get it. (*At door*) Come right in. Old Slowpoke George isn't down yet. (NANCY, BOB, BETSY *and* STEVE *enter.* TRUDY *and* ANNE *take coats, exit, and return.*)

NANCY: Oh, look at the table. Isn't it pretty?

BOB: I hope we eat soon. I'm starved.

BETSY: Bob Freeman! What would Mother say?

STEVE: My mother gave me such a lecture on manners, I'm afraid to move. (MRS. SMITH *enters.*)

ALL: Good afternoon, Mrs. Smith.

MRS. SMITH: I'm glad to see all of you. (*Looking around*) Isn't George down yet? What can be keeping him? (BETTY *enters right.*)

BETTY: Where in the world is George? He isn't in his room. (GEORGE *enters from left.*)

GEORGE: Hello, everybody. Sorry I'm late.

ALL: Happy Birthday, George.

BETTY: Better find your places at the table. I made place cards for everybody. (*Children start to walk around table, looking for their place cards.*)

MRS. SMITH: I'll need you to help with the refreshments, Betty. (*Each child sits down as he finds his place card.*)

BETTY: All right, Mother. (MRS. SMITH *and* BETTY *exit.*)

NANCY: Look! The place cards have a rhyme, but the last word is missing. See if you can guess what mine is. (*Reads*)

Mistress Nancy, take this chair,
And have a lot of fun.
This is a double party
For George and—

ALL: Washington!

TRUDY: This is like a game. Let me read mine. (*Reads*)

Welcome, little Trudy,
Upon this happy day,
And give three cheers for Washington,
Hip-hip, hip-hip—

ALL: Hooray!

BOB: Now it's my turn. (*Reads*)

This place is for our Robert.
We hope he is content.
Who knows but someday, years from now,
He may be—

ALL: President!

BILLY: I can tell you right now I'm not going to vote for him. (*Laughs*) Now I'll read mine. (*Reads*)
This place reserved for Billy,
A very special guest.
I know he thinks these colors,
Red, white and blue, are—

ALL: Best!

BETSY: My turn! (*Reads*)
Here sits a girl named Betsy.
Her spirits never lag.
A lady with a name like hers
First made our country's—

ALL: Flag!

HARRY: I have a funny one. (*Reads*)
Harry, you're the next in line,
So sit where you are beckoned.
Harry has a birthday too,
But not on the—

ALL: Twenty-second!

ANNE: These rhymes took a lot of work. Here's mine. (*Reads*)
Anne is such a pretty name,
We're glad to have her here.
She knows the name of Washington
Is one to make us—

ALL: Cheer!

FRED: My rhyme is about the table decorations. (*Reads*)
Howdy, Fred, please take a seat,
And look around and see
The hatchet with which little George
Cut down the cherry—

ALL: Tree!

STEVE: I guess I'm the last one. (*Reads*)
Our friendly Steve will sit right here

And help to celebrate
The birthday of a famous pair
Born on this lucky—
ALL: Date!
BILLY: Don't you have a rhyme, George?
GEORGE: Yes, mine has two verses. (*Reads*)
And here's our host whose name is George.
He waits for cherry pie,
And like that other famous George,
He cannot tell a lie.

His name will always make him think
Of that inspiring youth—
The other famous Washington
Who always told the—
ALL: Truth! (BETTY *enters carrying large birthday cake, decorated with a ring of red cherries on white frosting. She sets cake on table in front of* GEORGE.)
GEORGE (*Excitedly*): A cake! A birthday cake! (MRS. SMITH *enters with plates of ice cream on tray, which she sets down on small table at side.*)
MRS. SMITH (*As she begins to distribute ice cream*): I hope the cake is all right.
TRUDY: I'm sure it's wonderful, Mrs. Smith. You're such a good cook.
ANNE: Let's all sing "Happy Birthday"! (*All join in singing of song.*)
BILLY (*Eyeing cake hungrily*): This cake looks great, but nobody can bake cherry pies like yours, Mrs. Smith.
BOB: Cherry pies! Yum! That's one reason I always like George's birthday parties. We always have cherry pie!
BETSY: Bob Freeman! What a thing to say!
MRS. SMITH: That's all right, Bob. We were going to have cherry pie today, but a terrible thing happened—

GUESTS: What?

STEVE: Did you burn them?

MRS. SMITH: No, but I was late in baking them, and I set them out on the back porch to cool. When I went for them, they were gone—just disappeared.

ALL: How awful!

MRS. SMITH: I simply can't understand it. Nothing was ever disturbed before. The porch is screened in.

ANNE: That's too bad, Mrs. Smith, but don't worry. We all love cake.

BOB: But think of all those cherry pies!

NANCY: How did you ever manage to bake a cake in such a short time?

MRS. SMITH: I didn't. Betty had to run up to the bakery and buy one. I couldn't disappoint George and his guests.

BETTY: Aren't you going to cut the cake, George?

GEORGE (*Pushing the cake away from him*): I—I can't. I don't think I feel very well.

MRS. SMITH (*Running to him*): What's the matter, George? Are you sick?

GEORGE: Yes—er—that is—no—no, I'm not sick. (*Throwing down his napkin in disgust*) What chance does a fellow have of doing anything dishonest when his name is *George Washington Smith!*

BETTY: Dishonest?

MRS. SMITH: What are you talking about?

GEORGE: I'm talking about the pies. Oh, Mom, I'm so ashamed of myself. But—well—I've always hated having cherry pie and ice cream for my birthday, when all the other kids have a birthday cake, so I—I sneaked out on the porch when I was supposed to be getting dressed, and—

MRS. SMITH: George Washington Smith! What did you do with those pies?

GEORGE: I hid them. I took them down to the cellar and hid them on the top shelf behind the strawberry jam.

BETTY: George! What a terrible thing to do!

GEORGE (*Ashamed*): I know, and I'm sorry, Mom, honest. I never dreamed you would go out and buy a cake.

MRS. SMITH: And I never dreamed you wanted a birthday cake so badly that you would do a thing like that. Maybe I was thinking too much about George Washington and the cherry tree.

STEVE: Our teacher says that story didn't really happen anyhow.

GEORGE: I don't care if it really happened or if somebody made it up. I'm glad I know about it because it helped me to tell the truth and get that funny feeling out of my stomach.

MRS. SMITH: So am I, dear. It's a wonderful story to grow on.

BETTY: And I'm proud of you for remembering it.

BOB: I always wished I had been named for somebody famous, but maybe it's pretty hard to live up to a great name.

GEORGE: From now on, I'm going to try to live up to mine. Maybe some day George Washington Smith will be a great name, too.

MRS. SMITH: I'm sure it will, son. But, Betty, what are we waiting for? Now that we know where the pies are, we can serve them.

TRUDY: But this lovely cake!

BOB: I vote for the cherry pie!

ALL (*Ad lib*): So do we! Me, too! We want cherry pie! (*Etc.*)

MRS. SMITH: Don't worry about the cake, children. We'll save that for supper and we'll have our birthday pie after all.

STEVE (*Rising*): Let's have a song in honor of Mrs. Smith. Do you all know "Billy Boy"?

ALL (*Ad lib*): Sure. That's a good song! (*Etc.*)

STEVE: Then here we go! (*Children rise and sing to tune of "Billy Boy".*)

ALL (*Singing*):
She can bake a cherry pie, Georgie Boy, Georgie Boy.
She can bake a cherry pie, Mister Georgie.
She can bake a cherry pie quick as you can wink your eye
Not a baker can ever beat your mother! (*They continue singing, as curtain falls.*)

THE END

A Matter of Health

Characters

CHAIRMAN OF THE BOARD OF EXPERTS, *a girl*
MARY ⎤
SARAH ⎟
RUTH ⎟
LOUISE ⎬ *members of the Board of Experts*
SUE ⎟
BILLY ⎟
FRED ⎟
JOHN ⎦
PROBLEM PATTY
PROBLEM PAUL
PROBLEM PEGGY
PROBLEM PETE
PROBLEM POLLY
PROBLEM PATRICK

SETTING: *The meeting room of the Board of Experts.*
AT RISE: *Members of the Board of Experts and* CHAIRMAN *are sitting around large table.* PROBLEM PATTY *is sitting in the consultant's chair.*

CHAIRMAN: Hello there and welcome. Today we are about to discuss some important health problems. Here is Problem Patty with question number one.

PROBLEM PATTY: Thank you, Madam Chairman. I really do need help. I am called Problem Patty because it is such a problem for my mother to get me off to school on time.

MARY: A great many mothers have that same problem, Patty.

PROBLEM PATTY: Yes, I know. But mine seems to be extra-special. You see, in the morning, I am always in a hurry. But Mother insists I take time out for breakfast. My problem is how to stop wasting time on breakfast and get to school before the bell rings.

SARAH: The answer to that one is very simple. You'll just have to get up earlier.

PROBLEM PATTY: But I'm too sleepy! Anyhow, why should I bother with that silly old breakfast?

RUTH: It looks as if we'll have to educate Problem Patty about breakfast. Breakfast isn't a bit silly, you know. In fact, it's terribly important because it gets you off to a good start for the whole day. What do you usually eat for breakfast?

PROBLEM PATTY: Whatever I can grab on the run. (*Experts shake heads in disapproval.*)

CHAIRMAN: That will never do! Let's give her the formula for the right kind of breakfast.

EXPERTS (*Singing to tune of "Twinkle, Twinkle, Little Star"*):
Get out the juice, get out the toast,
That's what children love for breakfast most.
Get out the dishes for the oatmeal, too,
Good hot cereal's the dish for you!
Get out the cocoa, get out the milk,
Breakfast will make your skin like silk.
Get out the bacon and get out the eggs,
They'll build you sturdy arms and legs!

CHAIRMAN: Give yourself plenty of time for a good breakfast, Patty, and see if your problem doesn't have a happy ending.

PROBLEM PATTY: Very well, I'll try. But I'll bet my mother will say, "I told you so!" (PATTY *exits as* PAUL *enters.*)

CHAIRMAN: Mothers have a way of being right about a lot of things. But here comes Problem Paul. He looks as if he has a very tough problem to solve.

PROBLEM PAUL: My problem is really difficult. In fact, you'll have to be good in arithmetic to answer it.

BILLY: We'll do our best. But I do hope it doesn't involve fractions.

PROBLEM PAUL: If you have twenty-eight teeth when you're eight years old, how many will you have when you're eighty years old?

BILLY: That answer doesn't depend on arithmetic. That depends on you.

PROBLEM PAUL: What do you mean?

RUTH:
Your teeth depend on daily care,
And proper foods to eat.
Of too much candy, please beware!
There's danger in a sweet!
Your teeth will last a good long while,
If you take care, you bet!
At eighty you will have your own,
Or buy another set!

CHAIRMAN: Here's the formula that should solve your problem, Paul.

EXPERTS (*Singing to the tune of "She'll Be Comin' 'Round the Mountain"*):
You should clean and scrub your grinders after meals, after meals,
You should clean and scrub your grinders after meals, after meals,
If you're heedin' our reminders,

You'll be scrubbin' all your grinders,
And you'll soon begin to know how good it feels!

So be sure to brush your teeth five times a day, times a
    day,
So be sure to brush your teeth five times a day, times a
    day,
Every night and every morning,
After meals, and that's a warning—
You will find that brushing teeth prevents decay.

CHAIRMAN: I guess you'll have to solve your own problem
    by taking care of your teeth, Paul. No one else can do it
    for you.

PROBLEM PAUL: All right. I'll try to remember. When I'm
    eighty years old, I'll write you a letter and let you know
    how your advice worked out. (PAUL *exits as* PEGGY
    enters.)

CHAIRMAN: And now we're ready for our next Problem,
    and this time, it's Problem Peggy. Make yourself com-
    fortable, Peggy, and tell us your troubles.

PROBLEM PEGGY: My problem is also about teeth, but it's
    quite different from Paul's. You see, my problem is
    toothpaste. Each of us uses a different kind at our house,
    and I'd like to know how to tell which one is best.

LOUISE: Even the best toothpowder or toothpaste has to be
    mixed with elbow grease.

PROBLEM PEGGY: Elbow grease! That would taste horrible.
    I like a toothpaste that tastes good.

LOUISE: Elbow grease doesn't have any taste at all. It just
    means that you should scrub your teeth good and hard
    when you brush them.

PROBLEM PEGGY: That sounds like a good idea. Elbow
    grease and toothpaste, you say? That's a pretty good
    formula . . . and not at all expensive.

SARAH: But the main idea is to remember to use it four times a day.

PROBLEM PEGGY: Thank you. I'll be sure to take your advice. (*She exits and* PROBLEM PETE *enters.*)

CHAIRMAN: Dear me! Look at this dirty fellow. It must be Problem Pete.

FRED: Yes, that's Pete all right. You'd hardly believe he's a nice-looking fellow when he's cleaned up. His problem must be terrific.

CHAIRMAN: Let him state his case.

PROBLEM PETE:

I live near a laundry,
But I'm in a quandary.
I guess I'm a guy without hope!
I love to see dirt
On my face and my shirt.
I hate to use water and soap!

The water's so wet,
And the soap that I get,
It always throws suds in my eye!
But my friends are so few
I am hoping that you
Will give me advice I can try.

My mother is worried,
My father is flurried,
That I'm such a terrible "dope"!
I go out to play,
And my friends fade away,
Because I hate water and soap!

CHAIRMAN: Dear me! This *is* a problem!

LOUISE: Maybe he should send himself away to be dry-cleaned.

JOHN: Maybe he should get a girl. My dad says there's nothing like a girl friend to make a fellow spruce up and take pride in his appearance.

MARY: Humph! What girl would want to be with him? Just look at his face and hands.

SUE: And I'll bet his hair hasn't been combed in a week.

CHAIRMAN: But soap and water are his main problem. How can we solve that?

BILLY: There just isn't any other way to cleanliness.

FRED: Or to health, either. My dad's a doctor, and he says disease germs love dirt. He lent us this microscope so we could really see bacteria at work in a single drop of dirty water. Want to have a look, Pete? (*Motions for* PETE *to come to microscope on large table*)

PROBLEM PETE: I've seen lots of dirt in my day, Fred.

FRED: But nothing like this, I'll bet. Take a good look. (PROBLEM PETE *looks into microscope.*)

PROBLEM PETE: What are all those squirmy little things?

FRED: I'd have to be a scientist to name them for you, Pete. But that's the sort of wildlife you find in dirt, whether it's in a drop of muddy water or on your face and hands.

PROBLEM PETE: Golly! I'd hate to think that those things are crawling all over me.

FRED: And every time you put your finger in your mouth or put the end of a dirty pencil in your mouth, you get a dose of those little bugs.

PROBLEM PETE: Maybe there's a reason for soap and water after all.

FRED: It's our best weapon against these little killers, Pete.

PROBLEM PETE: O.K., I surrender! I'm a soap and water boy from now on.

SUE:
We've scouring pads for pots and pans,
And cleansers for the sink,
And polish for the silverware,

So bright it makes you blink!
There's cleaning wax for kitchen floors
That really is a joy,
But only soap and water will
Shine up a dirty boy!

PROBLEM PETE: I guess you have something there, and the next time you see me I'll be all shined up like a new penny from head to foot. (PROBLEM PETE *exits*.)

CHAIRMAN: I think Problem Pete is going to be all right. Now, who is next on our list?

LOUISE: I have the name of Problem Polly as our next consultant (PROBLEM POLLY *enters*.), and here she is.

PROBLEM POLLY: Oh, dear! I'm really worried! My problem is candy. I have what is known as a *sweet tooth*. I can't pass by a dish of chocolates or gumdrops without taking a handful. What can I do?

SARAH: Plenty of people, old and young, have your problem, Polly. It's all a matter of self-control. Try eating a piece of candy after meals instead of between meals, and see how it works.

BILLY: Set up a candy budget for yourself—three small pieces a day, one after each meal—and see if you can stick to it. Put yourself in training the way athletes do.

MARY: If you drink enough milk and eat plenty of fresh fruit and vegetables, maybe you won't be so hungry for candy.

PROBLEM POLLY: Oh, dear! There's that word *milk* again. How much are you supposed to drink?

MARY: Three or four glasses a day. You really need a quart a day to measure up to good health standards.

PROBLEM POLLY (*With a sigh*): Very well, I suppose I'll have to give it a fair trial. But what about all those fruits and vegetables? Why are they so important?

ALL: Vitamins! Eat vitamin foods! Vitamins taste better in food than in medicine!

PROBLEM POLLY (*Laughing*): I guess you're right about that.

EXPERTS (*Singing to the tune of "Skip to My Lou"*):
Choose all your vitamins, skip to my Lou,
Choose all your vitamins, skip to my Lou,
Choose all your vitamins, skip to my Lou,
Skip to my Lou, my darling!

Without any vitamins, what would I do?
Without any vitamins, what would I do?
Without any vitamins, what would I do?
What would I do, my darling?

You'd be a sick-a-bed, boo, hoo, hoo!
You'd be a sick-a-bed, boo, hoo, hoo!
You'd be a sick-a-bed, boo, hoo, hoo!
Boo-hoo to you, my darling!

Eat 'em in oranges, a grapefruit'll do,
Eat 'em in oranges, a grapefruit'll do,
Eat 'em in oranges, a grapefruit'll do,
Grapefruit'll do, my darling.

Lettuce and lima beans have a lot, too,
Lettuce and lima beans have a lot, too,
Lettuce and lima beans have a lot, too,
They have a lot, my darling.

Eat all the dairy foods, do, do, do!
Eat all the dairy foods, do, do, do!
Eat all the dairy foods, do, do, do!
And drink your milk, my darling!

PROBLEM POLLY: You've presented some very convincing arguments. From now on, I promise to be a real vitamin girl with plenty of fresh fruits, green vegetables and milk. I'll put the lid on the candy box and keep it on tight. (PROBLEM POLLY *exits.*)

CHAIRMAN: We have one more problem boy to see, but he seems to be late.

SARAH: If it's Problem Patrick, he's always late.

RUTH: He's getting slower and slower.

FRED: No pep at all.

SUE: Look, here he comes . . . dragging along at a snail's pace.

CHAIRMAN: Hurry up, fellow, you're keeping us waiting.

PROBLEM PATRICK (*Entering and yawning*): I'm sorry. I just stayed in bed for a little extra snooze, and I must have slept longer than I planned. (*With another yawn*) Excuse me, please.

CHAIRMAN (*With a yawn*): Please try to stop yawning, or you'll have us all doing it.

PROBLEM PATRICK: But that's my problem. I yawn all the time. In fact, I'm so sleepy right now I can hardly keep my eyes open.

CHAIRMAN: What time did you go to bed last night?

PROBLEM PATRICK: I don't remember. It must have been after eleven . . . or maybe closer to twelve. (*Experts shake heads in disapproval*)

CHAIRMAN: No wonder you're sleepy.

PROBLEM PATRICK: Oh, that's nothing for me. I'm a regular night owl.

FRED: Do you eat mice?

PROBLEM PATRICK (*Startled*): What did you say?

FRED: I asked you if you ate mice. That's what night owls eat.

PROBLEM PATRICK: Don't be ridiculous.

FRED: I'm not being ridiculous. If you want to be a night owl, you should follow his eating habits as well as his sleeping habits. A diet of mice would be just about as good for you as the owl's sleeping habits.

JOHN: If you want to be an owl, you should grow feathers.

PROBLEM PATRICK: You're making fun of me. I came here to get help with my problem of yawning. It's very embarrassing. I yawn all the time, whether I want to or not. I can't seem to help it.

LOUISE: Ten hours of sleep each night would soon fix that.

PROBLEM PATRICK: Thomas Edison got along on only three or four hours' sleep a night.

JOHN: First he's an owl, now he's Thomas Edison.

PROBLEM PATRICK: I'm getting out of here. You're just trying to make a dunce of me.

BILLY: You've already done that yourself, boy, by yawning your way through life.

MARY: You need all the rest you can get to build up your energy.

BILLY: It takes more energy than you have now just to grow.

PROBLEM PATRICK: That's a funny statement.

BILLY: But it's true. When you were six years old, you probably weighed about forty-three pounds, and were about forty-three inches tall. In five years, if you kept up to other boys of your age, you gained thirty pounds and added twelve inches to your height.

FRED: Boy, that's work. From the time you're six till you're fourteen—that's only eight years—you're supposed to gain sixty pounds, and grow about twenty inches. You can't do that by yawning, brother.

PROBLEM PATRICK: No wonder I feel tired all the time. Mom says I'm growing like a weed.

CHAIRMAN: Why don't you give your body a square deal, Patrick?

PROBLEM PATRICK: I've never thought of it that way before. I've always wanted to be big and strong, but, well . . . I thought it was kid stuff to go to bed early.

JOHN: Then all big-time athletes must be pretty silly. They always get a good night's sleep.

PROBLEM PATRICK: Maybe you're right about my needing more sleep.

CHAIRMAN: Of course, we're right. That's why we're experts.

PROBLEM PATRICK: You sure know all the answers.

CHAIRMAN: No, we don't know all the answers, Patrick. Nobody knows all the answers to health problems. But we do know that it always pays to follow the rules . . . and we know our health rules backwards and forwards. Maybe we should give you a copy of the list we compiled in class.

FRED (*Handing* PATRICK *the list*): Try to stop yawning long enough to read these. You'll find they solve most of our daily problems. (PROBLEM PATRICK *reads list of health rules that have been compiled by class.*)

PROBLEM PATRICK: These rules should be easy to follow.

CHAIRMAN: Of course. Most of them are just plain, common sense, and I am sure our Problem Pupils will agree with me. (PATTY, PAUL, PEGGY, PETE *and* POLLY *enter.*)

PROBLEM PATTY:

A hearty breakfast every day
Will start me on my healthy way.

PROBLEM PAUL:

A toothbrush, though it's not so weighty
Will save my teeth till I am eighty.

PROBLEM PEGGY:

No toothpaste ever can compare
With elbow grease and dental care.

PROBLEM PETE:

Soap and water are the foe
To fight the germs and lay them low.

PROBLEM POLLY:

Vitamins are fine and dandy
In place of too much cake and candy.

PROBLEM PATRICK:

From now on, I will use my head

And get sufficient rest in bed.

ALL (*Singing to the tune of "For He's a Jolly Good Fellow"*):

We'll all be healthy and happy, we'll all be healthy and happy,

We'll all be healthy and happy, and you can be just the same.

And you can be just the same, and you can be just the same,

If all these rules you will follow, if all these rules you will follow,

If all these rules you will follow, then you can be just the same!

(*Curtain*)

THE END

The Forgetful Easter Rabbit

Characters

MOTHER RABBIT
FATHER RABBIT
HUFFY
PUFFY
RUFFY
TUFFY
FLUFFY } *bunnies, their children*
DUFFY
MCGUFFY
GOOFY

LESTER
SYLVESTER } *two boys, dressed as bunnies*

JACK
BOBBY
EDDIE
BILL
MIKE
DOROTHY } *their friends*
SUE
RUTH
MARY
SALLY

THE FORGET-ME-NOT LADY

TIME: *Easter morning.*

SETTING: *A forest glade. At right are ten toy wheelbarrows or small wagons, nine of which have Easter baskets in them. At center is a large kettle labeled* EASTER EGG DYE.

AT RISE: MOTHER *and* FATHER RABBIT *and seven bunnies (all except* GOOFY) *are dancing around kettle. They all carry baskets on their arms and are singing to the tune of "The Mulberry Bush."*

ALL (*Singing, as they pretend to dip eggs into kettle*):
This is the way we dye the eggs, dye the eggs, dye the eggs,
This is the way we dye the eggs,
So early Easter morning.
(*As they replace eggs in baskets*)
This is the way we fill the nests, fill the nests, fill the nests,
This is the way we fill the nests,
So early Easter morning.
(*They march to their wheelbarrows and put their baskets into them.*)

MOTHER RABBIT: Well, children, is everything finished and ready to go?

BUNNIES (*Singing*):
Everything's ready and tippety-top, tippety-top, tippety-top,
So let us be off with a hippety-hop,
So early Easter morning.

FATHER RABBIT: Just a minute! Do you have your lists? (*Bunnies take lists from their pockets.*)

BUNNIES (*Holding up lists*):
Names and addresses of children galore,
Waiting for Bunnies to come to their door!

MOTHER RABBIT: Splendid! Now remember—deliver your baskets and come straight home.

FATHER RABBIT: And be sure to obey the rules. (*He takes scroll from his left pocket and unrolls it. As he reads the rules, the bunnies soberly nod their heads after each one.*)
No dilly-dallying!
No shilly-shallying!
No lettuce nibbling!
No dewdrop dribbling!
No time a-wasting!
No carrot tasting!
No garden looting!
No turnip rooting!
In short, behave yourselves and be a credit to your Easter upbringing.

BUNNIES:
We promise, Father, we'll be good,
And act the way all rabbits should!

FATHER RABBIT: Very well then, follow me. (*He starts to push his wheelbarrow off right.*)

MOTHER RABBIT: Wait! Wait! Call the roll! Someone is missing! (FATHER RABBIT *takes list from his right pocket.*)

FATHER RABBIT (*Putting on his glasses and reading from list*): Fluffy and Tuffy!

FLUFFY *and* TUFFY: Here!

FATHER RABBIT: Huffy and Puffy!

HUFFY *and* PUFFY: Here!

FATHER RABBIT: Duffy, Ruffy, McGuffy!

DUFFY, RUFFY *and* McGUFFY: Here!

MOTHER RABBIT: We might have known—Goofy is missing!

FATHER RABBIT: But where is he?

HUFFY: I'll bet he forgot!

PUFFY: He's always forgetting something.

FLUFFY: Maybe he forgot to set his alarm clock.

TUFFY: Or forgot to get up.

RUFFY: Or forgot to get dressed.

DUFFY: Maybe he forgot where to meet us.

McGUFFY: Maybe he even forgot that today is Easter.

MOTHER RABBIT: McGuffy! How can you say such a thing! Even the most forgetful rabbit in the world couldn't forget about Easter.

FATHER RABBIT: We'll have to go without him. We can't keep the children waiting for their Easter baskets.

MOTHER RABBIT: But someone must wait for him and see that he gets on his way.

FATHER RABBIT: Huffy and Puffy are the speediest! They can easily catch up with us.

HUFFY: Oh, dear!

PUFFY: How long must we wait?

FATHER RABBIT: If Goofy isn't here in ten minutes, you may leave without him. Now, everyone line up and follow me. Here we go! (*They march off right pushing their wheelbarrows and singing.*)

ALL (*Singing*):
Hippety-hop, we're on our way, on our way, on our way,
Hippety-hop, we're on our way,
So early on Easter morning!

HUFFY: That Goofy! He'd forget his head, if his ears didn't hold it in place.

PUFFY: I don't see why *we* always have to wait for him. (SYLVESTER *and* LESTER, *dressed as rabbits, enter.*)

LESTER: Hello! Aren't you going to be late with your Easter eggs?

HUFFY: We have to wait for our brother.

SYLVESTER: *We're* finished.

LESTER: We filled all the nests on our lists.

PUFFY: You must have had an early start.

SYLVESTER: Every year there are more and more children, so every year we start earlier and earlier.

HUFFY: You must be new around here. I don't think we know you.

LESTER: Surely you've heard of your cousins, Lester and Sylvester.

SYLVESTER: I'm Sylvester.

LESTER: And I'm Lester. Why don't you hop along and deliver your Easter eggs? We'll wait for your brother.

HUFFY: Would you really?

LESTER: Sure.

PUFFY: But Goofy might be terribly late.

LESTER: Oh, we don't mind, do we, Sylvester?

SYLVESTER: Not at all, Lester! Not at all! We'll take care of Goofy.

HUFFY: Thanks, thanks a lot.

PUFFY: Maybe we can do you a favor sometime, in return. Come along, Huffy. (HUFFY *and* PUFFY *exit with their wheelbarrows.*)

LESTER (*Laughing uproariously as soon as* HUFFY *and* PUFFY *are out of sight*): We'll take care of Goofy all right! (*They shake hands and push back their rabbit hoods.*)

SYLVESTER: Congratulations, Lester. We really fooled them!

LESTER: They really thought we were rabbits. Hurry up! Let's call the others. (*They run to left and call.*) Come on, everybody! The coast is clear. (*Ten children enter.* EDDIE *carries a long rope with him.*)

BOBBY: We were hiding in the bushes and heard every word.

SALLY: You fooled those silly rabbits all right.

JACK: They really believed you were their cousins.

LESTER: Of course, they believed it!

MARY: Now we can catch that forgetful rabbit and teach him a lesson he'll remember.

SUE: But are we sure he's the one?

SYLVESTER: Of course, he's the one! You heard them say

he'd forget his head if it weren't fastened between his ears.

MIKE: Well, he certainly has forgotten all about us. I haven't had an Easter basket for years.

ALL: Neither have I!

DOROTHY: And it's all his fault!

RUTH: What shall we do to him when we catch him?

EDDIE (*Holding up long rope*): First we'll tie him up, and then we'll think of something really dreadful.

BILL (*Pointing to kettle*): Look! Look! A kettle of hot water! Maybe we could make us some rabbit stew!

ALL: Rabbit stew!

LESTER: That's not a bad idea, Bill, but first we'll have to catch our rabbit.

SYLVESTER: Sh! I think I hear him coming. You'd better run and hide till I blow the whistle.

DOROTHY: Are you sure you can fool him?

RUTH: He'll know you're not his brothers.

LESTER: Don't be silly! (SYLVESTER *and* LESTER *put rabbit hoods back on.*) All rabbits look alike. Now clear out of here! Fast! (*Children run off right, as* GOOFY *enters left. He carries a basket of Easter eggs on each arm and one in each hand.*)

GOOFY: Quick! Quick! Come take these baskets before I drop them! (LESTER *and* SYLVESTER *put baskets in empty wheelbarrow.*) Thank you. (*Looking about*) Where is the rest of the family?

LESTER: They've all gone.

SYLVESTER: What made you so late?

GOOFY: It's a long story!
    I forgot my hat,
    I forgot my tie!
    I forgot my watch,
    So the time went by.

I then sat down
To rest my legs,
And, bless my stars,
I forgot the eggs!

I forgot the road,
And I walked right past,
But I turned around,
And I'm here at last!

SYLVESTER: And it's about time!

LESTER: Where is your list?

GOOFY: I have it here somewhere. (*Feels in pocket*) Here
it is! (*Unfolds paper and reads*)
A bunch of parsley,
A hot cross bun,
A dozen eggs—
That's not the one!

LESTER: That's a market list, stupid!

GOOFY: It must be in my other pocket. (*Takes out an-
other paper; reads*)
"In adding fractions, what is the rule?"
My arithmetic paper I brought from school!

LESTER: I'll bet you forgot it.

GOOFY: Oh, no! It's here someplace. (*Taking bits of
paper from his pocket one at a time*)
A ticket stub,
The milkman's note,
An excuse for absence that Mother wrote.
Some trading stamps . . .
Oh, dear, oh, dear,
My Easter list
Just isn't here!

LESTER: What are you going to do?

SYLVESTER: You can't deliver the eggs without your list.

GOOFY (*Digging into last pocket*): Wait! Wait! Here it is!

LESTER: Let me see that!

SYLVESTER (*Looking on as* GOOFY *hands list to* LESTER): It's an Easter list all right, but look at the date.

BOTH: 1954!

LESTER: You can't use that!

GOOFY: Sure, I can. It's the same one I used last year, and the year before and the year before that. . . .

SYLVESTER: We have him! We have him! (*Blows whistle and children rush in and seize* GOOFY)

GOOFY: Hey! What is this? What's the matter? Who are you?

ALL: We're the forgotten children!

BOBBY: We haven't had an Easter basket for years.

SUE: And now we know why.

DOROTHY: It's all your fault!

GOOFY (*Calling*): Huffy, Puffy! Do something! Make these children let go of me.

LESTER: Huffy and Puffy have gone with the others. (*Throwing back rabbit hood*) My name is Lester. I'm a real live boy (*Pointing*), and this is my brother, Sylvester.

GOOFY: But what are you going to do?

MIKE: We're going to punish you for neglecting us.

GOOFY: Oh, dear! I'm sorry I forgot, but I'll add your names to my list.

JACK: And then forget all about it by next year!

BILL: Nothing doing! We're out for revenge!

EDDIE: Tie him up, boys!

GOOFY (*As boys tie him up*): Help! Help! What are you going to do to me?

CHILDREN (*As if giving a cheer*):
Put him in the pot!
Put him in the stew!
Now, Forgetful Easter Bunny,
We'll fix you!

(THE FORGET-ME-NOT LADY *enters from left, wearing a long, old-fashioned dress. She carries a basket filled with artificial forget-me-nots, and a bucket. A small metal ladle hangs from her sash.*)

FORGET-ME-NOT LADY: Wait a minute, children. What seems to be the trouble?

GOOFY: Oh, Lady, please help me! They're going to put me in a pot and make me into a stew!

LADY: But who are you, and what have you done to deserve such a terrible fate?

GOOFY: I'm only a poor, innocent little Easter rabbit.

LESTER: He's neglected all these children for years and years.

SYLVESTER: They haven't had any Easter baskets since they were tiny tots.

GOOFY: I didn't mean to forget them, honest I didn't. Every year my father makes out a new list, and every year I forget where I put it . . .

JACK: He forgets everything.

LADY: Tell me, Jack, did you shine your shoes this morning?

JACK: How did you know my name?

LADY: I know the names of all children. I never forget a single one.

JACK: But who are you?

LADY: I'm the Forget-Me-Not Lady of Memory Lane. But you haven't answered my question. Did you shine your shoes?

JACK: No, ma'am. I forgot.

LADY: Bobby, you look very nice in your Easter suit, but where is your tie?

BOBBY: My goodness! I forgot it!

LADY: And how about you, Eddie? Did you brush your teeth this morning?

EDDIE: I'm sorry. I forgot.

LADY: Dorothy, aren't you supposed to make your own bed every day?

DOROTHY: I was in a hurry this morning. I forgot it.

LADY: Mike, have you done your homework for this weekend?

MIKE: I forgot to bring my books home.

LADY: Last night I heard a little dog crying for some fresh water.

BILL: Oh, dear! That was Rover. I forgot to fill his dish.

LADY: I believe Sue and Ruth and Mary have library books that are overdue. Is that right?

GIRLS: I guess we forgot! (SALLY *sneezes.*)

LADY: Bless you, Sally! Where's your hanky?

SALLY: I—I forgot to bring one.

LADY: Here, take one of mine. (*Gives her one from basket*) It has a forget-me-not in one corner.

SALLY: Thank you.

LADY: Well, children, it looks to me as if you and Goofy are very much alike.

BILL: But Goofy forgot something important. He made us unhappy.

LADY: Rover was unhappy when you forgot his water dish, and parents and teachers are unhappy when children forget.

EDDIE: I still think Goofy should be punished.

LADY: Wouldn't it be better to cure him instead?

ALL: Cure him? How?

LADY: Let me give him a dose of my forget-me-not tea. See! I'll put in some fresh forget-me-nots (*Puts some flowers in bucket*), fill the dipper with water (*Takes ladle from sash and fills it*), and it's ready to drink. (*Goes to* GOOFY) Here, Goofy, try this. (*As* GOOFY *tries to reach the dipper*) Untie him, boys, so he can drink. (*Boys untie him.*)

GOOFY: Thank you. (*Inspects dipper*) Is it bitter? How does it taste?

LADY: Try it and see.

GOOFY (*Tasting "tea"*): Um-m-m! It's good. (*Drinks it down*) Thank you.

LADY: How do you feel?

GOOFY: Just fine . . . only . . . I'm beginning to remember things. I remember where I put the new Easter list. It's under the clock in the parlor. And the list from last year! I put it in my copy of *Peter Rabbit* for safekeeping. It's between pages four and five! (*Holding his head*) Oh, dear! My head is buzzing! I'm remembering everything I've forgotten for years.

DOROTHY: Is he really cured?

LADY: Of course, he is. Goofy will never forget again as long as he lives.

MIKE: Please, Lady, could we have some of that tea?

LADY: I'm sorry, Mike. It's good only for rabbits. It won't work with children. You see, children are human beings, and it's only human to forget things once in a while.
Show me the child who never forgets,
And show me the grown-up, too,
And you will be doing a magical trick,
Not even a wizard can do!

DOROTHY: But isn't there some way to help us?

LADY: Of course. My forget-me-nots will help you remember. (*Gives a bunch to each child*) Pin these on, and wear them every day. When you look at them, they will remind you to stop and think. The more time you spend in remembering, the less time you'll have to forget.

GOOFY (*Pushing wheelbarrow center stage*): And help yourselves to the Easter eggs, my friends. (*As children crowd around*) Take as many as you want. I've just remembered where I hid an extra supply, so I'll have plenty for all the children on my list.

CHILDREN (*Taking eggs*): Thank you! Thank you!

LADY: One moment, boys and girls. Isn't there something you've forgotten?

BOBBY: We remembered to say thank you.

LADY: Yes, but there's something else. Look at your forget-me-nots and you'll remember.

ALL: I know! I know!

BOBBY: We forgot to wish everybody a Happy Easter.

ALL (*Singing to tune of "London Bridge," as they skip in a circle around* FORGET-ME-NOT LADY):

Happy Easter, one and all,

One and all, one and all,

Happy Easter, one and all—

This day we'll long remember! (*Curtain*)

THE END

Peter Rabbit Volunteers

Characters

MAMMA RABBIT
PAPA RABBIT
PETER ⎫
FLITTY ⎪
FLIGHTY ⎪
PINKY ⎪
FLOPPY ⎬ *their children*
HIPPETY ⎪
HOPPETY ⎪
THUMPER ⎪
BUMPER ⎭
MAZO THE MAGICIAN

TIME: *The day before Easter.*
SETTING: *The Rabbits' home in the forest.*
AT RISE: MAMMA RABBIT *is dipping white eggs in a kettle at center.* FLITTY, FLIGHTY, PINKY *and* FLOPPY *are sitting at a worktable at right painting designs on eggs.* HIPPETY *and* HOPPETY *work at other end of table, arranging grass in Easter baskets, which they pass to* THUMPER *and* BUMPER, *who tie bows onto handles.*

MAMMA RABBIT (*Dipping white eggs in and out of kettle*): If this batch doesn't turn out right, I'll give up.

FLITTY: If at first you don't succeed, try, try again.

MAMMA RABBIT: This is no time for smart sayings, Flitty.

FLIGHTY: But that's what you're always telling us, Mamma.

PINKY: Keep quiet, Flighty.

FLOPPY: Mamma Rabbit has an important job to do.

HIPPETY: I guess Easter Rabbits are the most important rabbits in the world.

MAMMA RABBIT: I can't understand these eggs! (*Holding up a basket of white eggs*) Just look at them! Not a drop of color!

PINKY: We're having the same trouble. My colors don't seem to stick.

FLITTY *and* FLIGHTY (*Ad lib*): My dye won't dry. The design is smeared. (*Etc.*)

HIPPETY: When Papa comes home, he'll know what to do.

HOPPETY: He always has the answers.

THUMPER: Maybe you're using the wrong coloring formula.

MAMMA RABBIT: It's the same mixture I use every year.

FLITTY: Maybe you're leaving the eggs in the dye too long.

FLIGHTY: Or maybe not long enough.

MAMMA RABBIT (*Crossly*): Maybe! Maybe! Maybe! If you can't offer any practical suggestions, you'd better hold your tongues.

THUMPER: Just the same, I wish Papa would come home.

BUMPER: So do I, Thumper. He and Peter went off somewhere together.

HIPPETY: From the way his nose was twitching when he left, I think he smelled danger.

HOPPETY: Don't be silly, Hippety!

FLIGHTY: We're always safe at Eastertime. (PAPA RABBIT *runs in left, very much excited.*)

PAPA RABBIT (*Waving his arms and shouting*): Quick! Down the rabbit hole, every one of you!

ALL (*Ad lib*): What's the matter? What's wrong? (*Etc.*)

PAPA RABBIT: Don't ask questions! Run for your lives!

MAMMA RABBIT: Now, Papa, don't get so excited. Tell us what's wrong.

PAPA RABBIT: It's Mazo the Magician. He's on the prowl. Peter and I just saw him heading this way. And he's out looking for a new rabbit.

PINKY: But why does he want a rabbit?

PAPA RABBIT: For his rabbit trick, of course. Mazo's most famous act is pulling a rabbit out of a hat.

HIPPETY (*Amazed*): A real live rabbit?

HOPPETY: Wow! I'd like to see that.

PAPA RABBIT: You don't know what you're saying, Hoppety. How would you like to see one of your brothers or sisters being pulled out of a hat by the ears, six nights a week, plus Wednesday and Saturday matinees? It makes me shiver and shake to think about it. Now, do as I tell you and scamper down that rabbit hole.

MAMMA RABBIT: But I haven't finished coloring the eggs. There's something wrong with the dye.

PAPA RABBIT: No matter. The eggs can wait.

MAMMA RABBIT: But tomorrow is Easter, Papa, and we can't disappoint the children.

FLOPPY: We're not afraid with you and Peter to protect us, Papa.

MAMMA RABBIT (*Looking around*): Where is Peter? (*To* PAPA) I thought he was with you!

PAPA RABBIT: And so he was. (*Calling*) Peter! Where are you? Drat that youngster! I told him to stay close at my heels. Now he's gone off by himself.

MAMMA RABBIT: Now, now, my dear! You know our Peter is the venturesome one in the family.

PAPA RABBIT: I thought he had learned something from his sad experience in Mr. MacGregor's garden. (PETER *enters left, carrying a volleyball net.*)

PETER: Look, look, Papa! Wait till you see what I have!

PAPA RABBIT: Peter, you little rascal! I'll teach you to run off by yourself when I told you to stay with me.

PETER: Please, Papa! Let me explain.

MAMMA RABBIT: Wait a minute, Papa. Give Peter a chance.

PAPA RABBIT: He'd better talk fast!

PETER (*Holding up net*): I found this net on the playground down by the lake in the park.

PAPA RABBIT: I've told you a hundred times not to go near that playground.

PETER: But, Papa, I had to go. This is our only chance to catch Mazo the Magician and put an end to his rabbit tricks.

PAPA RABBIT: I don't see how that net will help.

PETER: We'll use it as a trap. People are always trapping rabbits. Now we can trap people. We stretch this net across the path, cover it with leaves, and when Mazo comes along, he'll bang straight into it and get so tangled up, he'll be completely helpless!

MAMMA RABBIT: What do you think, Papa?

PAPA RABBIT: Hm-m! It's worth a try. I'm warning you, Peter. If it doesn't work, I'm going to be angry.

PETER: It will work, all right. Come on now, everybody. Give me a hand. (*Rabbits stretch net between trees at left.*) Are we all set?

PAPA RABBIT: Ready and waiting!

PETER: Let's call his name. All together now (*Calling*), Ma-zo!

ALL (*In a singsong*): Ma-zo! Ma-zo the Magician!

PETER: Hold tight, everybody. Here he comes. (MAZO *enters left wearing black suit, cape, and high hat. He carries a wand, and has a pair of long, outsized ears concealed in a pocket. He blunders into the net and rabbits wrap it around him. In the struggle, his hat falls off.*)

MAZO: Help!

PETER (*Pulling net*): Hold on! Don't let go!

PAPA RABBIT: We have him. (*Rabbits drag* MAZO *to center, where they finally let him sit up, completely wrapped in the net.*)

MAZO: What is all this?

PAPA RABBIT: It's a people-trap, my dear fellow, and you are our first victim.

MAZO (*Indignantly*): Do you know who I am?

PETER: You're Mazo, the Mighty Magician.

PAPA RABBIT: And now we have you in our power.

MAZO: But, what have I done?

MAMMA RABBIT: I could cry my eyes out when I think of all those poor little rabbits.

MAZO: What poor little rabbits?

FLIGHTY: The rabbits you've been pulling out of hats for years and years.

BUMPER: But you've played your last rabbit trick, you wicked man!

THUMPER: Now it's *our* turn!

MAZO: There must be some mistake! I *like* rabbits!

PINKY: Then why do you hurt them?

MAZO: I never hurt a rabbit in my life!

HIPPETY *and* HOPPETY: Oh, no?

PETER: Let's give him a dose of his own medicine! We need Grandpa Jack Rabbit's great big hat.

MAMMA RABBIT: I know right where it is! Come along, Flitty. We'll get it. (*She and* FLITTY *exit right*)

THUMPER: How would you like to be pulled out of a hat by your ears?

MAZO: Listen to me, please! Let me explain! I'm a professional magician . . .

FLIGHTY: Then use your magic to get yourself out of this! (MAMMA RABBIT *and* FLITTY *re-enter from right pushing a tall upside-down top hat large enough to conceal* MAZO. *They move beside him.*)

PAPA RABBIT: Careful now, children. We'll have to loosen the net enough to get him inside the hat.

MAZO: But this is terrible! I'm innocent! (*Rabbits pretend to put* MAZO *into the hat, actually pushing him behind it, where he kneels, out of sight.*)

PAPA RABBIT: We'll need something to stand on. We're not tall enough to get a good grip. (THUMPER *and* BUMPER *bring two chairs from the worktable.* PAPA RABBIT *and* PETER *stand on them, reaching into hat.* NOTE: MAZO *puts on outsized ears, unseen by audience.*)

PETER (*Reaching into hat*): I can hardly get hold of his ear. It's so little.

THUMPER: Pull, when we count three.

ALL: One . . . two . . . three—pull! (PAPA RABBIT *and* PETER *pretend to pull* MAZO *up by his ears.*)

MAZO: Ouch! My ears! You're stretching them.

MAMMA RABBIT: That's enough! I can't bear to look!

PAPA RABBIT: Now, Mazo, you know how the rabbits must have felt.

MAZO (*Holding his ears*): I told you I never hurt a rabbit in my whole life.

PETER: But you admit you pulled them out of your hat.

MAZO: Of course, I did. But never by the ears. Never! And I swear to you, I never pulled a rabbit out of a hat without holding it properly.

MAMMA RABBIT: And how is that?

MAZO: By the thick fur at the back of the neck, just as you do with kittens.

BUMPER: Great bunches of parsley! He really does know how to pick up a rabbit.

MAZO: If I didn't, I wouldn't be an Easter magician.

THUMPER: A what?

MAZO: An Easter magician. It's my job to show boys and girls the trick of handling and caring for their Easter pets. That's why I go around pulling rabbits out of hats

—to show them the proper way to pick up their pets.

MAMMA RABBIT: We've made a terrible mistake.

PAPA RABBIT: We had no idea.

MAZO: That's what the children say. They have no idea their pets might get sick or die without proper care. It takes a lot of magic to teach human beings the tricks they need to know about animals.

PAPA RABBIT: Help me, Peter. We must help Mazo out of there at once. (*They help* MAZO *out of the hat.* MAMMA RABBIT *exits right.*)

THUMPER: You'd better sit down, Mazo.

BUMPER: I'll get you a chair.

MAZO: Thank you, Thumper and Bumper.

THUMPER *and* BUMPER: How did you know our names?

MAZO: I know the names of all the rabbits in this forest. I wonder if Flighty and Floppy could find my hat.

FLIGHTY (*Handing hat to him*): Here it is, sir.

FLOPPY: I hope it isn't dented.

MAZO: It's all right, thank you. Pinky, my magic wand, if you please.

PINKY (*Picking it up*): Here it is, Mazo.

MAZO: Thank you. Now if Hippety and Hoppety will just lend me a hand, I believe I will sit down. (HIPPETY *and* HOPPETY *help him to sit in chair held by* THUMPER *and* BUMPER.)

PETER: I guess you don't want me to do anything for you, Mazo. I'm the one who thought up the idea of the net and the hat.

MAZO: I must admit, Peter, you're a very clever rabbit. In fact, if I could choose any rabbit in the world to pull out of a hat, I'd pick you. (PETER *smiles and quietly exits right.*)

MAMMA RABBIT (*Entering right, carrying towel*): Now do let me wrap your ears in a nice hot towel to unstretch them. (FLITTY *and* MAMMA *wrap* MAZO's *ears in towel*)

FLITTY: How does that feel, Mazo?

MAZO: That feels fine, Flitty. I can almost feel them going back to normal.

MAMMA RABBIT: As soon as you feel stronger, we'll help you to bed.

MAZO: No, indeed. The show must go on! Easter is almost here.

PAPA RABBIT: You're right, Mazo, and *our* show must go on, too. It's almost time to deliver the Easter baskets.

MAMMA RABBIT: But the eggs aren't ready. There's something wrong with the dye. (*Moves to kettle*) See! No color at all. (*Holds up white eggs*)

MAZO: I can fix that with one sweep of my magic wand. Changing colors is one of my best tricks. (*Starts to rise*)

PINKY: No! Please don't get up.

MAZO: But I feel fine now. I think my ears are back to normal. (*Rises and removes towel from head, removing false ears at same time*) Look! They're as good as new, and they don't hurt a bit. (*Approaches kettle*) Now, let's have a look at that Easter egg dye. Hm-m-m! All it needs is a touch of magic. (*Waves wand over kettle and chants*)
Ali kazee, kazoo, kazan,
Abracadabra, too.
Purple and red, yellow and green,
I summon to color the brew!

THUMPER *and* BUMPER (*Looking into kettle*): It's working!

MAMMA RABBIT (*Placing basket of white eggs in kettle, and taking out another basket containing colored eggs*): I've never seen such beautiful Easter eggs.

FLOPPY: The colors are perfect!

HIPPETY: Is that the way you color the baby chicks that are sold at Easter?

MAZO (*Angrily; pointing his wand at* HIPPETY): Just for

that, Hippety Rabbit, I'm going to turn you into a big, fat, ugly toad. Abraca—

PAPA RABBIT (*Seizing his arm*): No!

HIPPETY: Why are you so angry, Mazo? I only asked a question.

MAZO: But what a question. To think that an Easter magician would ever be guilty of coloring baby chicks. Those colored chicks always make me sad on our happy Easter holiday.

HOPPETY: Why? Does the dye make them sick?

MAZO: Not the dye, but the way they are treated! Poor, frightened little things, all huddled together, half smothered. It's part of my Easter magic to teach children and their parents to stop this custom.

PAPA RABBIT: Mazo, you're a true friend of all Easter animals. We'll never forget you.

MAZO (*Rubbing his ears*): And I'll never forget you. (*Putting on his hat*) But now it's time to get my show on the road. Too bad I don't have a rabbit to pull out of my hat. (PETER *enters right with a stick with bright bandanna bundle on the end.*)

PETER: Oh, yes you do, Mazo. I've come to offer my services.

ALL (*Ad lib*): Peter! Where are you going? (*Etc.*)

MAZO: You mean you're volunteering to help me with my act?

PETER: If you will have me, sir.

MAZO (*Clapping him on the shoulder*): You're just the rabbit I'm looking for. Clever, brave, strong, daring. . . .

MAMMA RABBIT: But, Peter, you're too young to leave home.

PAPA RABBIT: Now, Mamma! You said yourself that Peter is the most venturesome of all our children. We can be sure he'll be safe with Mr. Mazo.

MAZO: Indeed he will. A good bed, plenty of fresh water, and all the crisp lettuce and carrots he can eat.

MAMMA RABBIT: But he was born to be an Easter rabbit.

PETER: I'll still be an Easter rabbit, Mamma, and every year I'm sure Mazo will let me come back to help with the eggs.

BUMPER: Golly, Peter, maybe you'll be a magician, too.

PETER: I'll keep my eyes open, and learn every trick of the trade.

PAPA RABBIT: We'll miss you, Peter, but just knowing you're out there making the world a safer, happier place for Easter pets is magic enough for me.

PETER: Thank you, Papa. What do you say, Mamma?

MAMMA RABBIT: I agree, Peter. Remember, stay out of trouble and always carry a clean handkerchief. Goodbye, son.

ALL (*Ad lib*): Goodbye, Peter. Goodbye and good luck! (PETER *and* MAZO *exit left as rabbits sing, to the tune of "Here Comes Peter Cottontail."*)
Goodbye, Peter Cottontail,
Hopping down the magic trail,
Hopin' he's hoppin' straight along your way.
If you get an Easter pet
Make sure of the care he'll get,
So he'll see another Easter day.

You can learn to care for bunnies
And to save those Easter chicks,
If you watch for Peter Rabbit
And his bag of Easter tricks.
Oh, here comes Peter Volunteer,
Brimming full of Easter cheer,
Magical, magical, happy Easter day!
(*Curtain*)

THE END

The Return of Bobby Shafto

Characters

BOBBY SHAFTO
LORD MAYOR OF FLORABELLA
LADY MAGNOLIA
LADY MARIGOLD } *his daughters*
LADY MORNING GLORY
MAID MARJORIE
MARJORIE'S FATHER
TWO SAILORS

SETTING: *A wharf in the port of Florabella. Several large packing cases are piled up right, and a small platform representing a pier is at left.*

AT RISE: TWO SAILORS, *carrying a large sea chest, enter left, followed by* BOBBY SHAFTO, *who is wearing a velvet cape and cap, and long white stockings with silver buckles at the knee. As they reach center, the* SAILORS *put down chest.* SHAFTO *draws a deep breath and stretches his arms above his head.*

SHAFTO: It's good to be home in Florabella again.
1ST SAILOR: But it's been a good voyage, too, Master Shafto, and you have great treasure to show for it.
SHAFTO: That's right. I, Robert Shafto, will be the richest

man in Florabella, and the happiest, as soon as I claim my promised bride.

1ST SAILOR: But why did you have us row you ashore here, so early in the morning?

2ND SAILOR: The Lord Mayor of Florabella has planned a royal welcome for you in the main harbor, and a great ball is arranged in your honor.

SHAFTO: I must attend to a few matters before my return is made public, lad. (*Offstage singing of "Bobby Shafto," to the traditional tune, is heard.*) Quick! Someone is coming! Drag that chest behind those packing cases, men, and keep out of sight. (SHAFTO *and* SAILORS *hide chest and duck down behind boxes as* LADY MAGNOLIA, *dressed in white and twirling a white parasol, enters and strolls up and down singing.*)

LADY MAGNOLIA:
Bobby Shafto's gone to sea,
Silver buckles on his knee.
He'll come back and marry me!
Handsome Bobby Shafto!
I can hardly wait for Bobby's return. His ship has been sighted, and it will be in on the morning tide. Just a few hours more, and he'll be here. (*Offstage singing of "Bobby Shafto" is heard.*) Who is singing? Who *dares* sing my song? (LADY MARIGOLD *enters left, dressed in yellow with yellow parasol.*)

LADY MARIGOLD (*Singing*):
He'll come back and marry me!
Handsome Bobby Shafto! (*Sees* MAGNOLIA)
Good morning, sister Magnolia. I see you're up early. What a bright, breezy, beautiful day it is!

MAGNOLIA (*Grimly*): And it will be a dull, dark, dangerous day for you, sister Marigold, if you keep singing that song. Everybody knows Bobby Shafto belongs to *me!*

MARIGOLD: Is that so?

MAGNOLIA: Yes, that's so. (*They stare at each other suddenly, as song is heard offstage.*)

MARIGOLD *and* MAGNOLIA: Who's that? (LADY MORNING GLORY, *dressed in purple and carrying a purple parasol, enters left, singing last lines of "Bobby Shafto."*) Morning Glory!

MORNING GLORY: Well, well, well! I never knew my dear sisters were such early risers! Are you planning to meet someone?

MARIGOLD: That song! That song you were singing just now!

MAGNOLIA: What right have you to sing of Bobby Shafto?

MORNING GLORY: Every right in the world! As the song says, "He'll come back and marry *me*, handsome Bobby Shafto!"

MAGNOLIA: He will not!

MARIGOLD: Indeed he won't!

MORNING GLORY: And why not, pray tell?

BOTH: Because he's going to marry *me*! (*All three glare at each other.*)

MORNING GLORY (*Folding her parasol*): Perhaps we should talk this over! Two of us are making a mistake.

MAGNOLIA: Not me!

MARIGOLD: Not me!

MORNING GLORY: And what makes you so sure Bobby Shafto will marry *you*, sister Marigold?

MARIGOLD (*Folding parasol and producing a note from a little bag she carries on her wrist*):
This is the note he wrote to me
On the very day that he went to sea!
(*Reading*) I promise you, dear Marigold,
More treasure than your arms can hold!

MAGNOLIA (*Also folding parasol and producing note*):

And this is the note he wrote to *me*
On the very day that he went to sea!
(*Reading*) Magnolia fair, I've gone to win
A fortune for you when my ship comes in!

MORNING GLORY (*Also producing note*):
He also wrote such a note to me
On the very day that he went to sea.
(*Reading*) Dear Morning Glory, bright and fair,
Some day my fortune you will share!

MAGNOLIA: I don't care what he wrote to you, Morning Glory! Or to you either, Marigold! I intend to marry Bobby Shafto the minute he sets foot on this shore.

MARIGOLD: Not if I see him first, sister mine!

MORNING GLORY: You'll see! Bobby Shafto belongs to me!
(*As sisters glare at each other, the opening lines of "Bobby Shafto" are sung offstage.*)

MAGNOLIA: Listen! Someone else is singing our song!
(MAID MARJORIE *enters, wearing a peasant costume, and pushing a cart piled high with fruits and vegetables*)

LADIES: It's Maid Marjorie!

MAGNOLIA: Stop that singing!

MARIGOLD: Stop it at once, you wicked girl!

MAID MARJORIE: What's the matter? What have I done?

MORNING GLORY: That song! We forbid you to sing it!

MAID MARJORIE: But I am so happy, I can't help singing, your ladyships. Today will be my wedding day.

LADIES: Your *what?*

MAID MARJORIE: My wedding day! (*Singing*)
Bobby Shafto sailed away,
Promised he'd come home to stay!
This will be our wedding day!
Darling Bobby Shafto!

MAGNOLIA (*Laughing*): You silly girl! What makes you think the rich and handsome Bobby Shafto would marry a miserable beggar maid like you?

MAID MARJORIE: But I am not a beggar maid, Lady Magnolia. I make my own living, selling these fruits and vegetables from my father's garden.

MORNING GLORY: *Your* father's garden, indeed!

MARIGOLD: It's *our* father's garden!

MAGNOLIA: Every acre of farmland in Florabella belongs to us—to the Lord Mayor and his family.

MAID MARJORIE: Alas, milady, that is true. But at one time, half of it belonged to our family. It is our dream to buy it back some day.

MAGNOLIA: Your dream is not likely to come true, Maid Marjorie.

MARIGOLD: It is only with the Lord Mayor's permission that you are allowed to sell the fruits and vegetables grown on *our* land.

MORNING GLORY: So you are really nothing but a beggar maid after all!

MAID MARJORIE: Beggar maid or no beggar maid, I will be Madam Robert Shafto before sunset!

MAGNOLIA: Hold your tongue, girl!

MARIGOLD: Such idle boasting will get you into trouble.

MAID MARJORIE: But it's true, milady! He promised.

MORNING GLORY: And what about his promise to me?

MAGNOLIA: And to me?

MARIGOLD: And to me?

MAID MARJORIE: I don't believe it!

MAGNOLIA: You'll believe it soon enough when the glad news is announced at the grand ball my father is planning for this evening.

MAID MARJORIE: He couldn't have promised anyone else but me!

MAGNOLIA: But he did! (*Displays letter*) And I have his letter to prove it.

MARIGOLD (*Showing letter*): And so have I!

MORNING GLORY (*Also showing letter*): And so have I!

MAID MARJORIE: No! It can't be true! And I was just now on my way to the main harbor to meet him. They say his crew is already starting to come ashore.

MAGNOLIA: What? The ship is here?

MARIGOLD: Quick! To the harbor.

MORNING GLORY: We must be there to greet him! (*Sisters rush off left.*)

MAID MARJORIE: Oh, Bobby! Bobby! How could you do such a dreadful thing! (*She pushes cart left and sinks down on the platform, leaning her cheek against the post, and sings sorrowfully*)
Ever since you left my side,
Sailing on the morning tide,
I've waited here to be your bride,
Darling Bobby Shafto!
(*Her* FATHER *enters right, passing in front of the packing boxes*)

FATHER: Marjorie! What are you doing here? Haven't you heard the news? Bobby Shafto's ship is sailing into the harbor.

MAID MARJORIE: I know, Father! I know!

FATHER: Then why aren't you there to greet him? What will he think of you?

MAID MARJORIE: I don't care what he thinks of me, Father. Not any more.

FATHER: But you are his promised bride.

MAID MARJORIE: All the girls are saying the same about themselves.

FATHER: What do you mean by that?

MAID MARJORIE: Well, maybe not *all* the girls. But all three of the Lord Mayor's daughters—Lady Magnolia, Lady Marigold, and Lady Morning Glory!

FATHER: Nonsense! Bobby Shafto is an honest lad. He would never make false promises.

MAID MARJORIE: That's what I thought, Father. But I was wrong. They showed me his letters.

FATHER: Did you read them?

MAID MARJORIE: No, but . . .

FATHER: Then do as I tell you. Dry your eyes and put on your brightest smile. (*Tucking her hand in his arm*) You and I are going to be on hand when he returns. (*They exit left. When the coast is clear,* SHAFTO *and* SAILORS *emerge from behind the boxes.*)

1ST SAILOR: Well, Master Shafto, you really do have yourself in a "picklement!"

2ND SAILOR: This is a pretty kettle of fish! Four young ladies, all thinking you'll marry them!

SHAFTO: Easy, mates, easy! I can straighten everything out in a few minutes.

BOTH: How?

SHAFTO: By keeping my promises, of course.

2ND SAILOR: But you can't marry all four of them!

1ST SAILOR: What are you going to do?

SHAFTO: Fetch my sea chest and I'll show you. Hurry! We don't have much time! (*As* SAILORS *follow his command,* SHAFTO *sits on floor to remove shoes and stockings, retaining the silver buckles. He then rises and removes cap and cloak.* SAILORS *bring sea chest onstage.*) Open the chest quickly! (*He stuffs his discarded clothing inside chest and takes out a ragged cloak and bandanna and an eye patch with string attached.*) Give me a hand, mates! (*They help him put on eye patch and bandanna. As soon as disguise is complete,* LORD MAYOR *enters left with his daughters.*)

LORD MAYOR: Where is he? Where is that scoundrel Shafto? How dare he insult the Lord Mayor by sneaking ashore without hearing my speech of welcome?

MAGNOLIA: Find him, Father!

MARIGOLD: Put him in irons!

MORNING GLORY: He's probably run away with that wretched beggar maid.

LORD MAYOR: What beggar maid?

MORNING GLORY: Maid Marjorie, the gardener's daughter. She thinks he is going to marry her.

MAGNOLIA: When he's already promised to marry me!

MARIGOLD: And me!

MORNING GLORY: And me!

LORD MAYOR: Wait till I get my hands on the wretch!

SHAFTO (*Advancing with a bow*): Perhaps I can help you, sir.

LORD MAYOR: If you know anything at all about this fellow Shafto, I will reward you handsomely.

SHAFTO: I know all about him, Your Lordship. It so happens that *I* am Bobby Shafto!

ALL: What!

SHAFTO: Bobby Shafto, at your service, sir.

LORD MAYOR: Is this supposed to be a joke?

MAGNOLIA: You're not Bobby Shafto!

MARIGOLD: Bobby Shafto's tall and fair!

MORNING GLORY: With bright blue eyes and golden hair!

LORD MAYOR: And besides, it has come to my ears that Bobby Shafto made a fortune on this last voyage. You look more like a beggar lad than a merchant prince.

SHAFTO: Nevertheless, sir, my name is Robert Shafto, as my mates can testify. Speak up, lads.

1ST SAILOR: Aye, aye, sir.

2ND SAILOR: He's really Bobby Shafto, Your Honor.

SHAFTO: And I stand ready to keep my promises. (*Bowing to* MAGNOLIA) Lady Magnolia, my compliments.

MAGNOLIA (*Turning her back on him*): Don't speak to me!

SHAFTO (*With a bow to* MARIGOLD): Lady Marigold . . .

MARIGOLD (*Turning away*): How dare you speak my name!

SHAFTO (*With a bow to* MORNING GLORY): Lady Morning Glory, surely you remember me.

MORNING GLORY: I never saw you before . . . nor do I wish to see you ever again! (MAID MARJORIE *enters left with her* FATHER. *At the sight of* SHAFTO, *she runs to him.*)

MAID MARJORIE: Bobby! Bobby Shafto! Oh, I was so afraid something had happened to you.

SHAFTO: I promised I would come home again, Marjorie, and here I am.

LORD MAYOR: This fellow is an impostor! You are mistaken, Maid Marjorie.

MAID MARJORIE: Oh, no, sir! I could never be mistaken about Bobby Shafto. I'd know him anywhere.

FATHER: And so would I. Welcome home, lad.

SHAFTO (*As they shake hands*): Thank you, sir. I knew my true friends would see through my disguise. (*Removes tattered cloak, revealing original costume*) Open the chest, lads. (*As they do so, he removes eye patch and bandanna, tossing them into the chest and donning his velvet cap*) Now, ladies, do I look more like the Bobby Shafto you were expecting?

LADIES (*Ad lib*): Bobby! Bobby! It's really you! (*Etc.*)

SHAFTO (*Pointing to chest*): And here is the gold I promised, the fortune I made while I was away at sea.

ALL (*Crowding to look into chest; ad lib*): Gold! Bags of it! He's rich! (*Etc.*)

LORD MAYOR: What's the meaning of this? What's going on here?

SHAFTO: Nothing right now, sir. But within the hour Maid Marjorie and I will be married in the village church. You are all invited to the wedding.

MARIGOLD: But you promised to marry me!

MAGNOLIA: And me!

MORNING GLORY: And me!

MAID MARJORIE: Alas, Bobby, how could you do such a thing?

SHAFTO (*Taking her hands*): But I didn't, Marjorie. I made only one promise of marriage, and that promise was to you.

LADIES (*Each brandishing her letter*): But your letters!

FATHER: A promise is not to be broken, lad.

LORD MAYOR: If you have made false promises to my daughters, you will spend the rest of your life in prison. (*To daughters*) Let me see those letters.

MAGNOLIA (*Handing her letter to* LORD MAYOR): Read it, Father.

LORD MAYOR (*Reading*):
Magnolia fair, I've gone to win
A fortune for you when my ship comes in!

MARIGOLD: Read mine, too, Father! (*She hands him her note.*)

LORD MAYOR (*Reading*):
I promise you, dear Marigold,
More treasure than your arms can hold!

MORNING GLORY: And this is what he wrote to *me*, Father. (*Hands him her note*)

LORD MAYOR (*Reading*):
Dear Morning Glory, bright and fair,
Some day my fortune you will share!
(*To* SHAFTO) Well, young man, what do you have to say for yourself?

SHAFTO: "Actions speak louder than words," Your Honor. (*Reaching into chest and producing two bags of gold which he presents to* MAGNOLIA)
My ship is in, as you have heard,
And with this gold, I keep my word!

MAGNOLIA: But, Father, he promised . . .

LORD MAYOR: And he's kept his promise, daughter, just as his letter said.

SHAFTO: And now, if my mates will give me a hand with those heavy bags, I'll keep the rest of my promises. (*Bowing to* MARIGOLD *and presenting her with two bags handed to him by* SAILORS)
I promised you, dear Marigold,
More treasure than your arms can hold! (*As he hands her a third bag, she drops one*)

LORD MAYOR: Again he's kept his word! (*Picking up the bag she dropped*) He's given you more than you can carry.

SHAFTO (*Receiving two more bags from* SAILORS *and bowing before* MORNING GLORY):
Dear Morning Glory, bright and fair,
Here is my gold for you to share!

FATHER (*Clapping him on the shoulder*): You're a brave lad, Bobby Shafto! And a man of honor!

SHAFTO: Thank you, sir! And now, with your permission, I will keep my promise to Maid Marjorie.

LORD MAYOR: Just a minute! Just a minute! Although you have kept your promises to my daughters, I don't understand why you made them in the first place. Why would you wish to share your fortune with Magnolia, Marigold and Morning Glory?

FATHER: I think I can explain that, Your Honor. (*Producing folded paper*) Perhaps you will remember this agreement we signed when you first became Lord Mayor of Florabella.

LORD MAYOR: Agreement? What agreement?

FATHER: A legal agreement, Your Honor. This document grants me the right to buy back my original orchards and farmlands if and when I ever have the money to do so. Since the property belongs not only to you, but to your daughters as well, Bobby Shafto has already paid them for their shares.

SHAFTO: And there's more than enough gold in that chest to meet your price.

LORD MAYOR: But what if I refuse to sell?

SHAFTO: A bargain is a bargain, sir, and a promise is a promise! I have kept mine. Now it is your turn.

MAGNOLIA: It's a trick, Father!

MARIGOLD: Don't let him fool you!

MORNING GLORY: He has deceived us!

LORD MAYOR (*Studying document*): Nonsense! This document is perfectly legal. And as for his promises to you, he has kept them to the letter.

MAGNOLIA (*Sniffling*): But he has broken my heart!

MARIGOLD (*Dabbing at her eyes*): And mine!

MORNING GLORY (*With a sob*): And mine!

LORD MAYOR: Poppycock! When you thought he was a penniless sailor lad, you turned your backs on him. Besides, I'm sure your broken hearts will soon mend when you meet the three handsome gentlemen I have invited to the ball.

LADIES: Handsome gentlemen! Who are they?

LORD MAYOR: None other than Lord Poppinjay . . .

MAGNOLIA (*With rapture*): Lord Poppinjay! Oh, Father! I've always wanted to meet him!

LORD MAYOR: Count Cashbox . . .

MARIGOLD: How I should love to be a countess!

LORD MAYOR: And the Duke of Bankchester!

MORNING GLORY: Oh, Father! Not a real, live duke!

LORD MAYOR: I would hardly invite a dead one, would I? Now, stop your sniffling and wish Bobby Shafto and his bride the happiness they deserve.

MAGNOLIA (*To* 1ST SAILOR): If you will relieve me of these heavy bags, I will be glad to make a proper curtsy to the happy couple. (*Handing bags to* 1ST SAILOR *and making a curtsy*) Maid Marjorie, my apologies! Master Shafto, my congratulations!

MARIGOLD (*Handing her bags to* 2ND SAILOR *and dropping a curtsy*): It seems my sisters and I read more into your promises than you intended, Master Shafto. Please accept my best wishes.

MORNING GLORY (*Handing her money bags to* LORD MAYOR): A long and happy life to you both!

MAID MARJORIE: Thank you! Then you will all come to our wedding?

LORD MAYOR: With pleasure, my dear. And after the ceremony, your father and I will transact our business. Your lands will be returned to you by due process of law.

FATHER: Thank you, Your Honor.

LORD MAYOR: On one condition! (*Pause*) That this evening's ball be considered a wedding reception for the bride and groom.

MARJORIE *and* SHAFTO: Delighted, Your Honor.

ALL (*Singing*):
Bobby Shafto's home from sea,
Home to wed Maid Marjorie!
Oh, how happy they will be,
Hail to Bobby Shafto!
(*Curtain*)

THE END

The Friendship Wheel

Characters

BARKER

LONESOME LUCY

SIX TRICK-OR-TREATERS

BILL ⎫

BOBBY ⎪

BARBIE ⎬ the Happy Hunters

BETTY ⎭

CAROL ⎫

JOY ⎭ Christmas Twins

FEBRUARY

MARCH

APRIL

MAY

JUNE

JULY

AUGUST

SEPTEMBER

SETTING: *The stage is bare, except for a large wheel of fortune of the type used at carnivals and fairs, mounted on back wall.*

AT RISE: *The* BARKER, *dressed in circus costume, is trying to drum up trade, and during his opening speech,* LUCY, *who has been crying and is still wiping her eyes, enters. She stops short as she sees and hears* BARKER.

BARKER: Hurry! Hurry! Hurry! Right this way, boys and girls! Right this way! Take a chance on the big wheel. (*Spins wheel*)
Round and round and round it flies,
And when it stops, you win a prize!

Spin the wheel and find your lucky number! You can't miss! Every number is a winner! Step right up and try your luck! (*Sees* LUCY) Hello, little girl. Want to spin the giant wheel?

LUCY: No, thank you, sir. I have no money.

BARKER: Money! You don't need any money. Just step up and (*As he spins wheel*) give the wheel a spin.

LUCY (*Surprised*): You mean it's free?

BARKER: Of course it's free. This is the Friendship Wheel, and there's never a price on friendship.

LUCY (*Crying in earnest*): Oh, dear! Oh, dear!

BARKER: Come, come! This will never do! What is your name, child? And why are you crying?

LUCY (*Between sobs*): My name is Lucy. "Lonesome Lucy," they call me.

BARKER: Lucy is a pretty name, but I don't care for that *lonesome* part. Why do they call you *Lonesome* Lucy?

LUCY: Because I don't have any friends.

Boo hoo, boo hoo,

I'm lonesome and I'm blue.

I wish I had a friend or two,

Boo hoo, boo hoo.

BARKER: In that case you really *must* spin the great wheel.

LUCY: Why? What will it do for me?

BARKER: It will give you a chance at friendship.

LUCY (*Brightening*): Will it? Really and truly?

BARKER: Really and truly . . . providing you do exactly what the wheel tells you. Want to try?

LUCY: Oh, yes! I'll try anything. (*Spins wheel*)

BARKER (*Calling out in excitement*): Zero! Zero! It stopped at zero. How lucky can you be?

LUCY: What's so lucky about zero? It means nothing . . . nothing at all.

BARKER: But that's where you're wrong! (*Pretending to*

pluck a note from the wheel) Here . . . (*Handing it to her*) Read this . . . the instructions that go with the number.

LUCY (*Reading*):
Dear Lonesome Lu,
Here's what to do:
To make a friend
Find someone else
Who's lonely, too!
I told you it wouldn't mean anything. Nobody else in the whole world is as lonely as I am.

BARKER: Don't be silly!
In Africa, India, France, and Peru
There are thousands of children as lonely as you!

LUCY: But I don't know anyone in those countries. I can't even speak their languages.

BARKER: The language of friendship is spoken and understood all around the world. Let me show you. Just give the wheel another spin. (*As* LUCY *does so*) Stopping at . . . number thirty-one! Thirty-one's the number, little lady. (SIX TRICK-OR-TREATERS, *in Halloween costumes with UNICEF badges and carrying milk-carton containers, run in.*)

TRICK-OR-TREATERS:
Trick or treat! Trick or treat!
Your Halloween money means children will eat!

1ST CHILD: Hello, Mr. Barker. We came when you called our number.

2ND CHILD: Lucky number thirty-one!

3RD CHILD: October thirty-first is a lucky day because it's Halloween.

BARKER: And I want you to show this little lady how to make it one of the friendliest days in the year.

1ST CHILD: That's easy. Just join the trick-or-treat gang for UNICEF.

4TH CHILD: The trick is to collect money that will mean a treat for children in other parts of the world.

5TH CHILD: Here at home we think of a treat as candy or ice cream. But in some parts of the world a treat is a glass of milk or a bowl of rice.

6TH CHILD: Or medicine to save a life and cure disease.

2ND CHILD: In many towns boys and girls become "Friendly Beggars" to collect sewing supplies for other lands.

LUCY: It all sounds like fun.

1ST CHILD: It's not only fun—it's friendly!

2ND CHILD: American children have friends all over the world because we take time to be friendly on Halloween.

3RD CHILD: Do you want to go along with us next year?

LUCY: I'd love to. My name is Lucy, and I'll give you my address.

4TH CHILD: Don't bother. We'll find you.

5TH CHILD: You can find anyone in the world when the password is "Friendship."

BARKER: And now it's time to say goodbye. Thanks for coming, boys and girls.

ALL (*Ad lib*): Goodbye, Mr. Barker. Goodbye, Lucy. See you on Halloween! (*They exit.*)

LUCY: I feel less lonesome already. (*With a sigh*) But it's so long to wait till Halloween.

BARKER: You can make the time go faster by spinning the wheel again.

LUCY: I'd love to. (*Spins wheel*)

BARKER: Lucky eleven is coming up! (*As wheel stops*) Yes, here it is! The eleventh month of the year!

LUCY (*Counting months on her fingers*): That would be . . . November!

BARKER: Right!

LUCY: But November is such a dreary month. I always feel more lonely than ever in November.

BARKER:

Remember November
Will never be dreary,
If *you* will be sure
To do something cheery!
I will introduce you to my Happy Hunters. They will show you how to make November the cheeriest month on the calendar.

LUCY: Oh, no! Please! I don't want to meet any hunters. I hate the hunting season. All that shooting and killing!

BARKER: Who said anything about shooting and killing? My hunters are different. Listen! (*Blows a blast on a toy horn, hanging from his belt, then sings to tune of "John Peel"*)

Oh, ye wait till ye see all their coats so gay,
Oh, ye wait till ye hear what they have to say,
And ye won't wait long, for they're not far away,
And they're coming to wish you good morning!
(*Blows another blast on the horn*)
Oh, the blast of my horn ringing loud and clear
Sounds the call of the hunt they are bound to hear,
And my shout "Hoo-Halloo" that will make them appear
At my side in the pride of the morning!
(BILL, BOBBY, BARBIE, *and* BETTY, *wearing red coats and caps, enter.*)

ALL: Hello, Mr. Barker.

BOBBY: We came as soon as we heard your horn.

BARKER: I knew I could count on you. Lucy, these are my Happy Hunters. (*Indicating children by name*) Betty, Barbie, Bobby and Bill.

ALL (*Ad lib*): Hello, Lucy. How are you? Glad to meet you. (*Etc.*)

BARBIE: Would you like to go along on our next hunt?

LUCY: Thank you, but I'm not sure. What kind of hunt is it?

BETTY: It's a friendship hunt.

BILL: November is open season for hunting new friends.

BETTY: Let's sing our Hunting Song so she will understand.

ALL (*Singing to tune of "A-Hunting We Will Go"*):
A-hunting we will go, a-hunting we will go,
We'll find a friend and keep him till the end,
And never let him go!

LUCY: New friends! I'd love to go!

BOBBY: Good! We start early in November with American
Education Week.

BETTY: You can help write invitations to our parents and
neighbors asking them to visit the schools.

BARBIE: We make a lot of new friends that way.

BOBBY: Then comes Book Week.

LUCY: Book Week? What does that have to do with finding
friends?

BILL: When you read about children in other lands, you
learn to be better friends.

BETTY: And we also share our books with boys and girls
at home and overseas who have no libraries of their own.

BARBIE: November is a wonderful month for sharing.

BOBBY: It's a good time to collect warm clothing and share
it with needy children everywhere.

BILL: In our churches we celebrate Harvest Home festivals
by sharing fruits and vegetables with our neighbors.

BETTY: And best of all is Thanksgiving Day.

BARBIE: A day for thanks and a day for giving! What a
combination!

BILL: A day to thank,

BOBBY: A day to think,

ALL:
A day to forge
A friendship link!

BETTY:
A day of praise,

BARBIE:
  A day of prayer,
ALL:
  A day of blessings
  We can share!
BILL: And sharing always means friendship!
BARKER: Well, Lucy, how about it? Do you want to sign up for the Friendship Hunt in November?
LUCY: I certainly do.
BARBIE: Fine!
BETTY: We'll be looking for you.
BOBBY: Don't forget.
ALL (*As they exit*): Goodbye, Mr. Barker.
BARKER: Goodbye, boys and girls, and good hunting!
LUCY: I'm feeling better and better, Mr. Barker.
BARKER: One more spin and you'll be on top of the world.
LUCY: I can hardly wait. (*Spins wheel*)
BARKER (*Slowly*): It's stopping at . . . number twelve!
LUCY: No, no! Wait! It's still spinning.
BARKER: But now it stops! Right smack on number twenty-five.
LUCY: Twelve and twenty-five. That must be the twenty-fifth of December! Christmas Day!
BARKER: Listen! Do you hear something? (*Offstage singing of "Jingle Bells" is heard as* JOY *and* CAROL, *the Christmas Twins, enter. They are dressed alike in red sweaters and green skirts.*)
CAROL *and* JOY (*Singing to the tune of "Jingle Bells"*):
  Jingle bells, jingle bells, jingle all the way,
  Oh, what fun it is to find a friend on Christmas Day.
  (*They repeat song, then greet* BARKER.) Merry Christmas, Mr. Barker.
BARKER: And a Merry Christmas to you!
LUCY: But it's not time for Christmas.

CAROL: Who says it isn't time for Christmas?

JOY: It's always time for Christmas.

CAROL: We've already started our holiday projects for this year.

JOY: Making candles to sell at our Christmas Bazaar.

CAROL: Writing greeting cards.

JOY: Collecting articles for our Junior Red Cross boxes.

CAROL: Dressing dolls and repairing toys.

JOY: Filling scrapbooks with Christmas cards and carols for children overseas.

CAROL: Making favors for hospital trays.

JOY: Cutting out green paper trees so that everyone on our block will have a windowpane Christmas tree.

CAROL: It's a good thing Joy and I are twins, or we couldn't manage.

LUCY: There's only one of me, but I'd like to help.

BARKER: Good for you, Lucy! I'm sure our Christmas Twins could use an extra pair of hands. How about it, Joy? What do you say, Carol?

CAROL: I say Merry Christmas, Lucy.

JOY: And a Happy New Year!

LUCY: The same to you! May I really help with your Christmas projects?

CAROL: You can begin right now.

JOY: Come along to our Junior Red Cross meeting.

CAROL: That's where we work on our Christmas ideas.

BARKER: I'll send her along in a few minutes, girls, after she gives the Friendship Wheel another spin.

LUCY: Thank you, Mr. Barker, but I don't think I need to spin the wheel any more.

BARKER: You mean you've caught on to the secret?

LUCY: I believe so. (*Spinning wheel*) Look!
No matter where it stops
Or where it stays,

It always points
To Friendship Days.

BARKER: That's right, Lucy. And do you know why?

LUCY: I'm not quite sure how to say it, but I think it's because . . .

CAROL (*Singing to the tune of the verse from "Jingle Bells"*):
On every single day
Of every single year,
There's something we can do
To fill the world with cheer.

JOY (*Singing*):
A birthday card or gift,
A greeting we can send,
Or you can smile and shake a hand,
To make a brand-new friend.

LUCY: And that's what I'm going to do from now on.

BARKER: Then you'll never be Lonesome Lucy, not ever,
not ever again.

LUCY: Before I go, I'd like to spin the wheel one more
time, just to see what happens. (LUCY *gives the wheel
a hard spin, and before it stops, eight children, representing* FEBRUARY, MARCH, APRIL, MAY, JUNE, JULY, AUGUST,
and SEPTEMBER, *rush in.*)

FEBRUARY: What's going on?

MARCH: Someone pushed the panic button!

APRIL: All our numbers flashed at once.

MAY: We came as fast as we could.

BARKER: Take it easy. There's no need for alarm.

JOY: Our new friend, Lucy, was just experimenting.

CAROL: I never saw the wheel spin so fast!

LUCY: I'm sorry if I made you hurry, but I can't wait to
hear more about friendship days and friendship ways.

ALL (*Ad lib; excitedly*): Let me tell her. Let me! Let me!
(*Etc.*)

BARKER: One at a time. Who will speak for February?
FEBRUARY: I will, because February is my favorite month.
  There's Washington's Birthday and Abe Lincoln's, too,
  And Valentine's Day with candy for you,
  And Brotherhood Week, a time set apart
  To know all your neighbors and open your heart.
MARCH:
  When wild March winds begin to blow,
  And springtime melts the ice and snow,
  St. Patrick has a special day
  For friendly things to do and say.
APRIL:
  April brings both rain and shine.
  We share our joys at Eastertime.
  And Arbor Day's the day that we
  Should plan to plant a Friendship Tree.
MAY (*Singing*):
  A-tisket, a-tasket,
  A pretty May Day basket!
  Just hang it on your neighbor's door,
  And you'll be friends
  Forever more!
JUNE:
  Hurrah, hurrah for Flag Day!
  The date is June Fourteen.
  Let other countries learn from us
  What freedom's flag can mean!
JULY:
  July the Fourth for freedom!
  Our fight is fought and won.
  So let's help other nations
  Whose task is not yet done.
AUGUST:
  Vacation days in August
  Are days to make new friends,

And when we write them letters,
Vacation never ends.

SEPTEMBER:

September soon will come again
With schoolrooms strange and new,
But when you know the secret
There'll be new friends for you.

LUCY: And thanks to you and Mr. Barker, I have discovered the secret for myself.

I've learned by spinning Friendship's Wheel,
(And every chance a free one)
The surest way to make a friend
Is try your best to be one!

ALL (*Singing to tune of "Sing a Song of Sixpence"*):

Sing a song of friendship, everywhere you go.
When you meet a stranger, please just say "hello."
No one need be lonely, no one need be blue.
When you stop to make a friend,
Then you will have one, too. (*Curtain*)

THE END

Production Notes

ONE TO GROW ON

Characters: 10 male; 9 female; 6 male or female for Children.

Playing Time: 20 minutes.

Costumes: Court dress for members of the Court. The Queen has a small bell in a pocket. The Prince's crown hangs around his neck on an elastic band. Mr. Jolly wears a brightly-colored jester's costume, and the Godmother's costume should be green. The maids and Mrs. Custard wear aprons. The Children all wear everyday, modern dress. When Bill and Betty first enter, they are blindfolded.

Properties: Notebook for Mr. Jolly, books for Bill and Betty, bicycle, candle for maids, two tea wagons. One wagon holds a pile of wrapped presents: bird cage containing toy bird, map, jar of vitamins, three books, tape measure. The other holds a large birthday cake with 11 candles, and a silver cake knife.

Setting: The Court of King Kinross. Two thrones and a high stool are on a raised platform at center. There are folding screens at right and left of platform, concealing two "cages," each large enough to hold three children. Cushions and low stools or hassocks placed near the platform complete the furnishings. Exits are at right and left.

Lighting: No special effects.

Sound: Offstage fanfare, as indicated.

SHIRLEY HOLMES AND THE FBI

Characters: 9 male; 5 female; 1 male voice (from radio).

Playing Time: 25 minutes.

Costumes: Curly and Baby Face wear old clothes and have on half masks. Under their sweaters they wear shirts with "SPHS" printed on them. The officers wear uniforms. The others wear everyday dress.

Properties: Flashlights, paper of instructions, pails, mops, folder of papers, recipe, heavy canvas bag, ledger, coffee can, cigar boxes, money, boxes containing pans, bowls and ingredients for fudge, white flag on stick.

Setting: An abandoned garage-workshop with cement-block walls. Against one wall are two stepladders, a packing box, and some lumber, which conceal a cupboard. On a table are a hot plate and a radio. A baseball bat, canoe paddle, tennis racket, and volley-

331

ball net are piled in a corner. There is one exit, near which is a light switch.

Lighting: Lights are switched on as indicated.

Sound: Offstage sirens, voice from radio.

THE CASE OF THE GIGGLING GOBLIN

Characters: 11 male; 7 female; 8 male or female for Hobgoblins.

Playing Time: 30 minutes.

Costumes: Appropriate Halloween costumes and make-up, except for Pete and Joe, who wear old clothes. Judge wears spectacles, orange wig and robe, and orange make-up.

Properties: Gavel, two jack-o'-lanterns (one grinning and one frowning), two trays, notebook, book, black doctor's bag containing cardboard skeleton and short pointer, sticks of "dynamite," flashlight, camera.

Setting: Judge Jack-o'-Lantern's underground courtroom in the abandoned Bloody Bones Mine. A high desk with chair is on a raised platform up center. To the right of the desk is the prisoner's box, and to the left is the witness stand. A long table with four chairs is placed diagonally at right, and fifteen chairs are arranged in rows diagonally at left. Exits are at right and left.

Lighting: If desired, there may be a blackout as Pete and Joe enter, or lights may dim. Lights come up when they exit.

Sound: Recorded music for ballet, as indicated in text.

SIMPLE SIMON'S REWARD

Characters: 9 male; 7 female; 2 boys or girls for Children.

Playing Time: 20 minutes.

Costumes: Countess and Lord Ajax wear rich-looking costumes. Lord Ajax has a thick, bushy beard, in which the earring is concealed. The Countess wears one earring. The Herald wears a uniform with rich trim. All other characters may wear traditional Mother Goose costumes: smocks or loose shirts for the men, and long dresses, aprons and kerchiefs or mobcaps for the women. All should have pockets for coins. Simple Simon carries a handkerchief in his pocket. If desired, everyday clothes may be worn in place of Mother Goose costumes.

Properties: Flyswatter, about 36 small pies or tarts (real or cardboard), cart, staff for Herald, handkerchief, coins, two "diamond" earrings, purse.

Setting: The road to the Fairground. At center is an open booth, with many pies on the counter. On it hangs a sign reading PIES FOR SALE. Two tables with chairs or benches are at each side of the booth. Exits are at left and right.

Lighting: No special effects.

CIRCUS DAZE

Characters: 12 male; 3 female.

Playing Time: 25 minutes.

Costumes: Children wear jeans. Mr. Darnum and Mr. Cummings wear business suits. Clancy wears an old-fashioned policeman's uniform, false nose and mustache, and carries a rubber billy club. Others wear appropriate circus costumes. Leon and Hugo have torn jackets, and Hugo's face is smudged with soot. Sancho's long cloak conceals a sword.

Properties: Cardboard weight labeled 2,000 lbs., paper, pencil,

plates, baton, sword handle,
sword, sheet of cardboard with
outline of girl drawn on it, stuffed
snake, covered reed basket, passes,
camera.
Setting: Mr. Darnum's office. Several
folding chairs and a table with
circus props are at one side. A
weight labeled 2,000 lbs. is on the
floor. At center are a desk and
chair. Brightly colored circus post-
ers may complete the setting.
Exits are at right and left.
Lighting: No special effects.
Sound: Offstage circus music, as
indicated in text.

CAPTAIN CASTAWAY'S CAPTIVES

Characters: 13 male; 4 female. Spies
may be played by girls.
Playing Time: 30 minutes.
Costumes: Captain and crew wear
appropriate pirate costumes.
Wing Foo wears a cook's white
coat and hat. Lady Dorinda wears
a long gown and coronet, and
carries a small can of talcum
powder in a pocket. Children
wear everyday clothes.
Properties: Spyglass, wood and blunt
knife for whittling, six notebooks,
school books, folding stand, tea
tray, plate of fortune cookies, teapot and cups, toy pistols and
cardboard cutlasses, slip of paper
for grocery list.
Setting: A pirate ship. Helm is on
platform right. There is a coil of
rope at center, and canvas on floor
near it. Up left is a keg labeled
POWDER, up center a chest labeled TREASURE, left a barrel labeled APPLES, and a pile of crates
down left. Nets and ropes may be
hung to complete the effect. Exits
are left and right.
Lighting: No special effects.

AN ALL-AMERICAN THANK YOU

Characters: 4 male; 5 female.
Playing Time: 25 minutes.
Costumes: Modern, everyday dress
and Pilgrim costume. Betty, Fred,
Aunt Priscilla, Mrs. Tilly, and
Mrs. Abbot wear Pilgrim dress,
and Mary later puts on Pilgrim
costume. When she first enters,
Aunt Priscilla wears a coat. Corny
has a bandage on his leg.
Properties: Red gummed paper,
paper punches, Pilgrim dress, box,
papers, pencils.
Setting: The living room of Aunt
Priscilla Alden's home. A small
table is at center, and on it is a
small mirror. Chairs are placed
about the room, and a telephone
is at one side. Exits are at right
and left.
Lighting: No special effects.
Sound: Telephone and doorbell, as
indicated in text.

THE RABBIT WHO REFUSED TO RUN

Characters: 3 male; 1 female; 5 boys
or girls for Briar Patch bunnies.
Playing Time: 15 minutes.
Costumes: Robbie wears sport
clothes and a red baseball cap.
Others wear appropriate animal
costumes.
Properties: Lettuce leaf.
Setting: A forest glade with several
tree stumps and bushes.
Lighting: No special effects.
Sound: Recording of "I Whistle a
Happy Tune," barking, loud
bang, as indicated in text.

THE TOMBOY AND THE DRAGON

Characters: 3 male; 2 female; 7 boys
or girls for Guards, Dragon Keepers, and Pages.
Playing Time: 25 minutes.
Costumes: The King and Queen
wear royal robes and crowns. The

Queen carries a perfume atomizer in her pocket. Gloria and Michael are dressed alike in white, long-sleeved shirts, bright blue slacks, and blue shoulder capes. They wear blue berets trimmed with white plumes and golden crowns or emblems. Michael wears a pageboy wig, and Gloria carries a nail file in her pocket. When Gloria enters at end of play she wears a pink ruffled dress. The child playing the Dragon wears a dragon costume, with a cord in the tail which enables him to swing the tail. The Three Pages wear traditional pageboy outfits, with pageboy wigs and plumed berets. The Guards wear matching uniforms with gold trim, and the 1st Guard carries a newspaper clipping in his pocket. The Dragon Keepers wear plainer, matching uniforms, and carry cardboard spears.

Properties: Newspaper, handkerchief, tennis racquet, empty perfume atomizer, newspaper clipping, alarm clock, nail file.

Setting: The kingdom of Glockenspiel. The stage is divided into three sections. The right stage area is the throne room of the palace; two chairs stand at center, representing thrones. The center stage area contains a large "rock," a small table covered with gray fabric. Chains hang from either side of the rock. The left stage area contains a long couch or table. Exits are left, center, and right.

Sound: Offstage sound of bells, and gong, as indicated in text.

Lighting: If desired, appropriate stage area may be spotlighted as action takes place.

THE PAPER BAG MYSTERY

Characters: 6 male; 7 female.

Playing Time: 25 minutes.

Costumes: Girls wear Girl Scout uniforms; Miss Enders has leader's uniform. Brainy and Brawny change into coveralls. Officers wear policemen's uniforms.

Properties: 7 large paper lunch bags (there should be a banana in one bag, and some grapes in another); 1 large paper bag (same size as others) filled with fancy necklaces, rings, bracelets, and pins; 2 pairs of coveralls; dust mop; dustpan; carton containing pack of paper bags, box of Life Savers, pack of powder puffs, ballpoint pens, crayons, nail polish, purse-size Kleenex, fancy pencils, beads, bracelets, pins, ball of string, and scissors; bags and packages for Miss Enders; long-handled mop for Foxy.

Setting: A school office. At left is a safe with a combination lock. Desks, chairs, a table, typewriter, and telephone complete the set. Doors are at left and right.

Lighting: No special effects.

Sound: Offstage pounding, as indicated in text.

S.O.S. FROM SANTA

Characters: 7 male; 4 female; 5 male or female for elves and tailors.

Playing Time: 30 minutes.

Costumes: Mrs. Santa wears long dress. Santa first appears in bathrobe and high black boots, then changes into improvised Santa suit. Elves and Snip and Snap wear brightly colored elf suits. King and Queen wear red outfits; Queen has a red coat, and King has red trousers and cloak, and wears a crown. Rabbits wear appropriate masks with long ears.

Pilgrims wear traditional costumes; Uncle Sam has a long scarf, top hat, and white gloves. April Fool wears red jester costume and has a pointed red cap. Ghost wears a sheet.

Properties: Bundle of laundry containing pillowcases, small basket containing pair of socks, small book, cotton batting, watch, red box tied with green bow.

Setting: Santa's sitting room. A fireplace with chairs on either side is at back, and a sofa and other chairs are placed about the room. A bell-pull made of sleigh bells hangs by door at right, and there is also an exit at left.

Lighting: No special effects.

THE TOY SCOUT JAMBOREE

Characters: 10 male; 11 female; boys or girls for Two Swiss Children, Chinese Children, Child.

Playing Time: 20 minutes.

Costumes: Santa wears traditional costume; six Holly Berry Sisters wear red raincapes and hoods. Others wear appropriate national costume. French Toy Scout has key to wind-up dolls in his pocket.

Properties: Golden gavel, red umbrellas, red and green pinwheels, cardboard clock face, accordion, music box, kite, empty green burlap bag, letters, Reindeer Scout emblem.

Setting: Club House of the Toy Scouts. There is a long table at center with a Christmas tree on it. Reindeer Scout emblem is upstage.

Lighting: If desired, Christmas tree may light up, as indicated in text.

THE CHRISTMAS PEPPERMINTS

Characters: 9 male; 5 female.

Playing Time: 25 minutes.

Costumes: Dr. Fix and Nurse wear white, and Nurse may wear cap. Santa Claus is in traditional costume and wears spectacles. Fifi wears a full skirt, bodice, and peasant blouse, and, if possible, wooden shoes. Dolly Dimples wears a short, full-skirted dress. Toy Soldier and Drummer Boy wear appropriate uniforms. Scotty is dressed in a black outfit, with paper ears and tail. Jack-in-the-Box wears a pointed cap and fluted collar. Japanese Doll wears kimono; the Clown, a clown's costume. Consult storybooks for costume suggestions for Raggedy Ann, Pinocchio, and Mickey Mouse Doll.

Properties: Bandage, scissors, hand mirror, clipboard with several papers attached, striped bag filled with peppermint candy, red and green handkerchief, letters, brightly decorated box for Jack-in-the-Box, small hand cart, brightly wrapped Christmas packages, small Christmas tree.

Setting: Dr. Fix's consulting room at the New Hope Doll Hospital. A desk and chair are at one side. A chair and a cabinet or table containing doctor's equipment are at center.

Lighting: No special effects.

SANTA CALLS A CONFERENCE

Characters: 17 male; 15 female; 6 boys or girls for elves.

Playing Time: 25 minutes.

Costumes: Appropriate Christmas costume. Children of the World wear appropriate national costumes.

Properties: Place cards, red and green folders, pencils and scratch pads, gavel, piece of paper for Santa.

Setting: Christmas Convention Hall at the North Pole. At center are a long conference table and chairs. Two armchairs are at either end of table; a stool is also near table.

Lighting: No special effects.

Sound: "Jingle Bells," played as accompaniment to entrance of Children of the World, if desired.

THE GENTLE GIANT-KILLER

Characters: 7 male; 10 female.
Playing Time: 25 minutes.
Costumes: Modern, everyday dress. Mr. Mason wears overalls.
Properties: Application form, pencil; attaché case containing pointed cap, sword, cloak, pair of fancy bedroom slippers; long-handled mop.
Setting: Two chairs and a desk with telephone and index-card file are brought onstage for the first scene. For Miss Goode's classroom, set consists of desks and chairs for children and for Miss Goode. At one side of room is screen with names of parts of speech on large signs, pasted on the front. Behind screen is a pile of straw, under which is envelope containing song sheets and note. A bookcase and other appropriate furnishings complete the set. A door is at right.
Lighting: No special effects.
Sound: Offstage roaring and banging, sounds of fight, as indicated in text.

CUPID IN COMMAND

Characters: 6 male; 5 female.
Playing Time: 10 minutes.
Costumes: Children wear school clothes; Cupid wears red and white costume with baldric labeled "Dan Cupid." He has a quiver of arrows hanging from a cord over one shoulder and a golden bow fastened to his belt. He wears a coat over his costume when he enters.

Properties: Colored paper, paste, scissors, assorted hearts, paper doilies, and other materials for making valentines.

Setting: A long worktable covered with valentine card materials stands at center stage. A large valentine box is at center of table.

Lighting: No special effects.

THE TRIAL OF MOTHER GOOSE

Characters: 11 male; 8 female; 12 boys or girls for Children.
Playing Time: 25 minutes.
Costumes: King Cole and Queen wear royal robes and crowns. King has papers in his pocket and Queen carries a large handkerchief. Mother Goose wears a long skirt, apron, shawl, spectacles and a puckered cap. The characters from Mother Goose wear appropriate costumes. They may carry a prop suggesting their poem. The Fiddlers are dressed alike, and each carries a toy violin. Soldiers and Herald wear uniforms. Prince George wears peasant costume and a big hat; he carries a crown in his pocket. Cook and Mary wear aprons. Children may wear everyday clothes or costumes of countries around the world.
Properties: Spoon, silver-colored bowl, pipe and pipe-cleaners, fiddles, teacup and pot, saucepan, papers, scroll and pen.
Setting: The kitchen of King Cole's palace. Up right is a fireplace with an iron pot and stool nearby.

A worktable and chair are at left. A long table at center has a cloth that hangs to the floor; the table must be easy for Mother Goose to shake and move. Benches are on either side of it, and a high-backed chair is at the head, facing audience. Exit at right leads to the palace, and left exit to the outside.
Lighting: No special effects.
Sound: Loud knocking on door, and recorded violin music, as indicated in text.

THE MOUNT VERNON CRICKET

Characters: 5 male; 5 female.
Playing Time: 25 minutes.
Costumes: Modern, everyday dress. All wear outdoor clothing when they first enter. Mr. Harvey has a briefcase containing papers.
Properties: Old-fashioned wooden footstool, two large ugly vases, tray with coffee cups, spoons, etc.
Setting: The living room of the Bailey home. A sofa is at center, with a coffee table in front of it. Armchairs, tables, and a telephone complete the furnishings. Exit at left leads to front door, and exit at right leads to rest of house.
Lighting: No special effects.
Sound: Doorbell, telephone, as indicated in text.

THE BIRTHDAY PIE

Characters: 6 male; 6 female.
Playing Time: 15 minutes.
Costumes: Appropriate modern dress. Coats for guests.
Properties: Red, white and blue napkins, centerpiece (hatchet, American flags), place cards, birthday cake decorated with white frosting and red cherries, plates for ice cream, tray, radio, wrapped presents.
Setting: The Smith living room. Suitable living room furniture, couch, chairs, tables, etc. Table large enough to seat 10 people; 10 chairs.
Lighting: No special effects.
Sound: Doorbell.

A MATTER OF HEALTH

Characters: 6 male; 9 female.
Playing Time: 20 minutes.
Costumes: Everyday dress. Problem Pete may be dressed in dirty play clothes.
Properties: A list of health rules compiled by the class.
Setting: The meeting room of the Board of Experts. The Board members sit at a large table. There are a small table and chair for the Problem Pupils. A microscope and list of health rules are on the large table.
Lighting: No special effects.

THE FORGETFUL EASTER RABBIT

Characters: 9 male; 7 female; 7 boys or girls for Goofy's brothers and sisters.
Playing Time: 15 minutes.
Costumes: Boys and girls wear party dresses and suits; Lester and Sylvester wear rabbit costumes with hoods. The Forget-Me-Not Lady wears a long, old-fashioned dress and has a ladle hanging from her sash. Others wear rabbit costumes. Father Rabbit wears glasses and carries a list of the bunnies' names in his right pocket and a scroll in his left pocket. Goofy carries lists, papers, and trading stamps in his pocket. Other bunnies have Easter lists in their pockets.
Properties: Easter baskets, Easter

lists, eggs, rope, basket containing forget-me-nots and handkerchief, whistle, bucket.
Setting: A forest glade. At right are ten toy wheelbarrows or small wagons, nine of which have Easter baskets in them. At center is a large kettle labeled EASTER EGG DYE.
Lighting: No special effects.

PETER RABBIT VOLUNTEERS

Characters: 7 male; 5 female (four of the rabbit children are girls).
Playing Time: 15 minutes.
Costumes: All except Mazo wear rabbit costumes with long ears. Boy and girl rabbits may wear shorts and skirts, and Mamma Rabbit may wear an apron. Mazo wears a black suit, cape, and high hat. He carries a wand, and has a pair of long, outsized ears concealed in a pocket.
Properties: Volleyball net, tall upside-down black top hat, towel, bandanna bundle on stick.
Setting: The Rabbits' home in the forest. A worktable and chairs are at right, with eggs, paints, brushes, green paper grass, Easter baskets and ribbons. A large kettle is at center, containing two wire baskets of eggs, one basket of white and one of dyed eggs. Several trees form an exit at left, and there is another exit right.
Lighting: No special effects.

THE RETURN OF BOBBY SHAFTO

Characters: 5 male; 4 female.
Playing Time: 20 minutes.
Costumes: Bobby Shafto wears a velvet cape over rich-looking nautical costume. He has on long white stockings with silver buckles at the knee, and wears a velvet cap. Later he removes shoes and stockings and replaces cape and cap with a ragged cloak and bandanna and puts on an eye patch. Sailors wear appropriate dress. Magnolia is dressed in white, with white parasol; Marigold is in yellow, and Morning Glory in purple. Each has a small purse containing letter. Maid Marjorie and her Father wear peasant costumes. Lord Mayor wears an elaborate robe and hat.
Properties: Sea chest containing ragged cloak, bandanna, eye patch, seven bags of gold; letters; document for Father; cart piled with fruits and vegetables.
Setting: A wharf in the port of Florabella. Several packing cases, large enough to conceal Shafto and Sailors, are piled up at right. A small platform, representing a pier, is at left. Exits are at right and left.
Lighting: No special effects.

THE FRIENDSHIP WHEEL

Characters: 3 male; 5 female; 14 boys and girls for Trick-or-Treaters and Months.
Playing Time: 15 minutes.
Costumes: Barker wears a circus costume. He has a toy horn hanging from his belt. Trick-or-Treaters wear Halloween costumes with UNICEF badges and carry milk-carton containers. The Happy Hunters are dressed in red coats and caps, and the Christmas Twins wear red sweaters and green skirts. The children representing the months may have appropriate costumes. Lucy wears school clothes.
Setting: A bare stage, with a large wheel of fortune of the type used at carnivals and fairs mounted on the back wall.
Lighting: No special effects.

The Recycled Citizen

The Recycled Citizen

CHARLOTTE MACLEOD

G.K.HALL &CO.
Boston, Massachusetts
1989

Published in Large Print by arrangement with
Warner Books, Inc. and The Mysterious Press.

G.K. Hall Large Print Book Series.

Set in 18 pt Plantin.

Library of Congress Cataloging in Publication Data

MacLeod, Charlotte.
    The recycled citizen / Charlotte MacLeod.
        p.   cm.—(G.K. Hall large print book series)
    "Published in large print"—T.p. verso.
    ISBN 0-8161-4777-9 (lg. print).
    1. Large type books.   I. Title.
[PS3563.A31865R4   1989]
813'.54—dc20   89-38094